LANDOWNERSHIP
UNDER COLONIAL RULE

A STUDY OF THE EAST ASIAN INSTITUTE

LANDOWNERSHIP UNDER COLONIAL RULE

Korea's Japanese Experience, 1900–1935

EDWIN H. GRAGERT

HAWAI

UNIVERSITY OF HAWAII PRESS
HONOLULU

94 95 96 97 98 99   5 4 3 2 1

Studies of the East Asian Institute, Columbia University

The East Asian Institute is Columbia University's center for
research, publication, and teaching on modern East Asia.
The Studies of the East Asian Institute were inaugurated in 1962
to bring to a wider public the significant new research on
modern and contemporary East Asia.

Library of Congress Cataloging-in-Publication Data
Gragert, Edwin H., 1948–
Landownership under colonial rule : Korea's Japanese experience,
1900–1935 / Edwin H. Gragert.
p.   cm. — (A Study of the East Asian Institute)
Includes bibliographical references and index.
ISBN 0–8248–1497–5
1. Land tenure—Korea—History—20th century. I. Title.
II. Series: Studies of the East Asian Institute.
HD920.5.G73   1994
333.3'23'0951909041—dc20   93–36258
CIP

University of Hawaii Press books are printed on acid-free
paper and meet the guidelines for permanence and durability
of the Council on Library Resources

Designed by Ken Miyamoto

To
the Korean people,
may they be one again soon

CONTENTS

ACKNOWLEDGMENTS

THERE ARE a number of persons to whom I am grateful and without whose assistance and support this book would have remained a mere idea, or at the most countless boxes of note cards.

In Korea, the scholarship of Professors Kim Yong-sŏp at Yonsei University and Pak Pyŏng-ho and Sin Yong-ha at Seoul National University provided invaluable direction and collegial support during my research. Wŏn Yŏng-hŭi at the Taehan Chijŏk Hyŏphoe was responsible for revealing that the land records needed for such a study existed and were waiting to be researched.

In the United States, I express my appreciation to Susan Shin, Bruce Cumings, Gari Ledyard, Carter Eckert, Carole Ryavec, and Karl Moskowitz, all of whom provided vital criticism, comments, encouragement, patience, and friendship. Eugene Ch'oe, Amy Lee, Kenneth Harlin, and John McClure assisted me immeasurably at the East Asian Library of Columbia University. Above all, I thank Edward J. Baker at Harvard University, with whom I undertook much of the research for this study, and to whom I have looked for inspiration and consistent commitment toward integrating work on behalf of justice with scholarship.

Most important, I thank Patricia Kozu for her support over many years, her more than occasional nudging, and her persistent belief that any mission, even one of this magnitude, can be accomplished.

I assume full responsibility for the content of this book, including any mistakes and scholarly shortcomings. I welcome the controversy this book may generate and will be gratified if it stimulates others to challenge and explore modern Korean history.

CHAPTER 1

THE SETTING

IMPERIALISM and colonialism are subjects that evoke deep passions among observers of modern world history. Almost all contemporary nations have been either colonizer or colonized, most within living memory. It is no exaggeration that, more than any other phenomenon, the colonial experience has determined the social, political, and economic development of the twentieth-century world.

Asia is no exception: The history of modern East Asia is that of Asians coming to grips with external colonial control and subsequent independence. For some, both colonialism and independence came through military action; others entered into and took leave of the colonial experience almost passively, their fates determined by forces beyond their control. In most instances, colonizers in Asia were Europeans seeking to expand their territory and control over resources, but in other cases—as in that of Korea—colonizers were fellow Asians, a fact that flavored the nature of the colonial experience. Nonetheless, it is clear that the experience has affected the course of events in every contemporary Asian nation.

Japanese imperialism and colonial administration, which extended from 1895 through 1945, are subjects rarely analyzed dispassionately and with scholarly objectivity. This is especially true in the case of Korea, which came under Japanese control in 1904 and was annexed outright six years later. Financial, political, and social control, which was exerted over all aspects of Koreans' lives, attained intense and often brutal levels. Korea presents the potential for a comparative analysis of the impact that an intense colonial experience has on the social, economic, and political development of an Asian nation struggling to assert its identity. The impact was graphic, the legacy deep, and the historical record extensive.

When Japan annexed Korea in the first decade of the twentieth century, it absorbed a nation with a homogeneous people, language, culture, and a highly developed political tradition in which a strong central government had long-established modes of bureaucratic administration. Korea's borders had been defined and generally agreed upon for centuries. Dependent on agriculture for national revenue and livelihood, Korea developed labor-mobilization and produce-distribution systems that produced agricultural surpluses through most of the Yi (or Chosŏn) dynasty (1392–1910). Korean artisans produced daily necessities for the nation's citizens as well as specialty products for its upper class and those in neighboring China and Japan.

Korea had a unique national identity when it was confronted by imperialism in the late nineteenth and early twentieth centuries. As a result, from the outset the antagonism produced by Japan's imperialist expansion assumed the character of a confrontation between nations rather than a conflict between a nation-state and racial or tribal groups or heterogeneous ethnic peoples. Korea's boundaries were not arbitrarily drawn by colonial armies, linking disparate groups without regard to linguistic or cultural differences; they had been intact and had been diligently guarded against foreign encroachments for centuries.

Indeed, the very economic and political institutions developed during the Yi dynasty enabled Japanese colonial administrators and commercial entrepreneurs to assume control over Korea's resources without having to establish new modes of administration. Japan did not introduce new agricultural modes of production, build plantations using slave labor, or establish a bureaucratic government for the first time. Colonial Japan did not need to implant alien institutions to control Korean agriculture; they simply had to dominate and manipulate preexisting institutions. In fact, Japan scrapped early plans to redistribute landownership from Korean to Japanese hands (mainly corporate) in favor of using the existing system. Land ownership patterns remained intact and were not significantly altered until the depression of the 1930s.

Rather than radically change Korean land tenure, the Japanese colonial administration accelerated ongoing economic forces. The concept of individual ownership was clearly developed, with land deeds frequently passing from one person to another. By the beginning of the twentieth century, certain areas of the Korean peninsula, principally those near major population centers, produced for a market economy and were controlled by economic interests in those centers. High rates of absentee landlordism and tenancy and a marked concentration of landholdings in the hands of a few wealthy landowners characterized land tenure in such areas. As more areas of the Korean peninsula produced for (and became controlled by) the population centers during the colonial period, they acquired similar characteristics. And as investments in Korean agriculture accelerated, stimulated by the infusion of capital and colonists from Japan, so did the penetration of the Korean countryside by external economic forces.

It is clear, however, that massive agricultural dislocation occurred under Japanese colonial rule. Thousands of poor farmers left rural areas for urban areas; some migrated to Manchurian farms and factories and to Japan itself. The migration was a result of improved agricultural technology, higher production, and market forces affecting labor rates. Although less easy to document, the migration seems also to have been a result of the loss of traditional "farming use rights," which, while legally recognized, were also a vital part of Korea's rural tradition—particularly on commonly farmed land.

Japan's agricultural policies did not represent a sharp break from Yi dynasty development patterns; rather, they were characterized by selective use of traditional Korean institutions to pursue economic and political goals. The primary goals of Japanese agricultural policy were two-fold: to establish Korea as a provider of inexpensive rice and other commodities for Japan, and to ensure that Korea would be politically "pro-Japan." To accomplish the first goal, Japanese colonialism had two objectives: to rationalize and systematize the land registration system and to make land—particularly agricultural land—a secure and easily marketable item for anyone, whether Korean or foreign.

These objectives were compatible with Korean tradition and, seen in their historical context, were, with the policies implemented to attain them (particularly those dealing with land surveying and ownership registration), extensions of earlier Yi dynasty policies. Since the 1860s Korean intellectuals and some politicians had concluded that changes in the land registration system were desirable and necessary. Korean efforts at partial reform of this registration system came in the late 1890s, when land was investigated, and during the Kwangmu period (1896–1906), when land registers were compiled. In these waning years of the Yi dynasty the Korean government sought to ascertain the ownership, productivity, and size of all agricultural fields in the peninsula, all in an ultimately futile effort to increase land tax revenue. Although much of Korea's agricultural land was presumably surveyed at this time, the project ran out of funds and came to a halt in 1902. In addition, although the land registers created at this time accurately depicted land-ownership at the time of the Kwangmu survey, they failed to correct a major deficiency in the Yi dynasty land registration system in general: They did not provide for systematic recording of subsequent changes in ownership. Like others before them, the registers became obsolete shortly after being compiled.

Although Japan's colonial administration ultimately sought to co-opt preexisting economic and political institutions, there were several early attempts to radically alter Korean land tenure. The first occurred in 1904, when plans were made to expropriate all land controlled by the Korean royal family and court institutions and lease it to Japanese farmers. Fortunately for the thousands of Korean families relying on income and food from these lands, public opinion against this Nagamori scheme resulted in its demise. Other efforts to settle thousands of Japanese farmers on Korean agricultural land were initially more successful but eventually fell short. Adverse Korean public opinion, lack of interest among the Japanese populace, and the basic impracticality of the idea resulted in a Japanese colonial style of co-optation and accommodation. Abrupt change was rare; continuation of past traditions and patterns was the rule. This unmistakable feature can be seen in landownership statistics presented in subsequent chapters.

This interpretation of early Japanese colonial patterns, while consistent with other colonial experiences in Asia, contradicts virtually all previous analyses of land tenure change in colonial Korea. Conventional wisdom, originating from both research in the early 1930s and personal experiences in the 1930s and 1940s, holds that significant and rapid change in Korean land tenure occurred when Japan annexed Korea in 1910. According to this school of thought, the principal instrument of this change was the Japanese-created Provisional Land Survey Bureau (PLSB), said to have been explicitly established to provide a legal mechanism for the transfer of massive amounts of agricultural land from Korean to Japanese landowners.

This traditional interpretation of land tenure change under Japanese colonial rule has been widely accepted within the academic community and among the general public. However, this study demonstrates the fallacy of that argument. No abrupt change in Korean landownership patterns accompanied the cadastral survey during the first decade of Japanese colonial rule. Analysis of land records reveals that the land-distribution patterns observed by earlier scholars emerged only after the sharp economic dislocations of the depression of the 1930s, not during the early years of colonial administration of Korea.

The Historiographic Record

East Asian peoples have a propensity to record the present and revere what others have written previously; they are, to use John Fairbank's term, "historical minded." As a result of careful preservation and consciousness of the "historical judgment of the future,"[1] both Korea and Japan have bequeathed a rich legacy of historical resources with which to study their past. Among those resources are records pertaining to land

and landownership, particularly land registers from the late Yi dynasty, documents of land transfers, and cadastres from the period of Japan's rule of Korea (1910–1945), which contain information of significant breadth and value. Scholars of Yi dynasty land tenure have only recently begun to examine and analyze the statistical and social data contained in the land registers *(yang'an)*.[2] And, only in the past decade have legal scholars initiated pioneering studies of the thousands of documents of land sale, inheritance, mortgage, and commendation available in the archives of Seoul National University and other collections.[3]

The present study relies principally on three government registers of landownership, each compiled in a different period and for a different purpose: the Kwangmu *yang'an,* landownership registers compiled after the cadastral investigation by the Yi dynasty government during the Kwangmu period (1896–1906); the *t'oji taejang,* registers drawn up after the nationwide survey undertaken by the Japanese colonial government between 1910 and 1918 (and completed by 1914 in the villages studied); and the *t'oji tŭnggibu,* records of voluntary registration of ownership title and contractual agreements regarding individual pieces of land, initially compiled around 1917.[4] Both the *t'oji taejang* and *t'oji tŭnggibu* were maintained through 1945 and are still in use today in local government offices in most parts of the Republic of Korea.

KWANGMU *YANG'AN*

The value of the Yi dynasty *yang'an* lies in the breadth of information contained in their pages. The Kwangmu *yang'an* drawn up by the Korean government between 1898 and 1903 record the following information for each piece of land surveyed: the type of land, its owner, its cultivator (if different from the owner), its size in both linear measurements and in the volume of seed needed to sow it (a traditional Korean farming measurement), its quality in grade measurements, its productivity, a rough diagram of its shape, and the names of owners of surrounding pieces of land.

The Kwangmu *yang'an* contain more data on each piece of land than all previously compiled *yang'an* in the dynasty. Prior registers recorded the owner of a farm, but none registered the cultivator. Consequently, an analysis of tenancy in a village or even in an entire county became possible for the first time in Korean historiography. Concentration of land— whether in the hands of owners or of renters—the role of tenancy, and geographic differences in levels of tenancy can all be quantified and measured.

In addition, previous registers, which were compiled to determine taxes on agricultural land, omitted any record of residential land. The Kwangmu *yang'an* provide detailed data on the sizes of homes, their construction (whether made with tiled or thatched roofs), and the amount of landlordism in home ownership. Statements can be made about family size and the capacity of agriculture to provide a livelihood for the rural villages that comprised 85 percent of Korea's population in 1900.

Finally, the Kwangmu *yang'an* assist the historian in analyzing Korea's landless class, individuals who neither owned nor rented agricultural land but worked for wages. Previously, statements have been made on the existence of wage labor in Korean society at the turn of the century, but now it is possible to measure the size of this group in various locations throughout the Korean peninsula.[5]

The Kwangmu registers are disappointing in some respects, however. Although the data seem reliable, two glaring omissions make the historian's task more difficult. For one, the Kwangmu *yang'an* lack indications of traditional social status—that is, *yangban* (privileged elite), *sangmin* (commoner), and *ch'ŏnmin* (outcast). The only indicators of social class are absurd names, which signify slave origins.[6]

The second omission is a lack of information on the place of residence of individuals named on the *yang'an*. This is characteristic of all Yi dynasty *yang'an*. Village residents present no problem because they are recorded as either owner-dweller or tenant of village homes, but individuals living outside the villages are problematic. Unless one happens to recognize a particular individual (for example, a Seoul bureaucrat, entrepreneur, or local office holder) or devotes time and patience to a painstaking scrutiny of *yang'an* from all neighboring villages, it is impossible to know whether an absentee landowner or tenant walked to his fields from a nearby village or lived in a distant town and commissioned an agent to handle day-to-day operations. This is not to say that rates of absentee landlordism cannot be calculated; it simply means that many individuals cannot be fully identified without additional source material.[7]

The *T'oji Taejang*

The *t'oji taejang* (*tochi daichō* in Japanese) document landownership in Korea under Japanese colonial rule. Initially created to record the findings of the nationwide cadastral survey, the *taejang* continued to be maintained as the official register of landownership throughout the colonial period. They are the ultimate products of "reportism" (the process of reporting landownership claims during the survey), which some historians have identified as the means by which Japanese colonists fraudulently acquired ownership over Korean land.

The procedure for compiling the *taejang* was relatively straightforward.[8] Within a village, survey officials announced that individuals claiming to own land in the village should report such claims within a fixed period, usually sixty days. While each plot was being surveyed, the owners' reports were compiled *(t'oji chosabu)*[9] and compared to *yang'an* records. Most disputes, whether over ownership or boundaries, were settled at this time, using documentation and testimony provided by parties in the dispute and other members of the community. The relatively small number of disputes that could not be settled locally, together with appeals of local rulings, were referred to a higher judicial body within the survey bureaucracy.[10] After the lists of ownership reports were revised to take into account disputes that had been settled, the *taejang* were compiled, with an entry for each plot of land in the peninsula. Each entry contains the following information: plot number, name of owner (in Chinese characters), address, type of land, its area measurement in *p'yŏng*,[11] its grade, its assessed value in yen, and the date on which it was surveyed. In addition, space was allocated for recording approximately ten subsequent changes in any of these items. For plots of land undergoing less than six or seven ownership changes, which was the bulk of land, the same *taejang* are in daily use today.

Once compiled, the *taejang* were kept in the office of the county governor *(kunsu)* for use in determining both the amount of the land tax assessment and the person responsible for its payment. The accuracy of *taejang* data and of the measurements on the accompanying cadastral maps *(chijŏkto),* is unquestioned by even current Korean county officials who diligently guard the ninety-year-old registers.[12] Because most plots of land have not changed hands more than five or six times since the time they were first surveyed, the original page contains not only the name of the owner in 1914, but also that of the current owner.[13]

The *taejang* are invaluable as a historical resource. Not only is it possible to learn who was awarded ownership of a given parcel during the controversial cadastral survey, but each successive owner's name, address, and date of ownership transfer is also recorded. For the first time in Korea's history, the official register of ownership provides for changes over time. Because each plot of land, regardless of its size, has its own *taejang* page, changes other than ownership that affected the tax assessment of the plot are also recorded on the same page. For example, if a plot of upland was changed to paddy land through irrigation, the plot's type, grade, and assessed value would change on the *taejang*.

With one exception, the *taejang* are extremely helpful in analyzing changes in land tenure in the colonial period when used in conjunction with the earlier Kwangmu *yang'an*. Although *taejang* record owners from the time of the initial colonial survey, they contain no information about the actual cultivator. Thus, the extent of landlordism must be determined from the overall size of an individual's landholdings. If an individual owns more land than can possibly be cultivated by an extended family and a few laborers, it is assumed that the owner is a landlord. Similarly, if an owner lives a great distance from the land owned, the person is assumed to be an absentee landlord.[14]

As valuable as the *taejang* are in comparing land tenure patterns and changes in the late Yi dynasty and colonial period, this comparative analysis would be difficult without the *chijŏkto,* or cadastral maps, drawn at the time of the Japanese cadastral survey.[15] These maps enable the historian to compare individual plots with those crudely drawn on the Kwangmu *yang'an.* Because administrative units and geographic place names were changed radically by the colonial government, without the *chijŏkto* it would be difficult, if not impossible, to identify the same village on the two registers. In addition, these maps facilitate our understanding of village layout, particularly the positioning of individual fields relative to water supply, means of transportation, and residential sites.

THE *T'OJI TŬNGGIBU*

Whereas registration of all land in the *taejang* was compulsory, inclusion in the *t'oji tŭnggibu* was voluntary. Created in 1916, the *tŭnggibu* is a record certifying legal title and contractual agreements concerning a given plot of land. It was placed under the jurisdiction of the colonial judicial system and remains within the court structure of the South Korean government. The *tŭnggibu* system was modeled after that of Japan, which itself was patterned after the German land registration system of the late nineteenth century. Any outstanding contractual agreement involving a particular piece of land can be ascertained by examining the *tŭnggibu*—provided, of course, that the information was submitted.

The *tŭnggibu* consists of three pages for each piece of land registered: an identification page locating the land by its *taejang* plot number, the type of land, and its area measurement; an ownership page recording the owner at the time of registration, the date of registration, each subsequent owner, and date and mode of ownership transfer (for example, sale, inheritance, or foreclosure); and a contract page detailing primarily mortgage agreements but also liens and long-term tenancy contracts and the terms of these agreements.[16] (See Appendix.) Contractual agreements that involved using land as collateral were not officially recognized by the colonial government unless they were registered in the *tŭnggibu.*[17]

Because registration was voluntary and occurred if and when an owner desired the legal protection offered by registration, plots of village land appear in the *tŭnggibu* in the order in which they were registered, some early in the colonial period but others in the 1930s and 1940s; a few do not appear at all. Therefore, data on mode of ownership transfer and on mortgage contracts are available only after registration in the *tŭnggibu.* Fortunately, most landowners chose to register their land in the *tŭnggibu* early in the period.

With these three land registers, Kwangmu *yang'an, t'oji taejang,* and *tŭnggibu,* it is possible to analyze the ownership history of an individual parcel of land from the late Yi dynasty through the entire colonial period. The parcel's life during the forty-five-year period is available for scrutiny. In fact, the ownership history of an entire village or group of villages may be ascertained. The histories of five such villages appear in the following pages.

Five Rural Korean Villages

Availability of landownership data and diversity of geographic setting were the criteria used in selecting villages for study.[18] Since both the *taejang* and the *tŭnggibu* traditionally have been maintained in local government offices, the records for areas of the Korean peninsula north of the 38th parallel are not available. In addition, many areas in southern Korea were involved in the bitter fighting of the Korean War or were occupied by troops of the North Korean army. In many such areas local government offices and their contents were destroyed by the occupying troops, by subsequent Allied attacks, or by persons not wanting to be identified as landlords.

Even a complete set of land records from the colonial period is of little help, however, if one is attempting to analyze land tenure changes between the late Yi dynasty and the colonial years. Complete Kwangmu *yang'an* records are also required. Because of a major fire that burned most of these *yang'an* in 1907 and the colonial policy of destroying land records once the *taejang* were compiled, very few Kwangmu *yang'an* remain.[19] From the areas having the most complete *yang'an* and *taejang,* five villages were selected: Kongsu-ri in South Ch'ungch'ŏng province, Asan-gun, Paebang-myŏn; Paeksŏng-ni in South Ch'ungch'ŏng province, Nonsan-gun, Yŏnsan-myŏn; Songsan-ni in South Ch'ungch'ŏng province, Sŏch'ŏn-gun, Hansan-myŏn; P'albong-ni in North Chŏlla province, Iksan-gun, P'albong-myŏn; and Se-ri in Kyŏnggi province, currently within the city limits of Suwŏn (see Figures 1 and 2). Several of these villages were greatly influenced by the town-based market economies that emerged during the colonial period. For some, change came early; for others, traditional patterns persisted long into the colonial period.

In that the villages changed over time, they are representative of the Korean peninsula as a whole during the colonial period. New cities arose at the intersection of improved roads and newly established railroad lines. New financial and business institutions reached out from urban centers and swept previously self-sufficient villages into the new national and even international economic order. Korean farmers increasingly produced for markets far from their rice fields and became dependent on prices and consumption patterns far removed from Korea. Changes in

FIGURE 1
Provinces in which the
villages studied are located

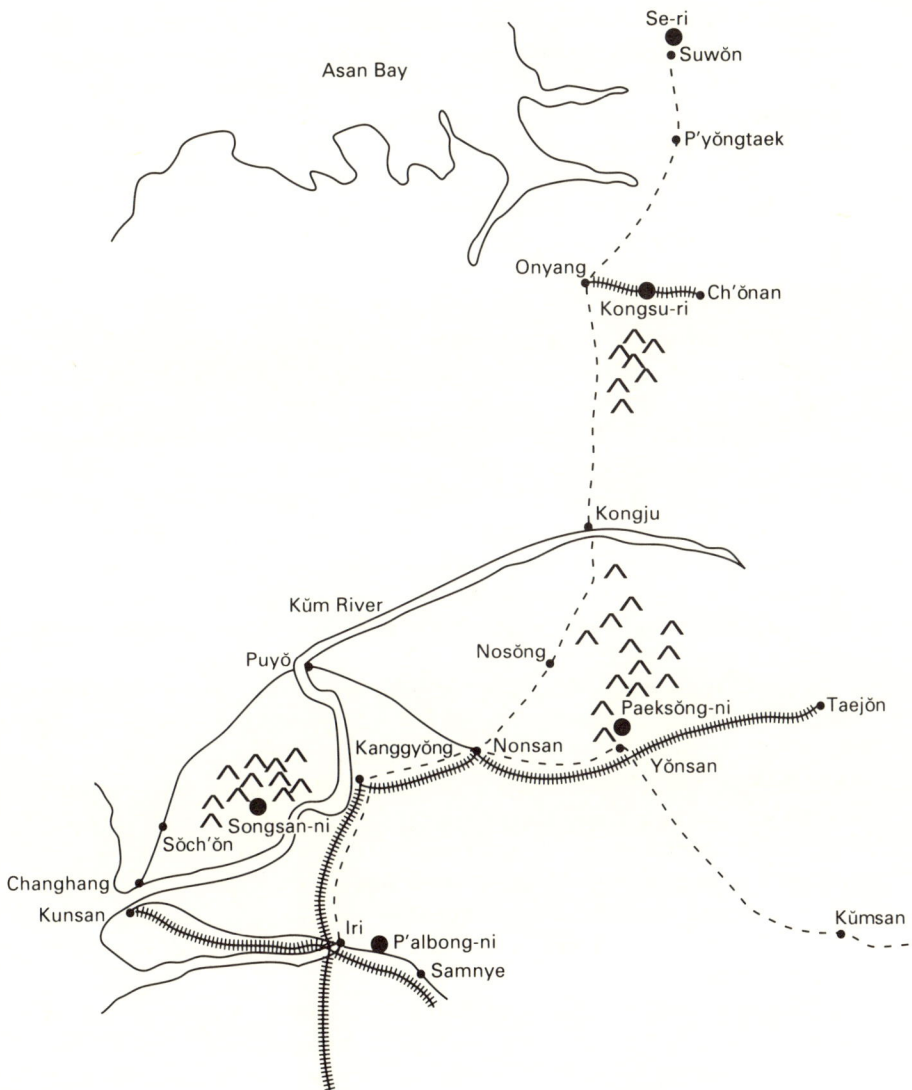

FIGURE 2
Location of the five villages studied

these patterns and the Japanese desire to control rice production eventually significantly altered landownership in each of the villages.

Because of the absence of land records for much of the country, we cannot say that the villages are a random sample of Korean villages or are somehow typical of Korean villages. However, among the areas with extant land records, the villages represent different types of geographic and economic settings. In the future, perhaps other scholars will be able to analyze data from other parts of the peninsula. I hope this study will motivate such research.

In order to examine the landownership situation in these villages, it is imperative to visit each village—at least on paper—and experience its location and characteristics.

KONGSU-RI

In 1900 anyone traveling south from Seoul encountered the small hamlet of Kongsu-ri. The village lay adjacent to the principal north-south road, which at the turn of the century was no more than a dirt path running through Suwŏn, P'yŏngt'aek, Onyang, and Kongju, the administrative and commercial center of Ch'ungch'ŏng province. Many Yi dynasty officials visited the Onyang hot springs, barely an hour's walk west of Kongsu-ri, on their way to and from Seoul. To help provide for these officials' pleasure and to finance the government offices in Onyang, the Korean government designated certain fields as *kongsujŏn* (land for official use). Many such fields were located in Kongsu-ri, which acquired its name from these fields.

Kongsu-ri grew rapidly during the early twentieth century. When the Seoul-Pusan railroad was completed in January 1905, new towns sprang up along its length. One of these new commercial towns was Ch'ŏn'an, located less than 10 kilometers from Kongsu-ri. Since the road between Ch'ŏn'an and the hot springs of Onyang ran directly through Kongsu-ri, the transportation orientation of the village, previously north-south, changed to east-west. Throughout the colonial period this road was widened and improved to accommodate motorized vehicles, leading to the establishment of a number of eating and drinking places in Kongsu-ri that catered to passing tourists.

Although Kongsu-ri had been relatively accessible even in the late Yi dynasty, the construction of the Kyŏngnam railroad line, from Ch'ŏn'an to Changhang on the Kŭm River opposite Kunsan, opened the village to increased economic enterprise and external influence. After the Mosan station in Kongsu-ri was completed in 1922, village produce could be shipped by rail directly to Seoul or to Japan-bound ships at Pusan or Changhang/Kunsan. The increase in commercial activity in and around Kongsu-ri led to a population increase from ninety households in 1914 to approximately two hundred households by the 1940s.

Today, almost half of Kongsu-ri's 2.5 square kilometers of land is cultivated; the remainder is primarily forest and residential land. Rice is still the principal crop, but fruit orchards, soy beans, barley, and mulberry leaves for a small silkworm industry are increasingly important truck farming crops. The village has a fairly reliable water supply from a natural reservoir that collects runoff from hills rising abruptly south of the village. Most village paddy fields are irrigated by streams that run from this reservoir and eventually drain into the Kobundari-ch'ŏn, a tributary of the Kokkyo-ch'ŏn, which itself flows into Asan Bay. In addition, because the village has a system of irrigation canals in its northern section, Kongsu-ri is much less affected by annual rainfall fluctuations than most Korean villages, resulting in a rice crop that, in an average year, is more than sufficient to feed village residents.

PAEKSŎNG-NI

In sharp contrast to Kongsu-ri, Paeksŏng-ni was extremely isolated and difficult to reach at the turn of the century. In the late Yi dynasty one had to walk four and a half days from Seoul to reach the nearest market community in Ŭnjin (present-day Nonsan), and another half day up the Nonsan valley to reach Paeksŏng-ni. All of the bustling commercial towns within easy traveling distance of Paeksŏng-ni are products of the colonial period.

Paeksŏng-ni's isolation enabled it to avoid the warfare of the Tonghak rebellion in the 1890s, which devastated much of the surrounding farm land. Although it was near the Tonghak stronghold of Ŭnjin, the village escaped undamaged because it was far from the major north-south transportation routes used by both the advancing and retreating armies.

In 1900 the village was self-sufficient and relatively unaffected by external economic forces. This remained the case even after the construction of the Yŏnsan station on the Honam railroad line, which was completed in 1911. This railroad connected Taejŏn, which would become the largest and most important commercial center in South Ch'ungch'ŏng province, with Iri and Kunsan, two centers of Japanese economic activity. Lying approximately 7 kilometers from Yŏnsan in the foothills of a mountain range, Paeksŏng-ni was bypassed by nearby economic development and remained virtually unchanged during the colonial period.

Almost all of Paeksŏng-ni's approximately 150 households (the same number as at the turn of the century) are engaged in agriculture, which is dominated by dry-field farms terraced up the hillsides. Paeksŏng-ni does well in years of average or above-average precipitation because it receives ample runoff from the hills. When rainfall is below average, however, there is no reliable source of irrigation because the village has no reservoirs, and the largest stream in the vicinity, the Yŏnsan-ch'ŏn, is 4 kilometers away at a lower elevation. As a result, little rice is grown in

Paeksŏng-ni. Instead, millet, tobacco, and ginseng make up the bulk of the village's agricultural production.

SONGSAN-NI

Like Paeksŏng-ni, Songsan-ni was extremely isolated in 1900. Traveling there from Seoul required five days of difficult walking over dirt paths and mountainous terrain. The village was near the Kŭm River, a major transportation route for agricultural produce during the colonial period, but at the turn of the century there were no commercial towns on the river's banks. In fact, no town of significant size or economic importance existed in the entire county except, possibly, for Hansan, located about 4 kilometers from Songsan-ni and believed to have had a sizable market in the nineteenth century.[20] All fifty of Songsan-ni's households were engaged in agriculture at the turn of the century, assisted by other families living in neighboring communities. Some of Songsan-ni's families lived in Hansan and walked to their fields.

Songsan-ni's fields were among the most fertile in Korea, and ample irrigation was available from Ch'uktong Lake on the village's northern boundary. This enabled Songsan-ni's farmers to concentrate on rice production in all but abnormally dry years. As a result, rice was and still is the village's dominant crop with 90 percent of the village's cultivated land devoted to its production.

During the colonial period Songsan-ni changed little, and the economic development of nearby market towns bypassed the village. However, as Kunsan became an increasingly important port for shipping rice to Japan, entrepreneurs and moneylenders began investing in agricultural land within the surrounding region. During the late 1920s and early 1930s investment capital in the form of mortgage financing increasingly flowed into Songsan-ni, much of it coming from Japanese businesspeople living in Kunsan. Several of these individuals became village landowners. Nonetheless, Songsan-ni remained a seemingly self-contained and isolated village retaining the landownership patterns that existed at the end of the Yi dynasty.

P'ALBONG-NI

The fourth village, P'albong-ni, also was rather isolated at the end of the Yi dynasty. The main road from the capital stretched south from Kongju in South Ch'ungch'ŏng province to Chŏnju in North Chŏlla province, passing through the village of Samnye, located 7 kilometers southeast of P'albong-ni. Little traffic ventured off this path and into P'albong-ni—which, as its name (Eight Mountain Peaks Village) suggests, was nestled among eight "mountains" with elevations of 100 to 200 feet.

Despite its isolated location, the village was intricately linked to the commercial activity network in North Chŏlla province that centered on Chŏnju, one of the most important commercial and political towns of the Yi dynasty. North Chŏlla province had the highest amount of land concentrated in the hands of a small number of individuals. Its wealthy landlords, however, lived not in Seoul but in Chŏnju and to a lesser extent in Iksan. High rates of tenancy and exploitation by officials in the province contributed to the high level of Tonghak activity in the area. One Tonghak uprising, in November 1894, is said to have involved as many as ten thousand farmers in the Iksan area, about 15 kilometers from P'albong-ni. A similar uprising in the neighboring village of Samnye involving five thousand farmers occurred in October 1894 and undoubtedly included farmers from P'albong-ni.

Early in the twentieth century Japanese businesspeople and colonial administrators recognized the value of the large agricultural plain on which P'albong-ni is situated. As early as 1905 Japanese corporate developers undertook large-scale land development projects in the region between Iksan (near present-day Iri) and Kunsan on the coast. In addition, the Oriental Development Company, the semiofficial Japanese development and immigrant settlement corporation, established a branch office in Iri in 1908. When the Honam railroad line and the branch lines connecting Chŏnju and Kunsan via Iri were completed in 1912, the town became the railroad junction for all commodity shipments to Japan via the port of Kunsan.

As transportation improved and as trade with Japan through Iri and Kunsan became more significant, P'albong-ni gradually became more closely linked with economic interests in these cities. Nonetheless, it continued to be dominated by regional landowners. P'albong-ni's residents, about 250 households in the 1930s, relied principally on agricultural production for their livelihood throughout the colonial period, but the village also housed several people who administered the *myŏn* (subcounty) bureaucracy and others who operated village shops.

Rice traditionally has been the principal crop of P'albong-ni; it is cultivated on about 70 percent of the village's land and is facilitated by fertile soil and ample irrigation. Central to the irrigation system is the large reservoir at the center of the village.

SE-RI

Unlike the other villages, Se-ri was transformed from an agricultural village into part of an urban center within a few decades. In 1900 Se-ri lay just outside the ancient walled town of Suwŏn, approximately 50 kilometers south of Seoul, but by the end of the colonial period it had been completely incorporated into Suwŏn. As a result of its proximity to

Table 1-1   Overview of Land in the Villages Studied

VILLAGE	1900	PADDY LAND 1914	1941	1900	UPLAND 1914	1941
Kongsu-ri						
Plots	201	226	250	194	225	286
Area	210,137	264,037	265,338	83,585	139,902	171,299
Value	*	41,910	42,264	*	13,852	15,642
Paeksŏng-ni						
Plots	127	105	113	191	203	200
Area	73,802	71,772	69,695	65,890	93,722	113,530
Value	*	9,773	9,704	*	7,208	7,454
Songsan-ni						
Plots	198	166	181	194	114	110
Area	162,478	148,710	149,038	35,818	35,944	33,696
Value	*	25,578	25,411	*	2,621	2,450
P'albong-ni						
Plots	*	86	96	*	147	137
Area	*	126,754	117,401	*	42,084	53,440
Value	*	24,778	22,695	*	3,538	4,089
Se-ri						
Plots	140	276	*	125	397	*
Area	180,907	395,074	*	75,547	322,516	*
Value	*	*	*	*	*	*
Total for all Villages						
Plots	666	859	640	614	1,086	733
Area	627,324	1,006,347	601,472	260,840	634,168	371,965
Value	*	102,039	100,074	*	27,219	29,635

* Figures not available
Note: Area measured in p'yŏng (one p'yŏng equals 35 square feet)
SOURCE: Kwangmu *yang'an* and *t'oji taejang*

Suwŏn and Seoul and its location within Kyŏnggi province and on the main north-south road, Se-ri was greatly influenced by political and economic developments in and around Korea's capital.

At the end of the Yi dynasty much of Se-ri's agricultural land, as in most villages in Kyŏnggi province, was controlled by various government agencies and royal family members. According to the *Kwajŏnbŏp*, a land distribution system established at the beginning of the Yi dynasty, the central government assigned certain plots of agricultural land to provide produce to support these agencies and individuals. The land was not owned by individual bureaucrats; instead, it remained in the name of the agency so that it might sustain succeeding officials and agency operations. This system enabled Korea to finance the government and prevent the growth of regional bases of economic power among government officials. Although this land was originally located only in Kyŏnggi province, additional land in other provinces was designated as "agency land" or "palace land" as the needs of the government increased and as the central government became powerless to stop individuals from abusing the

RESIDENTIAL			OTHER			TOTAL LAND IN VILLAGES		
1900	1914	1941	1900	1914	1941	1900	1914	1941
90	51	77	*	32	193	485	534	806
11,309	14,427	20,868	*	47,043	51,732	305,031	465,409	509,237
*	2,197	3,247	*	3,330	1	*	61,289	61,154
95	64	74	*	22	48	413	394	435
6,850	11,648	13,407	*	18,063	36,966	146,542	195,205	233,598
*	1,507	1,746	*	582	904	*	19,070	19,808
70	64	61	*	7	28	372	351	380
9,356	9,644	8,949	*	8,840	8,894	207,652	203,138	200,577
*	1,147	1,055	*	0	0	*	29,346	28,916
*	72	115	*	10	33	*	315	381
*	7,128	10,673	*	4,554	22,457	*	180,520	203,971
*	972	1,522	*	16	16	*	29,304	28,322
25	67	*	*	58	*	290	798	*
1,745	22,087	*	*	100,820	*	258,199	840,497	*
*	*	*	*	*	*	*	*	*
280	318	327	*	129	302	1,560	2,392	2,002
29,260	64,934	53,897	*	179,320	120,049	917,424	1,884,769	1,147,383
*	5,823	7,570	*	3,928	921	*	139,009	138,200

system by refusing to give up control after leaving the government. The agencies and royal family members frequently determined who cultivated their fields, sending representatives to oversee tenants and collect the rent, which was paid in kind. Hence, it is not surprising that Se-ri's agriculture became intimately linked with urban economics and politics.

The arrival of Japanese colonists in the first decade of the twentieth century reinforced Se-ri's integration into a larger economic system. Following the Russo-Japanese War (1904–1905) and Japan's establishment of a protectorate government, Japanese administrators recognized the agricultural value of the Suwŏn area and placed its experimental farm and agricultural school just north of the city.[21] The Suwŏn area was attractive because it was close to Seoul and had access to ample amounts of natural water, and because much of the land in the area was registered under a government agency or by members of the royal family.

Japanese individuals also acquired large amounts of Se-ri's land early in the colonial years. Although all *taejang* and *tŭnggibu* from the Suwŏn area were destroyed in the Korean War, the original worksheets from which the *taejang* were compiled still exist. These worksheets clearly reveal that Se-ri continued to be dominated by Japanese and Korean institutions and individuals in Seoul during the colonial period.

Physically, Se-ri was well suited to rice cultivation. In addition to being relatively free of hills, the village had an excellent supply of water from small lakes and streams. Transporting produce to markets in Suwŏn and Seoul was convenient even in 1900 and became more so with the completion of the Seoul-Pusan railroad line, which included a station in Suwŏn. Today the fields have been replaced by city streets and buildings, and what was once Se-ri is a short subway ride from downtown Seoul.

As shown in Table 1-1, the total area and the number of landowners in the villages were quite large. The total combined cultivated land area in the villages for which *yang'an* data are available was about 890,000 *p'yŏng* (about 735 acres), or about 90 percent of all land in those villages. When accurately measured in 1914, the total cultivated land area differed only slightly from the area recorded earlier, strongly suggesting that the *yang'an* statistics are more reliable than previously believed. Of the total land in the villages' *yang'an*, approximately 60 percent was paddy land and 30 percent was upland, with the remaining 10 percent consisting of residential, forest, cemetery, or other land.

By the final years of the colonial period total arable land had increased 7.9 percent over the 1914 total, the result of cultivating land that had earlier been of marginal agricultural value. Curiously, the area of paddy land actually decreased during the period as land that was not suitable for rice cultivation was converted to cash crop production for new urban and overseas markets. The increase in upland area was accompanied by a large increase in field number in each land category, reflecting the ever-decreasing size of the farms worked by Korean farmers.

Over the course of the forty-year period covered in this study, many individuals owned land in the villages described. Very few parcels of land remained in the same owner's hands throughout the entire period; most changed hands several times. Over 1,750 different individuals (110 of whom were Japanese) and corporations owned land in the villages at some point during the period. How the 1 to 2 million *p'yŏng* of land within the villages were divided among these 1,750 individuals and corporations is a much debated question that will be examined shortly. First we must examine Yi dynasty landownership to begin to clarify this debate.

CHAPTER 2

LEGACY OF THE PAST: RECORDS OF THE LAST YI DYNASTY CADASTRAL SURVEY

On June 22, 1898, the Korean Council of State hastily convened to discuss an urgent proposal drafted by the heads of the Ministry of the Interior and the combined Ministry of Agriculture-Commerce-Industry. Korea's economy was a shambles and many industries were contracted to foreign corporations and governments under threat of force. The ministries' joint proposal argued strongly for the implementation of a nationwide cadastral survey as a desperate measure to prevent national insolvency. In addition, the authors of the proposal questioned how Korea could become a modern state with a reformed government *(chŏngch'i yusin)* if it did not have a system of standard measurements of land area and distance, an important proposed by-product of the survey.

Within days of receiving this proposal, the Council of State, heeding the advice of the two ministries, created the Yangji amun (Bureau of Land Survey) to undertake the monumental and expensive task of surveying the entire Korean peninsula. Only the dire straits of the Korean government's financial situation could justify such an undertaking. Indeed, the primary purpose of this survey was to increase central government tax revenue by identifying untaxed and undertaxed land, accurately appraising the value of all land, and recording the name of the current owner-taxpayer. Taxes could be fairly assessed and collected only after the chaos of the Yi dynasty land registration system was corrected. This chaos resulted in part from conducting infrequent surveys despite the Yi dynasty mandate that such surveys be conducted every twenty years—or approximately one survey per generation.

Reflecting the importance placed on this endeavor by the Korean Council of State, the Yangji amun was headed by the ministers of the

interior, treasury, and combined agriculture-commerce-industry.[1] The
survey bureau's top-level staff came from among various reform-minded
bureaucrats who had argued for such a cadastral survey for many years,
led by Yi Ki who was responsible for drawing up specific plans for the
survey's implementation.[2] The Yangji amun also sought technical expertise from abroad. Shortly after its creation the amun hired Raymond
Edward Leo Krumm, a civil engineer from Columbus, Ohio, to oversee
the five-year survey project and train Koreans in cadastral surveying
skills.[3] Despite his antipathy toward Japan's control of Korea, ironically
Krumm hired a consultant from Japan who, upon arriving in Korea,
apparently found a better paying job in another government agency and
thus did not participate in the survey.[4] To actually survey the millions of
pieces of land in Korea and record them in the subsequent *yang'an,* the
amun hired a large number of trainees, giving preference to individuals
experienced in foreign language training—either English or Japanese—
on the assumption that they would be more open to new ideas and methods from abroad.

From July 1899, when the order to initiate the survey was issued,
through the following summer, Krumm organized his staff of forty-six
officials and twenty trainees to undertake Korea's first cadastral survey
since 1820.[5] Part of this organizational work involved a test survey of a
small district in Asan-gun in South Ch'ungch'ŏng province conducted
during the summer of 1899. Under the direction of Yi Ki, the reform-
minded Yi dynasty bureaucrat who had argued for such a survey since
the time of the Kabo Reforms[6] of 1894 and who provided technical
expertise on new survey techniques, the experimental survey proved successful.[7] As a result, the Yangji amun proceeded to survey much of the
peninsula's agricultural land during the next three years, halting in 1902,
when funds ran out.

The registers compiled after this survey, the Kwangmu *yang'an,* con-
tribute greatly to our understanding of late nineteenth-century landownership in Korea. They illuminate patterns of tenancy, absentee landownership, and land distribution in rural Korean villages at the turn of
the twentieth century. The Kwangmu *yang'an* demonstrate convincingly
that many land tenure patterns, thought to have been established by or to
have emerged from colonial land policies, have roots in rural economic
changes already underway in the late Yi dynasty. Indeed, it was these
very changes, particularly those affecting tax revenues, that generated
the urgency with which the Kwangmu survey was launched.

By 1898 many officials in the Korean government recognized that
Korea's land registration and taxation systems needed drastic overhaul-
ing. Those who originally advocated and eventually implemented the
survey correctly perceived that national revenue was insufficient to

undertake the institutional and social reforms they felt were required for Korea to become a modern state. As seen by these reformers, Korea's tax revenue shortage was due to both the dwindling amount of land registered as taxable on the *yang'an* and the undervaluation of even the recorded parcels. In short, the Kwangmu survey was a vital and desperate effort to provide the central government with adequate revenue for its operations.[8]

Pre-Kwangmu Land Registration Reform Efforts

Although the chief impetus for the Kwangmu survey was the government's financial crisis in the late 1890s, Koreans in and out of government had discussed the need for a new and accurate land survey since the seventeenth and nineteenth centuries.[9] While most scholars and officials advocated simply updating the current *yang'an,* other scholars of the *sirhak* (Practical Learning) school, already had proposed in the seventeenth century nationalizing all land in Korea and redistributing it to all farmers equally.[10] An early nineteenth-century proposal had even called for eliminating private ownership altogether and replacing it with communal ownership.[11] These radical proposals, though worded in terms of reestablishing ideal Chinese land tenure systems, found few sympathetic adherents in the Korean government.[12] None were acted on.

Following widespread peasant uprisings throughout the Korean peninsula in 1862, discussions of the need for change in Korea's land registry system took on an added urgency. Most reformers, however, favored simply altering the surveying process and opposed any major change in the landownership system. Problems with the taxation system were due to a corrupt ownership registration system, not to any fault in the distribution of land among farmers. Reformers felt that if an accurate cadastral survey could be undertaken, the tax burden would be more equitably distributed and the central government would increase tax revenue.[13]

Reform-minded scholars consistently criticized the *yang'an* because they simply recorded the size and productivity of plots, not clarifying the spatial relationship between various plots. The location of a person's land was not identified. Understandably, as a result numerous cases of boundary confusion and dispute arose throughout the Yi dynasty. To eliminate this inadequacy in the *yang'an,* most reformers advocated using the Chinese "fish scale" system.[14] This system, deriving its name from the scale-like pattern of plots drawn on a cadastral map, provided a clear boundary demarcation of individually owned pieces of land as well as cadastral maps depicting these boundaries, and the shape of each plot.

Also criticized was the common practice of "hiding" land; that is, not registering land in the *yang'an* in order to avoid taxation.[15] Individuals with financial means and/or political influence hid their landholdings by bribing local officials responsible for compilation and custody of the *yang'an*. These officials either omitted plots from the *yang'an* or, more frequently, registered the plots under a tax-exempt category (for example, as damaged due to natural disaster). Although it is difficult to estimate the amount of land hidden in this manner, as much as one-fifth to one-fourth of Korea's arable land may have been kept off the tax rolls in the latter years of the Yi dynasty. Revelations of this hidden land during the cadastral survey of the colonial period accounted for most of the large increase in registered arable land between 1910 and 1918.[16]

In addition to not registering land, owners were frequently criticized by reformers for registering land on the *yang'an* at less than its actual productivity. Traditionally, the Korean government assessed land by its productivity and area, a system established in the fifteenth century to make tax assessments more equitable.[17] Without accurate and periodic appraisal of this productivity, however, the system was extremely vulnerable to corruption. Registration of land at a lower grade meant a significantly reduced tax assessment. In noting this problem, many reformers suggested replacing the progressive tax assessment system with one that computed taxes simply on the basis of farm size, a "reform" that would obviously favor individuals owning higher quality land.

Based on the amount of attention Yi dynasty reformers have given this practice, one must conclude that fraudulent registration of agricultural land as "fallow" or "wasteland" on the *yang'an* was common.[18] Designed to stimulate redevelopment of land harmed by floods, drought, and other natural causes, such registration exempted the owner from taxation for a number of years or reduced the amount of tax to a minimum level. During the late nineteenth century large amounts of land had in fact been laid to waste by warfare or natural calamity, and its classification as "fallow" gave needed tax relief to many owners. However, this land tended to remain tax exempt long after its recultivation (particularly land owned by influential members of society), further limiting the central government's sources of tax revenue.

Korea's various royal family members and their relatives by marriage also abused the *yang'an* registration system by increasingly concentrating tax-exempt land in their own hands. Princes, royal concubines and their sons, princesses, and all other immediate royal relatives received income from specific parcels of agricultural land, registered on the *yang-an* as *kungbangjŏn*.[19] Although designed to provide a living stipend for these royal family members only during their lifetime, these *kungbangjŏn* designations were carefully guarded and remained in the control of the descendants even decades later, despite their no longer being closely related to the royal family. In addition, the various royal palaces increased their landholdings over the centuries through purchases, additional royal grants, commendations by small-scale landowners wishing to avoid taxation, and by outright expropriation. Throughout the latter centuries of the Yi dynasty reformers consistently proposed limiting the amount of land registered in the name of royal family members as a means of increasing state revenue. None advocated eliminating such royal land grants, however, in deference to the royal institution itself and to the political power of its members.

As increasing amounts of land came to be underregistered or removed from the tax rolls altogether, the tax burden fell heavier on tax-paying landowners, who responded by the thousands in the uprisings of 1862 throughout the Korean peninsula. In response to this rural discontent the Korean government issued a series of decrees ordering new cadastral surveys in various parts of the peninsula to correct registration abuses and ameliorate peasant conditions. Few of these decrees were actually enacted, however, partly due to the government officials' reluctance to alter the status quo of a registration system in which they had a vested interest.

Unexpectedly, some reformers resisted the new surveys, fearing they would result not in heightened accuracy, but in even more land taken off the tax rolls through bribery and falsification of the *yang'an*. Consequently, these reformers advocated radical changes in the registration system.[20]

During the rule of the Taewŏn'gun (1864–1873) the Korean government initiated measures to restore central government control over land owned by royal family members.[21] During this same period the Korean government also attempted to identify "hidden *kyŏl*" and to reevaluate land that had been improperly classified as fallow.[22] The extent to which these measures caused increased tax revenue is uncertain. Further, the success attained was at least partially offset by the withdrawal of additional land from the tax rolls during the last years of the nineteenth century. For example, in 1896 King Kojong designated specific plots of land to support his new wife, Lady Ŏm, and in 1899 set aside additional land for the crown prince totaling several hundred acres altogether.[23]

Natural calamities also set back the government's efforts to increase tax revenue. Two consecutive years of bad harvests caused by early frost and flooding in 1876 and 1877 led the government to classify increased amounts of land as fallow on the *yang'an,* exempting the land from taxation for a number of years. The damage to cultivated land was reportedly so severe that Kojong dispatched spies to each of the affected provinces to report on its extent. The spies reported that, while damage was indeed extensive, wealthy landowners had improperly taken advantage of the situation and withdrawn undamaged land from the *yang'an* as well.

They recommended that the government undertake a new cadastral survey to recover such land.[24] Other disastrous harvests occurred in 1888 and 1890, leaving so much land uncultivated that the government sent equal-field officers to the various provinces to see that fallow land was brought back into cultivation—and thereby be taxable—as soon as possible.[25]

These natural calamities, coupled with ineffective government action on the proposed reforms, intensified the debates over Korea's land policy. With a greater sense of urgency, many reformers felt that simply rectifying the classification of land on the existing *yang'an* would no longer suffice. Some, such as Yu Kil-jun in 1891, suggested that a completely new registration system was required to bring the nation back to financial solvency and at the same time "rescue our destitute farmers."[26] Yu advocated not only undertaking a new cadastral survey, but also changing the units of measure—issuing land deeds so that ownership would be clear even after the *yang'an* was out of date—and creating cadastral maps for the entire country detailing boundaries for each plot of land. Although most of these points were later incorporated into the Kwangmu cadastral reforms, they were too radical for implementation in 1891 and went unheeded.

Not surprisingly, unabated and unreasonable tax assessments and local government corruption culminated in the peasant rebellion of early 1894. Government officials sent to rural areas to inspect the situation during the uprising noted that tax collection had in fact continued in areas that had not yet been brought back into cultivation.[27] Other farmer grievances included corruption of the productivity grade system, boundary encroachments by large landowners, and abuse of political and economic power by county magistrates and *myŏn-jang* (subcountry administrators).[28]

Increased urgency over a new cadastral survey policy swept the highest echelons of government in Seoul in 1894–1895 as Tonghak warfare broke out throughout southern Korea. Proponents of change found the reform-minded government established in the summer of 1894 receptive to changes in the taxation system and financial administration. Although the reform government did not include a new cadastral survey in its many reforms, it did address problems in Korea's land registration system. In March 1895 the head of the newly created Ministry of the Interior issued a decree ordering that the names of owners and cultivators and the amount of paddy land and upland owned throughout the county be investigated and recorded on local land registers.[29] However, the fall of the reform government and the exile in 1896 of Pak Yŏng-hyo, interior minister and early supporter of a new cadastral survey, delayed implementation of these changes.

Although early advocates of a new cadastral survey came from the supporters of Western reforms, they were joined in 1895 by individuals opposed to Korea's growing economic dependence on Japan. Following negotiations in March 1895 between Korea and Japan for a three million yen loan to finance the proposed reforms, these individuals opposed the terms of the loan agreement on the grounds that they were potentially detrimental to Korea's financial well being. One opponent was Yi Ki, who was particularly concerned that the Korean government had agreed to use the national land tax revenue as collateral to guarantee the loan's repayment in case revenues from import duties were insufficient.[30] He argued that the reforms should be financed through domestic Korean capital resources and that these funds should come from increased tax revenue generated by a new cadastral survey. Yi was so incensed that he presented his survey ideas in a formal proposal to Ŏ Yun-jung, the minister of finance who had negotiated the Japanese loan on behalf of the Korean government.

In his proposal entitled "Absurd Thoughts on the Land System," Yi criticized those who advocated implementing the legendary Chinese "well-field" land system, calling it unrealistic and impractical.[31] Feeling that any attempt to limit the maximum amount of land an individual could own was doomed to fail due to the power and influence of large landowning scholar-officials, Yi strongly believed that Korea's revenue problems could be solved easily with a new cadastral survey. He was convinced, however, that survey and registration procedures had to be reformed to minimize corruption and clarify ownership of individual land parcels.

To lessen the chances of corruption Yi suggested that the productivity assessment units be changed. Rather than use only the officially determined and highly subjective *kyŏl-bu* tax assessment system, which Yi claimed farmers neither used nor understood, he also proposed that land area be registered using the traditional Korean productivity measurement of *turak*.[32] Farmers, he argued, would then be able to determine whether the assigned value was in accordance with farming reality. As another measure to minimize official corruption, Yi advocated recording the names of the surveyor and local officials on the *yang'an* and that they be held accountable for its accuracy.

Yi suggested procedural changes in the registration system to minimize ownership questions and disputes. In order to clarify boundaries and location of individual plots within a village, Yi called for drawings of fish scale pictures of all fields during the survey and for inclusion of these pictures on the *yang'an* with data on ownership and area. Yi felt that to record the owner and the cultivator of each plot would also help clarify ownership and accountability. Finally, Yi proposed that local government officials issue bills of sale whenever a piece of land was sold. He believed this would help clarify ownership in cases of landownership changes after compilation of the *yang'an*.[33] Yi also perceived that it would enable the government to more closely scrutinize land transactions for possible corruption by powerful landowners. Most of Yi Ki's proposals for specific changes were incorporated later into the Kwangmu cadastral survey, but political events between 1895 and 1898 dimmed hopes for immediate reform.

During these years economic and political reforms became deeply embroiled in the rivalry between Japan and Imperial Russia for dominance in Northeast Asia. As the two powers sought alliances with Koreans in and out of government, they inevitably involved themselves in domestic Korean politics, seeking to influence Korean policies toward the reform movement. For example, the Japanese minister and other officials, as well as representatives of other governments, actively supported and even directed many of the reforms implemented during the year of reform cabinet rule.[34] With each power attempting to install individual Korean reformers in positions of authority in hopes of gaining the allegiance of the Korean government, the reform movement itself lost considerable credibility.

On October 8, 1895, Japanese soldiers and legation officials killed Queen Min, sparking domestic and international protests against Japanese excesses in Korea. The targets of criticism within Korea, however, were not only Japanese officials, but also reform-minded Koreans thought to be pro-Japanese. When, soon after the Queen's death, the Japanese-supported reformers ordered that all Korean men cut off their topknots in accordance with Western (and modern Japanese) custom, anti-Japanese fervor was heightened,[35] and public response to the order —announced on January 1, 1896, according to the newly adopted Western calendar—was quick and decisive. Koreans throughout the peninsula opposed the order, Tonghak rebels attacked government offices and soldiers, and demonstrations broke out in Seoul and other urban areas. In the midst of this nationwide crisis, King Kojong, fearing for his life, secretly fled his palace on the night of February 11 and took up residence for the next year at the Russian embassy. The reform cabinet under Prime Minister Kim Hong-jip (1842–1896) was forced to resign the same day. Shortly thereafter he and former finance minister Ŏ Yun-jung were assassinated by anti-Japanese elements. Yu Kil-jun and Pak Yŏng-hyo, both supporters of the new cadastral survey in the reform government, fled to Japan for safety.

Because the social and political changes advocated by the cabinet under Kim Hong-jip had been associated with Japan, many were discredited and some discarded.[36] The succeeding conservative government, however, soon realized that in the face of tremendous financial difficulties some financial and technological reform was imperative if it were to function.[37] Turning to Western powers for assistance, the government hired many foreign advisors, mainly from Europe and the United States, to provide technical and financial expertise. In an effort to increase its revenue, the government awarded economic concessions to foreign companies, particularly Russian and American, to develop Korea's natural resources.[38]

Many of the reforms that had been shelved earlier were suddenly revived by the conservative government between 1897–1898. For example, proposals emerged from low-level government officials advocating a new cadastral survey to correct the abuses in the land registration and taxation systems—as if they were discovering for the first time what Yi Ki and others had been pointing out for decades.[39]

Outside of government, the newly established Independence Association (Tongnip hyŏphoe), led by reform-minded intellectuals educated abroad, became a major lobbying force for social, political, and economic change on the peninsula. Through its newspaper, the *Tongnip sinmun*, printed in both Korean and English, the association pressed for reforms but at the same time sharply criticized the Korean government's reliance on foreign capital and capitalists to finance and direct these reforms.[40] In May 1897, as part of its reform platform, the association called for new cadastral and population surveys to serve as the basis for Korean financial reform and increased tax revenue. Articles in the *Tongnip sinmun* called specifically for the government to reveal and register all "hidden kyŏl," abolish taxes on fallow land and thereby equalize the tax burden, increase national income by increasing the area under cultivation, and institute long-range economic planning.[41]

By 1898 the idea of a new cadastral survey had undergone a radical transformation in the minds of Korea's educated citizenry: The proposal was no longer considered an externally (Japanese) imposed threat to tradition, but rather a means by which Korea could establish financial independence from foreign powers. In addition to insuring economic solvency, some individuals hoped that a survey could identify and prevent illegal Japanese land acquisitions outside the 10 *ri* (approximately 3.3 miles) distance from the five consular ports proscribed by treaty. Korean farmers would thereby be protected.[42] The cadastral survey was by general consensus—both in and out of government—defined in terms of national interest and nationalism.

Acting on this consensus, the Korean government announced plans in June 1898 to establish the Land Survey Bureau (Yangji amun) and undertake a nationwide cadastral survey. This announcement was followed later the same month by the formal proposal to the Council of State (cited at the outset of this chapter), which shortly thereafter gave its approval for the establishment of the cabinet-level Land Survey Bureau to oversee Korea's first nationwide cadastral survey since 1720.

As noted earlier, following an experimental survey in South Ch'ung-ch'ŏng province in July 1898, Raymond Krumm and his Korean technical staff initiated the survey of Korea's provinces the following summer, a project estimated to extend over five years. The survey was well funded by the central government through 1901, revealing the high priority placed on the project. The national budget for that year included almost $130,000 for survey operations, one of the largest budget line items, with approximately $100,000 allocated for field survey work.[43]

Amidst a generally upbeat optimism toward the prospects of national solvency in 1901—buoyed by a favorable balance of trade and a record rice production and tax revenue the preceding year—the foreign community in Korea noted the benefits gained thus far from the ongoing survey and anticipated further positive results upon its completion. Homer Hulbert, an influential and longtime American resident of Korea, commented that the survey had cost the government under $200,000 by the fall of 1901 and yet had enabled the government to increase tax collection by $782,709, thereby showing "that the surveys were a paying investment."[44]

This optimism and enthusiasm was short-lived, however, as the Korean economy faltered in late 1901 and 1902. Due to a severe drought, only a fraction of the rice crop could be harvested in the fall of 1901, reducing significantly the revenue from the land tax and impoverishing many rural areas throughout the Korean peninsula. The national government was forced to curtail most of its funding for the survey project, allocating only $8,000 for field survey operations in 1902.[45] Even more damaging to the survey, county governments, which bore all costs of the survey teams while they were in each county, could no longer afford to assess local landowners to cover these survey-related expenses.[46] As a result of the ruinous harvests, throughout late 1901 and into 1902 local officials petitioned the government to halt the survey. In August 1901, for example, the county magistrate from Ch'ŏngju reported that he had been unable to collect enough to pay for the survey in his county.[47] Although the government subsequently cut the magistrate's salary in half for delivering such bad news, it had no choice, faced with its own financial crisis, but to grant these petitions.

By December 1901 most field surveying had come to a dramatic halt, and the remaining resources were used to compile the *yang'an* and draw up deeds to distribute to landowners.[48] This administrative and record-keeping work limped along for another year and a half, but little actual field surveying occurred after January 1902.[49]

The Kwangmu cadastral survey had come to an end. During its existence 124 counties—out of a total of 331—were either completely or partially surveyed.[50] Since counties in mountainous and isolated areas with little agricultural land were not investigated, more of Korea's agricultural area was actually surveyed than these figures suggest.[51]

The existing Kwangmu *yang'an* provide valuable data on the nature of Korean land tenure at the turn of the twentieth century, prior to the establishment of Japanese colonial legal and administrative changes. They provide the analytical basis from which to initiate a study of the colonial period. Statistical data in the *yang'an* will show that many of the Korean land-tenure characteristics thought to have originated under Japanese colonial rule actually had roots in the Yi dynasty.

A great deal has been written about Yi dynasty land tenure over the past decades, principally by Korean and Japanese historians. Until recently, however, most of this historiography has been based on Yi dynasty law codes and official court records of memorials directed at the Korean throne. These studies help to clarify Yi dynasty law regarding landownership and tenure by focusing criticism on the Korean land-distribution system for allowing poverty among farmers and for failure to live up to the concepts of legendary Chinese land tenure systems—usually equal-field or well-field. There is little question that the Korean government and people felt these ideal models provided the standards by which the Korean tenure system should be judged. Many scholars, however, fail to go beyond an analysis of the standards to determine their validity in light of Korean reality. Only in recent years have scholars looked beyond official decrees and memorials to the wealth of *yang'an* and other primary land records available.[52]

Yi Dynasty Landownership System

It is not within the scope of this study to provide a definitive statement on land tenure in Korea at the beginning of the Yi dynasty, much less on its development during the dynasty's five hundred year history. The focus here is on landownership patterns existing in Korea at the end of the dynasty—the start of the twentieth century—and changes in them during the subsequent colonial period. However, as these patterns were a legacy of earlier periods in the dynasty, they must be evaluated in part within the context of Yi dynasty land tenure in general. Thus, by necessity the premodern origins of late nineteenth-century landownership institutions must be examined.

In 1900, at the time of the Kwangmu cadastral survey, three main categories of landownership appeared in the *yang'an:* ownership by private individuals—comprising the bulk of all agricultural land in the country;

ownership by royal family palaces and institutions, often benefiting specific royal relatives; and ownership by agencies of both the central government in Seoul and local government in the region of the land owned.
In addition, a certain amount of land reportedly lay fallow, its ownership
and revenue status unclear due to long periods of noncultivation.

CONCEPTS AND PRACTICE OF PRIVATE LANDOWNERSHIP
IN THE LATE YI DYNASTY

Throughout the Yi dynasty private landownership was the predominant form of ownership and was already legally recognized for most
types of land in the early fifteenth century. An official prohibition against
the sale of land by individuals, included in the 1391 land reform *(kwajŏnbŏp)*, devised by Cho Chun and Yi Sŏng-gye, was lifted in 1424.[53]
This ruling followed royal approval of a memorial to the throne by the
governor of Kyŏnggi province that noted the hardships of the prohibition
on small-scale farmers and requested that transfer of ownership be
allowed.[54] This de jure recognition of private ownership permitted farmers to keep land within the family from one generation to the next, providing security from capricious government officials who might demand
land back to redistribute to another family whose cultivator died.

Later, the 1469 Yi dynasty law code, the *Kyŏngguk taejŏn,* formally
specified procedures for inheritance of privately owned land and for settlement of ownership disputes. The *Kyŏngguk taejŏn* also detailed the
process for buying and selling privately owned land: "In the sale of arable
or residential land [either party] has fifteen days in which to change his
mind and one hundred days within which to report the sale to the government and receive a certificate of sale. The same holds true for [the sale
of] slaves."[55] By requiring registration of each land purchase, the government hoped to control and limit such sales. This process soon became a
mere formality, however, as landowners throughout the dynasty bought
and sold land and other property openly without notifying the government or receiving certificates of sale.

The late fourteenth-century land reform, the *kwajŏnbŏp,* included a
multitiered taxation system with numerous classifications of privately
owned land, differing principally in the method of tax payments. Under
this system the producer, rather than the recipient of rent taxes, maintained ultimate disposition rights over the land, determined who would
cultivate it, and decided which crops would be grown. According to the
kwajŏnbŏp system, a landowner paid taxes to one of a variety of government and nongovernment institutions and individuals, depending on the
yang'an classification of the land owned. Most owners paid rent taxes
(se) directly to the central government. Many others paid taxes *(cho)* to a
specific individual, royal palace, monastery, or government agency that

had been granted tax collection rights *(sujogwŏn)*. These individuals and institutions, therefore, received stipends directly from the producers, usually in kind, rather than from the central government. In most cases, the government granted *sujogwŏn* for a predetermined number of generations, after which the right was granted to another individual or institution.[56] The rate of taxation differed depending on the type of recipient. Payments of *cho* to individuals and palaces averaged 50 percent of the crop, whereas *se* amounted to approximately 10 to 20 percent.

The *kwajŏnbŏp,* designed to provide stipends in kind for government bureaucrats in office and finance normal governmental operations, broke down during the economic and social dislocation after the Hideyoshi invasions of the late sixteenth century.[57] During this period the Korean government lacked the authority to enforce the redistribution of *sujogwŏn*. Rather than having a term limitation, this right to collect taxes directly from the producers remained permanently in the hands of numerous individuals and institutions. This new relationship between *sujogwŏn* holder and the land became institutionalized through registration on the *yang'an,* depriving the central government of available land to either tax directly or to use to support new government agencies and royal family members.

By implication, this turned the *sujogwŏn* holder into the equivalent of an owner. *Cho* payments became part of a complex system of tenancy rents. As generations and even centuries passed, this land came to be seen as the personal property of the individual or institution registered on the *yang'an;* it had become, for all intents and purposes, privately owned land. Between the seventeenth and twentieth centuries these new landowners, many of whom were absentee landlords living in Seoul, increased their holdings through additional government grants, purchases, fraudulent registration on the *yang'an,* and by commendation. By the end of the dynasty their total holdings were extensive in certain regions of the peninsula, as is evident from the Kwangmu *yang'an,* and as we have seen these holdings were the object of many attempts to reassert central government control over such land.

Individuals and institutions established legal ownership over land through a complex and irregular system of cadastres and land records in the the owner's possession. Landowners used the *yang'an* as the principal document to substantiate claims of ownership. While in theory the Korean government updated the *yang'an* through cadastral surveys conducted every twenty years, such surveys were expensive and seldom undertaken.[58] Even when the government initiated a new survey, it rarely extended over all of the three southern provinces—the core agricultural areas—but was limited to scattered sections of the peninsula. In the last three hundred years of the Yi dynasty, the Korean government undertook only four major cadastral surveys in 1663–1669, 1718–1720, 1820, and 1898–1903.

In order to compile a new *yang'an* at the time of each cadastral survey, the previous *yang'an* was the primary source from which to begin.[59] However, several generations and sometimes an entire century had elapsed since the compilation of the previous *yang'an*. In such cases ownership was established based on land records in the possession of the owner or multiple claimants. The individual possessing the most complete and accurate collection of certificates of sale and other land documents (known generically as *mun'gi*) dating back to the previous *yang'an* was awarded ownership recognition.[60] Each piece of land had its own bundle of *mun'gi*, which were literally tied up and passed from one owner to the next. If a complete set of *mun'gi* was not available, having been lost or destroyed, multiple claimants to landownership could settle their dispute by securing the testimony of landowners on each side of the land in question. The government then arbitrated the dispute. Thus, in addition to having codified legal recognition of private ownership, Korea developed a body of judicial decisions that strongly reflects the wide acceptance of the private ownership concept in daily life.[61]

Throughout the latter half of the Yi dynasty, private landowners owned the bulk of agricultural land in Korea. Kim Yong-sŏp found minimal amounts of land registered in the names of government agencies and palaces in his study of eighteenth-century *yang'an*.[62] This was particularly true outside of Kyŏnggi province. Figures from the early nineteenth century show that approximately 75 percent of the total registered land was in private hands, though much was registered as fallow or wasteland.[63] During the rule of the Taewŏn'gun (1864–1873), private individuals also owned a similarly high percentage of the total registered land.[64] In short, not only was private landownership legally recognized throughout the Yi dynasty, it was also a widely accepted principle and practice.

ROYAL PALACE OWNERSHIP

Throughout the Yi dynasty the Korean government designated certain agricultural land for the support of institutions such as temples, private academies, and royal palaces. The taxes *(cho)* from this land were remitted directly to the institutions by their local agents *(tojang)* or by the cultivator directly. *Kungbangjŏn,* or land set aside to support royal palaces, played a critical role in landownership in Kyŏnggi and two other provinces close to Seoul, Ch'ungch'ŏng and Hwanghae.[65] The *cho* from *kungbangjŏn* supported the many royal family members and the families of the royal concubines, many of whom received a palace name in which the land was subsequently registered.

Although government *kungbangjŏn* designations were of modest size at the beginning of the dynasty, palaces expanded their holdings considerably following the devastation of the Hideyoshi invasions (1592–1598) and Manchu attacks (1627 and 1636). By laying claim to and developing land abandoned during the warfare, the palaces were able to significantly increase acreage registered in their names.[66] Like other institutions, palaces did not receive outright ownership but actually received tax collection rights *(sujogwŏn)* for a period of time determined by the central government. However, over time they became the de facto owners of *kungbangjŏn* and collected tenancy rent from cultivators as other landlords did. By the late nineteenth century the Korean government recognized this de facto ownership and registered the palaces as the "current owner" *(siju)* on the Kwangmu *yang'an.*

Kungbangjŏn, like other land that deprived the central government of tax revenues, became the target of reform efforts late in the dynasty. During his reign, the Taewŏn'gun attempted to convert some of this land to privately owned status and tax it. Through his efforts in the 1860s and 1870s, he hoped to strip the palaces of their independent sources of income and replace their *cho* revenue with stipends from the central government. This bid to separate the royal family members from their financial independence achieved only limited success in the face of strong opposition from powerful individuals.[67]

Reformers made a similar effort in 1894 during the Kabo Reforms. The reform government under Kim Hong-jip attempted to place all royal household affairs, including financial support of numerous royal family members, under the newly created royal household ministry, the Kungnaebu—an effort apparently modeled after the establishment of the Kunaichō in Japan.[68] Although the palaces were to remain owners of their lands (a testimonial to their political power), they would be required to pay taxes on them to the central government. The Kungnaebu would then supply the household members with a living stipend, making them dependent on the government. This proposal, like the efforts of the Taewŏn'gun, met with little success. On the whole, royal household finances, including administration of the *kungbangjŏn,* remained in the hands of the various palaces until 1907 when the Japanese-controlled Korean imperial government stripped them of their land, part of a much larger process to reform and control the Korean economy.

At the turn of the century *kungbangjŏn* was registered in the names of seven large palaces (ch'ilgung), other smaller palaces, and the royal treasury (Naesusa).[69] Each province contained a certain amount of *kungbangjŏn* in 1900, but most of this land was concentrated in areas near Seoul. Although three of the research villages contained no *kungbangjŏn,* Se-ri and other villages near Suwŏn possessed a great deal. *Kungbangjŏn* in Se-ri totaled 26,977 *p'yŏng* of arable land, almost 10 percent of the village total in 1903.

GOVERNMENT OWNERSHIP

Government agencies, both national and local, owned tax-exempt land throughout the Korean peninsula at the turn of the century, but as with the *kungbangjŏn,* this land was concentrated in Kyŏnggi province. Estimates vary on the total area of government-owned land, but it probably did not exceed 4 to 5 percent of total arable land in Korea. Three of the villages studied from the Kwangmu period contained government land, but only one in any sizable amount. Overall, government land represented 7.7 percent of total arable land in the researched villages, and almost 22 percent of that was in Se-ri.

Government ownership and the forms it took were legacies of the tenure system established at the beginning of the Yi dynasty. Most of the various land categories recorded in the 1391 *kwajŏnbŏp* designated land from which produce was used to support specific government agencies and functions.[70] Similar to *kungbangjŏn,* the producer paid a *cho* payment directly to a particular agency and not to the central government's treasury. These payments provided rice and other commodities for a wide variety of government offices, including local military installations, schools, most bureaucratic agencies in Seoul, and hundreds of other local and national government offices and bureaus. The operations of the royal library (the Kyujanggak) were also supported by *cho* payments received from specifically designated parcels of land scattered throughout the peninsula.[71]

To say that this land was tax-exempt meant that the agency itself was granted the right *(sujogwŏn)* to collect taxes, *cho,* from its land, usually at a rate of approximately one-tenth to one-fifth of the harvested crop. Because the *cho* collected from the cultivators was frequently less than the tax collected by the central government from privately owned land, it was common for individual landowners to commend *(t'utak)* their land to these government institutions. In addition, agencies could and did purchase other agricultural land. Thus, although the Korean government initially designated modest amounts of land to support its various agencies, the agencies themselves steadily increased their holdings during the second half of the dynasty. Because the central government had no central budget or accounting procedures, it was never certain how much *cho* any one agency received beyond the officially designated amount.

During the 1860s and 1870s, the Taewŏn'gun attempted to establish central government control over the independent taxing power of government agencies but had little success. Bureaucrats in the various gov-

ernment agencies with their own vested interests were too well established for this reform to succeed and successfully fought to maintain
their fiscal autonomy. In addition, the central government lacked the
resources to implement a thorough investigation and reform of the land
registration system to determine the location and extent of agency lands.
As a result, most government agencies maintained control and therefore
taxing authority over their lands until 1908, when those lands were
brought under central government control by the Japanese residency-
general.[72]

As Korea neared the end of the nineteenth century, it carried forth a
legacy of a complex landownership situation that combined private ownership with ownership by royal family members and their palaces, and by
government agencies. Individual villages and sections of Korea were a
patchwork of ownership patterns, as will be seen as we examine the data
from the last cadastral survey records of the Yi dynasty.

CHAPTER 3

VILLAGE OWNERSHIP PATTERNS IN 1900: THE KWANGMU *YANG'AN* REVELATIONS

T HE *yang'an* compiled after the 1898–1903 cadastral survey reveal that on the village level in Korea private landownership was predominant, mirroring the national situation in the last years of the dynasty. In the villages examined in Chapter One (Songsan-ni, Paeksŏng-ni and Kongsu-ri in South Ch'ungch'ŏng province, and Se-ri near Suwŏn in Kyŏnggi province), the bulk of village land —a full 88.5 percent of total arable and residential land—was in the hands of private individuals.[1] As shown in Table 3-1, in contrast to the other three villages, the palaces and government agencies in the village near Suwŏn controlled a sizable amount of land, which is not surprising in light of the Kyŏnggi province's role in the early Yi dynasty *kwajŏnbŏp* system.[2]

Private Landownership in the Kwangmu Period

At the turn of the century individual landowners in each of the villages included residents of the villages themselves or of neighboring villages, as well as absentee landlords. Unfortunately, Kwangmu surveyors did not register addresses of nonresidents, making it difficult to determine whether they lived in Seoul, in provincial towns, or in a neighboring county.[3] Nonetheless, it is clear that absentee landownership was commonplace in the final decade of the Yi dynasty. The percentages of arable land owned by residents and nonresidents varied from village to village, as Figure 3-1 indicates, but in each instance nonresidents owned a sizable portion. Nonresident ownership was most pronounced in Se-ri (84 percent of total land) and in Kongsu-ri (over two-thirds), but even in the more isolated villages nonresidents owned over one-third of all arable land.

Individuals registered on the Kwangmu *yang'an* fall into two groups: the *siju* (current owner) and the *sijak* (current cultivator). Among those listed as *siju* were individuals who cultivated their own land, and therefore lacked a *sijak,* and landlords who rented land to others in exchange for rent payments, usually in kind. Further, as Kim Yong-sŏp found in other areas of the peninsula, many individuals cultivated part of their land and rented the remainder to *sijak.*[4] It was not uncommon for a person registered as a *sijak* on a large farm to also own land as a landlord in another part of a village—a phenomenon that Thomas C. Smith found in Tokugawa Japan and ascribed to ongoing changes in fundamental land-ownership and tenancy relationships.[5]

As seen in Tables 3-1 and 3-2, the structure of village landownership in the villages was quite complex and varied significantly from one to the other. In general, owner cultivation prevailed in the isolated villages, Songsan-ni and Paeksŏng-ni, while tenant cultivation *(sijak)* was predominant in the villages closest to urban centers, Kongsu-ri and Se-ri. In Kongsu-ri, for example, landlords owned two-thirds of all paddy land and over one-third of total upland in the village in 1900. Almost half of all paddy land in Se-ri was owned by landlords. If institutional landlords such as the various palaces are included, the percentage is higher still. Paeksŏng-ni contained less land registered in the name of landlords; Songsan-ni had almost none.[6]

In each village a sizable percentage of residents did not own or rent land, presumably working as day laborers or craftsmen. This pool of day laborers demonstrates that a person no longer needed to rent or own land to survive in rural Korea by the turn of the century. As Smith found in Japan, the availability of these day laborers indicates that the value of labor was increasing. Consequently, landowners found it cheaper to hire individuals for short periods of time rather than to lease land in tenancy in exchange for a percentage of the crop.

In the villages a small number of landlords controlled disproportionately large amounts of arable land. Overall the seventy-three individual landlords who did not cultivate their own land represented 17 percent of all registered landowners at the turn of the century but they owned approximately 29 percent of all individually owned arable land. In Kongsu-ri, where landownership was most imbalanced, forty-eight landlords (36 percent of all owners) owned over 57 percent of all privately owned land in the village. Similarly, fourteen landlords in Se-ri (14 percent of all village owners) owned 34 percent of all privately owned land.

Even among these landlords a sharp division existed. Many of them owned only small amounts of arable land in the villages, undoubtedly only part of their total agricultural landholdings throughout the Korean peninsula. Other individuals controlled large percentages of village land.

Table 3-1 Land Distribution in Four Villages ca. 1900 (in *p'yŏng*)

VILLAGE	LANDLORDS	LANDLORD-FARMERS	OWNER-FARMERS
Songsan-ni			
Residents	0	0	53
Land owned			103,992
Land rented			
Nonresidents	0	1	88
Land owned		2,611	86,744
Land rented		0	0
Palace land	0		
Government land	2,039		
Paeksŏng-ni			
Residents	0	7	52
Land owned		22,393	54,979
Land rented			
Nonresidents	11	5	29
Land owned	21,720	11,196	16,199
Land rented			
Palace land			
Government land			
Kongsu-ri			
Residents	2	3	20
Land owned	1,381	19,958	46,833
Land rented		2,566	
Nonresidents	46	3	37
Land owned	149,414	2,510	31,382
Land rented			
Palace land			
Government land	7,540		
Se-ri			
Residents		20	8
Land owned		12,642	22,156
Land rented			
Nonresidents	14	8	39
Land owned	56,335	22,161	32,826
Land rented			
Palace land	26,977		
Government land	60,543		
Totals			
Residents	2	30	133
Land owned	1,381	54,993	227,960
Land rented	0	2,566	0
Nonresidents	71	17	193
Land owned	227,469	38,478	167,151
Land rented	0	0	0
Palace land	26,977	0	0
Government land	70,122	0	0

*Includes 4,029 *p'yŏng* of fallow land
**Includes 24,065 *p'yŏng* of fallow land
SOURCE: Kwangmu *yang'an*

OWNER-TENANTS	PURE TENANTS	LANDLESS	TOTAL
1	0	10	64
2,910	0		106,902
1,229	0		1,229
0	2	0	91
	0		89,355
	2,039		2,039
			0
			2,039
13	7	14	93
9,519	0		86,891
9,585	13,836		23,421
8	12	0	65
3,686			52,801
3,403	6,367		9,770
			0
			0
16	23	27	91
25,940			94,112
40,379	50,921		93,866
8	46	0	140
3,997			187,303
7,954	70,711		78,665
			0
			7,540
5	18	9	60
10,443			45,241
21,828	40,826		62,654
7	25	0	93
9,838			121,160
13,401	39,587		52,988
			26,977 *
			60,543 **
35	48	60	308
48,812	0		333,146
73,021	105,583		181,170
23	85	0	389
17,521	0		450,619
24,758	118,704		143,462
0	0		26,977
0	0		70,122

FIGURE 3–1
Landownership of Village Residents in 1900 by Size of Land Owned

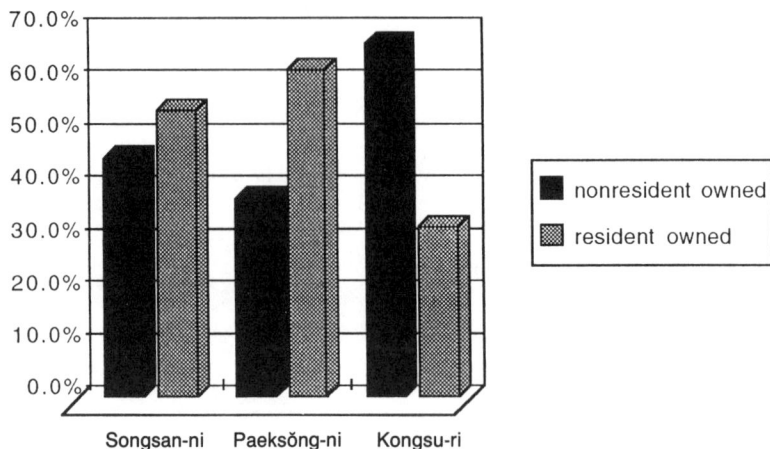

Breakdown of the Village Land Owned by Residents

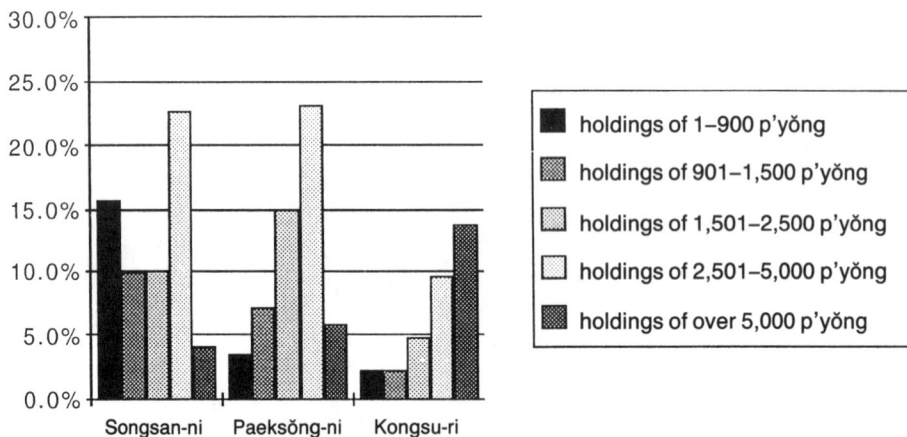

Source: Kwangmu *yang'an*

Table 3-2 Land Distribution among Landlords versus Cultivators (in *p'yŏng*)

VILLAGE	LAND OWNED BY LANDLORDS			LAND OWNED BY CULTIVATORS			TOTAL
	PADDY	UPLAND	HOUSE	PADDY	UPLAND	HOUSE	
Songsan-ni							
No. of plots	1	0	0	195	104	70	370
Area	1,279			159,160	35,818	9,356	205,613
Paeksŏng-ni							
No. of plots	42	30	16	85	161	79	413
Area	26,102	8,745	569	47,700	57,145	6,281	146,542
Kongsu-ri							
No. of plots	113	66	75	80	122*	15	471
Area	135,249	29,742	8,798	67,413	49,011*	2,511	292,724
Se-ri							
No. of plots	45	25	5	51	86	15	227
Area	46,534	9,682	411	53,089	57,096	834	167,646
Totals							
No. of plots	201	121	96	411	473	179	1,481
Area	209,164	48,169	9,778	327,362	199,070	18,982	812,525

*Includes two plots of cemetery land
SOURCE: Kwangmu *yang'an*

For example, of the forty-eight Kongsu-ri landlords mentioned above, seven owned a total of 94,199 *p'yŏng* of cultivated land, over one-third of all arable land in the village. Two of these individuals, Yi Chong-hong and Cho No-mi, owned a total of 45,196 *p'yŏng* of paddy land and 3,709 *p'yŏng* of upland, 17 percent of all village land and 22 percent of village paddy land.[7]

The other villages displayed similar, though not as skewed, land distribution patterns. In Paeksŏng-ni eleven absentee landlords (9 percent of all owners) owned approximately 15 percent of the cultivated land, but among these individuals three large-scale landlords owned most of this land—over 14 percent of the village total. Among the fourteen Se-ri landlords, three individuals controlled over 13 percent of all agricultural land in the village.

At the turn of the century landownership among local residents, whether landlords or owner-cultivators, was also skewed in each of the villages. As seen in Figure 3-1, a small number of individuals in each village owned a disproportionately large share of agricultural land. On the other hand, residents owning no more than 900 *p'yŏng* (less than one acre, but approximately the amount required for subsistence) made up a sizable percentage of village landowners, but they owned a small percentage of total arable land in the village.[8] In Songsan-ni, for example, 20.3 percent of all village residents owned no more than 900 *p'yŏng* each, and these individuals owned only 3.5 percent of village land. In Paeksŏng-ni almost half of all village residents owned no more than 900 *p'yŏng* each; many owned much less. Unable to support themselves with so little land, most undoubtedly rented land from landlords or worked as wage laborers for larger landowners.

Conversely, each village contained a small number of residents who owned relatively large amounts of arable land (over 5,000 *p'yŏng* each). These landowners were most evident in Kongsu-ri, where six landowners, only 6.5 percent of all village residents, owned 39,376 *p'yŏng*, or over 13 percent of all cultivated land in the villages. One of these landowners, Yi Kap-tŭk, owned over 13,000 *p'yŏng*, reportedly cultivating 5,542 *p'yŏng* himself and renting the remainder to local tenants. Interestingly, Yi cultivated another 1,040 *p'yŏng*, which he rented from another landlord. In addition to his arable land, Yi owned eight residential plots, renting seven to other village residents and living on one (the largest) himself. Yi typified the local gentry, who owned a disproportionate percentage of village land in each village.

The isolated villages, Songsan-ni and Paeksŏng-ni, were characterized by a relatively large group of medium-ranking landowners—those owning between 1,500 and 5,000 *p'yŏng*—who dominated local ownership. In Songsan-ni, where land was most equitably distributed, over 42 percent of village residents fell into this group. These twenty-seven residents, all of whom also owned their own homes, owned a total of 75,352 *p'yŏng,* or 38 percent of all cultivated land in the village. In Paeksŏng-ni twenty-two landowners (23.6 percent of all residents) were medium-ranking and owned a total of 45,679 *p'yŏng,* or 32.7 percent of all arable village land. Both villages included several individuals owning large amounts of land, but these landowners were a minority and did not dominate village landownership, as in Kongsu-ri.

Landownership was concentrated among members of several clans in the village, disproportionate to their percentage of the total village population. For example, members of three dominant clans in Songsan-ni owned 86 percent of all arable land owned by village residents.[9] Landowners belonging to ten different clans in the village owned the remaining arable land. Paeksŏng-ni's landowning residents were predominantly members of two clans, the Chŏnju Yi and Ch'ŏngju Han, together owning 76 percent of total arable village land. Members of at least fifteen other clans owned the remaining 24 percent of cultivated land. A similar situation existed in Kongsu-ri and Se-ri, but it was less pronounced because of the small percentage of arable land owned by village residents. Land concentrated in the hands of locally powerful clans continued and even increased during the colonial period.

Each village had a large supply of tenant and wage labor. Landowners with less than subsistence levels of arable land rented additional land from resident and absentee landlords to supplement their income. In addition, a large number of farmers in each village owned no land at all, either renting from landlords or working as wage laborers for village landowners. Overall, 108 residents of the villages, or 37.2 percent of all residents, owned no land. This percentage would probably be higher if others in the villages, living in homes owned by others not registered as the *siju,* were included. As seen in Table 3-1, Kongsu-ri, with its sharp division between owner and tenant, had the highest number of persons registered as living in the village but owning no land.

While each village had a pool of landless laborers, in Kongsu-ri and Se-ri these individuals formed the majority of all village residents—54.9 percent in Kongsu-ri and 59.5 percent in Se-ri. In these two villages absentee landlords owned large amounts of arable land and relied on local laborers to cultivate it. The high rates of tenancy and wage labor in villages like Kongsu-ri and Se-ri strongly suggest the rising value of labor in areas near or influenced by urban economies. This situation apparently made it possible to support oneself and one's family on labor alone. Similar to the *mutaka* in late Tokugawa Japan, these landless families supported themselves through by-employment and wage labor on village farms or in nearby towns.[10] These individuals, however, seldom earning more than a subsistence income, lacked the security that accompanied landownership. Because they were on the margin of the agricultural economy, in hard economic years they joined the waves of migrant farmers who started leaving Korea's southern regions in the late nineteenth and early twentieth centuries to seek a better life in northern Korea and Manchuria.[11]

In addition to owning most arable land in each of the villages, individual landowners (as opposed to institutions) possessed most of the residential land as well. Of the residential plots in the villages, individuals owned 98 percent; six homes in Se-ri were owned by a royal palace. One home had a tile roof, while the rest, like most rural homes in Korea, had thatched roofs.[12] These residential plots, usually consisting of a house, storeroom, and courtyard, varied considerably in size, ranging from under 20 *p'yŏng* (about 700 square feet) to over 830 *p'yŏng* (almost 30,000 square feet), and averaged about 100–150 *p'yŏng* each. The number of rooms in each house varied from two to twelve, but most homes consisted of two or three rooms. In general, the size of one's home and the number of rooms corresponded to the size of one's arable land-holdings. Individuals owning large amounts of cultivated land tended to also live in homes of above-average size. See Table 3-3 for this correlation.[13] Most tenants lived in small homes, though there were notable exceptions.[14]

On the whole, homeowners lived in their homes, and rates of tenancy in the housing market fell considerably below those for arable land. It was not uncommon for an individual who owned little or no farmland to own one's own home. As with tenancy rates for cultivated land, however, significant differences existed from village to village. As expected, the two isolated villages exhibited high rates of homeownership by local

Table 3-3   Correlation between Arable Landownership and Size of Homes, 1900

ARABLE LAND OWNED (IN *P'YŎNG*)	NUMBER OF ROOMS IN HOME										
	2	3	4	5	6	7	8	9	10	10+	TOTAL
Over 5,000	1	3	0	1	0	0	0	0	1	1	7
2,501–5,000	5	16	7	2	1	0	2	0	1	0	34
1,501–2,500	11	15	6	3	0	3	0	1	0	0	39
901–1,500	15	17	3	1	1	1	1	0	0	0	39
1–900	18	25	4	3	0	1	0	0	0	0	51
0	29	37	9	2	2	0	0	0	0	0	79
Total	79	113	29	12	4	5	3	1	2	1	249

Note: Unit is number of owners of arable land
SOURCE: Kwangmu *yang'an*

owner-farmers. In Songsan-ni, for example, only two individuals rented homes while the other sixty-two registered residents owned homes. Although not as dramatic, residential tenancy rates were also low in Paeksŏng-ni, where seventy-seven of ninety-three registered residents (83 percent) owned homes. In Paeksŏng-ni landlords owning the sixteen rented homes lived—with two exceptions—within the village itself. It was apparently unprofitable in both villages to own homes and rent them to village residents.

In Kongsu-ri and Se-ri, on the other hand, local and absentee landlords owned many village homes, suggesting that investing in residential land in these villages was lucrative as early as the turn of the century. Landlords owned 83 percent of Kongsu-ri's ninety-one homes. Some landlords, like Yi Pok-hŭng, even specialized in residential landownership. Yi, a local owner-farmer possessing 3,456 *p'yŏng* of arable land in 1900, owned thirteen homes in Kongsu-ri; one housed his family.[15] Similarly, of Se-ri's forty-two homes, twenty-six were owned by landlords who rented to Se-ri residents. One such landlord, Kim Kyŏng-bo, owned fourteen homes in addition to his arable landholdings.

The high rates of tenancy among Kongsu-ri and Se-ri residents could be due to the proximity of both villages to commercial centers. Possibly, in these villages improvements in agriculture late in the Yi dynasty produced sufficient wealth and productivity to guarantee a profitable return on investments in residential and arable land. In short, residents of Kongsu-ri and Se-ri could afford to pay rent for their housing and their fields. Just as in Japanese rural villages near Tokugawa commercial centers, by 1900 the relationship between tenant and landlord in villages such as these had clearly become a commercial one.[16]

Palace Land in Kwangmu Korea

Three palaces in Se-ri—the Myŏngnye-gung, Nudong-gung, and the Sŏnhi-gung—owned *kungbangjŏn*. Myŏngnye-gung, now Tŏksu-gung, housed Queen Min prior to her murder in 1895, and land under its control financed the substantial expenses of the queen, her relatives, and her entourage. Originally receiving 500 *kyŏl* of agricultural land from the Korean government in the 1640s, the palace reportedly expanded its landholdings to 1,700 *kyŏl* under Queen Min.[17] After the queen's death, King Kojong resided in the palace (Kyŏng'un-gung) from 1897 until his death in 1919, and the queen's relatives and entourage moved to another palace in the northern part of Seoul, transferring the name Myŏngnye-gung to their new home. This palace and those associated with the late queen were supported by the Myŏngnye-gung landholdings around the Korean peninsula in 1900; 2,200 *p'yŏng* existed in Se-ri.[18]

Another small palace in northeastern Seoul, the Nudong-gung, owned one plot of paddy land (about 1,250 *p'yŏng*) in Se-ri in 1900. At that time the Nudong-gung was under the control of Yi Hae-sŭng, a direct descendent of Yŏngjo and grandson of Royal Household Minister Yi Chae-sun, one of Ch'ŏlchong's nephews.[19] Statistics on the total land-holdings under the Nudong-gung are not available. Undoubtedly, many other distant royal relatives had similar *kungbangjŏn* scattered throughout the peninsula.

The third palace, the Sŏnhi-gung, owned most of the *kungbangjŏn* in Se-ri—about 23,500 *p'yŏng* of arable land (mostly paddy) and another 500 *p'yŏng* of residential land. Of these holdings, 4,029 *p'yŏng* were classified as fallow, presumably laid waste by the natural calamities of 1901–1902. The Sŏnhi-gung was established in 1762, during the reign of Yŏngjo, as a place for ancestral ceremonies *(chesa)* for Yongbin, Yŏngjo's fourth wife.[20] Although Yi dynasty law prohibited such palace land from remaining in clan hands more than four generations after a queen's death, the Sŏnhi-gung acquired official recognition of permanent ownership over its land in 1823.[21] During the eighteenth and nineteenth centuries the palace expanded its landholdings from about 1,000 *kyŏl* to 3,400 *kyŏl,* which was the total at the end of the dynasty.[22] At the time of the Kwangmu survey, the Sŏnhi-gung and its land were under the control of Yi Chae-sun, heir to the Yŏngjo-Yongbin Yi royal line.[23]

In 1900 the various palaces owning *kungbangjŏn* in Se-ri possessed the best land in the village. During the Kwangmu survey, a value from one to six in descending order was assigned to each plot of land based on productivity averages in recent years. This grade, as a reflection of the land's value, determined the amount of land tax to be assessed. Whereas most land in Se-ri was of relatively low quality (averaging grade five), land owned by palaces averaged one grade higher. No such correlation is found among private owners, regardless of the size of landholdings or type of cultivator (tenant versus owner).

Clearly, *kungbangjŏn* played an important role in late Yi dynasty land tenure, at least in provinces near Seoul. In addition to the three palaces owning land in Se-ri, various others owned land in villages near Suwŏn, occasionally owning almost all land in a village. This land provided income for the numerous royal family members and their staffs, and therefore guaranteed financial independence from the central government for Korea's ruling clans. Large amounts of *kungbangjŏn* also contributed to high rates of tenancy and absentee landlordism in the Suwŏn area, both at the turn of the century and into the colonial period. Se-ri tenants who farmed for the palaces in 1900 found themselves simply renting land from a new landlord in 1908—the head of the Mitsubishi Corporation.

Government-Owned Land in Kwangmu Korea

At the time of the Kwangmu survey, Se-ri contained government land registered in the names of the county school in Suwŏn, a public granary, and the wall maintenance storehouse. The Suwŏn county school, *hyanggyo*, was part of the Yi dynasty education system. According to this system the government established a school for classical education in each county *(kun)* and designated land *(hakchŏn)* in its vicinity to finance the school.[24] Until 1900 management of these lands was the responsibility of each school, but in April of that year the Korean government placed all *hakchŏn* under the control of county officials and theoretically deprived the schools of their right to directly collect taxes from it. The extent to which this policy changed taxation procedures at each local *hyanggyo* is not known, but when Se-ri was surveyed shortly thereafter, the Suwŏn *hyanggyo* continued to be the registered owner of over 16,000 *p'yŏng* of arable land in the village. Further, after the Japanese cadastral survey of 1910–1918, the school continued to own its land and did so until the creation of the public school system, when the government-general used the former *hakchŏn* to finance local public schools.

In addition to *hakchŏn*, Se-ri contained a small amount (1,303 *p'yong*) of public granary land *(konggojŏn)* designated by the Yi dynasty government to support local granaries throughout the peninsula. These granaries were created, in theory, to store surplus rice that could be loaned at nominal interest to destitute farmers in years of poor harvests. Local public officials also stored the annual land-tax rice in these granaries prior to shipment to Seoul or other markets. The category of *konggojŏn* was abolished in 1908, and the land was placed under the Ministry of Finance, the T'akchibu.[25] Because of the absence of data on local officials in late nineteenth-century Korea, it is impossible to know who in the Se-ri area received the produce from *konggojŏn* as payment for operating the granary—assuming it was still operational.

The *susŏnggo,* or wall maintenance storehouse, controlled most government-agency land in Se-ri at the turn of the century. This land, totaling 42,869 *p'yŏng,* (22,665 *p'yŏng* being registered as fallow) presumably financed repairs to Suwŏn fortifications. The storehouse, located in Suwŏn, was probably established in the fifteenth century when the Korean government created the Susŏng kŭmhwa togam, an agency responsible for repairing fire-damaged walls and bridges in Seoul and elsewhere in the peninsula.[26] This agency was abolished during the reign of Sŏnjo in the late sixteenth century, yet it apparently maintained its lands near Suwŏn. No later reference to this agency or to any other involved in wall maintenance can be found. It is impossible to determine who in the Se-ri area was receiving *cho* payments at the outset of the twentieth century. According to colonial records, ownership over all *sus-ŏnggo* land in the village was in the hands of the government-general.

In 1900 all agency land in Songsan-ni and part of that in Kongsu-ri, totaling 4,695 *p'yŏng,* was registered as *yanghyang tunjŏn,* or land under the control of the Office of Military Provisions in Seoul.[27] The Korean government created this office in 1593 and designated a modest amount of land (278 *kyŏl*) distributed throughout the peninsula to provide food for Korea's troops during the Hideyoshi invasions. Although reportedly expanding its land at one point to over 7,000 *kyŏl,* the Office of Military Provisions controlled only about 400 *kyŏl* in 1899—land that presumably still produced food for Korea's meager army. In July 1906 the residency-general placed all *yanghyang tunjŏn* under the T'ak-chibu, asserting for the first time central government control over army provisions.[28]

The situation in the villages represented on a smaller scale the complex decentralized system of government agency landownership. No overall government body or authority had the means or power to oversee this system of indirect government financing, much less reform it. No central agency was responsibile for monitoring agency land allocations and accurately recording government landownership. Not surprisingly, the Korean government was not able to reform this system easily; the task was staggering in its enormity.

Tenancy

Tenancy was a common feature of late Yi dynasty land tenure. Palaces, government agencies, and individual landlords used tenant farmers to cultivate vast landholdings throughout the peninsula. Tenancy rents and their collection methods varied around the country, but at the turn of the century the rents generally averaged about one-half of the land's produce in exchange for the right to farm the land.[29]

The amount of land farmed by tenants differed sharply from area to area. In his study of Kwangmu *yang'an,* Kim Yong-sŏp found that tenant-cultivated land comprised from 5 percent to 83 percent of a village's land.[30] The percentage of tenant households among village residents varied as greatly, with most tenants in Kim's study farming small amounts of land—less than 1.5 acres. Others, however, rented enormous estates from large-scale landlords and undoubtedly hired local laborers to help cultivate this land, or they sublet parcels to other tenants.[31] These wealthy tenants could have been a newly emerging group of individuals on the local level who had become managers of large amounts of accumulated arable land at the end of the Yi dynasty.

The Kwangmu data from the villages in this study reveal a similar disparity in the extent of tenancy in rural Korea in 1900. In the villages studied, the rate of tenancy-cultivated land varied considerably—from practically none to almost 60 percent of all land in the village—and averaged over 31 percent of all cultivated land. Tables 3-1 and 3-4 reveal the tenancy level in each village. Although many tenants owned part of the land they cultivated (owner-tenants), forty-eight of the 290 registered residents of the villages (12 percent) rented all of the land they cultivated. Another sixty residents did not own or rent land (other than the land on which their home was situated), making up a rather large pool of undoubtedly poor and available wage laborers that varied in size from village to village.

The two isolated villages contained relatively small percentages of tenant-cultivated land. In Paeksŏng-ni, for example, 75 percent of all land in the village was farmed by the owner; the tenants cultivated the rest. Songsan-ni, like one of Kim Yong-sŏp's villages, contained virtually no tenancy at all. Only two parcels of land, totaling 3,318 *p'yŏng,* were farmed by someone other than the registered owner. While it is possible that tenants were simply not recorded on the Kwangmu *yang'an* for Songsan-ni, this is unlikely because the *yang'an* from neighboring villages suggest that tenancy rates were low in the entire Hansan area of South Ch'ungch'ŏng province.[32] Supporting evidence for this comes from colonial-period tenancy data indicating that tenancy rates were lowest in this part of the province.[33]

In Kongsu-ri and Se-ri, which were closest to urban areas, between 45 percent and 60 percent of cultivated land was farmed by tenants. Not surprisingly, over half of the residents in these two villages did not own land; rather, they rented it from local and absentee landlords or worked as farm laborers. The relatively high tenancy rate in Kongsu-ri corresponds precisely with tenancy statistics for the same area during the colonial period. Asan-gun, in which Kongsu-ri lies, had the highest tenancy rate in South Ch'ungch'ŏng province later in the 1930s.[34]

In short, areas near Yi dynasty market towns or other centers of commercial activity were characterized by higher tenancy rates than more remote areas. This suggests that agricultural land in areas near towns, at least to some extent, had become a viable investment for urban residents and indicates that economic forces were already at work late in the Yi dynasty to create tenancy patterns similar to those found in the colonial period.

Farms cultivated by tenants tended to be small in each village, particularly since about half of the land's produce was paid to a landlord or a smaller amount to a government or palace agency in rent or taxes. As seen in Table 3-1, resident tenants who rented all of the land they cultivated rented an average of just over 2,000 *p'yŏng* (less than two acres) in

Table 3-4 Arable Land Cultivated by Owners versus Tenants (in *p'yŏng*)

VILLAGE	LAND CULTIVATED BY OWNER			LAND CULTIVATED BY TENANT			TOTAL
	PADDY	UPLAND	TOTAL	PADDY	UPLAND	TOTAL	
Songsan-ni	159,160	35,818	194,978 (98.3)	3,318	0	3,318 (1.7)	198,296
Paeksŏng-ni	47,700	57,145	104,845 (75.1)	26,102	8,745	34,847 (24.9)	139,692
Kongsu-ri	67,413	49,011	116,424 (40.3)	142,424	30,107	172,531 (59.7)	288,955
Se-ri	53,089	57,096	110,185 (48.8)	99,724	15,918	115,642 (51.2)	225,827
Total	327,362	199,070	526,432 (61.7)	271,568	54,770	326,338 (38.3)	852,770

Notes: Figures do not include residential land or land classified fallow
    Numbers in parentheses represent percentages of total
SOURCE: Kwangmu *yang'an*

each of the villages studied. Many of these individuals rented very small plots of land, but others rented large estates that were more than they could cultivate. These tenants presumably sublet part of the land to other tenants or hired farm laborers to help cultivate it.

An individual's economic well being was not determined solely by the amount of arable land one owned. One tenant in Kongsu-ri, Yi Sŏng-ch'il, did not own land and instead rented 8,500 *p'yŏng* (about 7 acres) of paddy land, more than any other farmer cultivated in any of the three villages in South Ch'ungch'ŏng province. Although he farmed the largest of such rented landholdings, Yi was not an isolated example.[35] Tenants like him were undoubtedly better off financially than many of the land-owners who possessed much smaller amounts of land. Kim Yong-sŏp concludes that such tenants were part of a small but growing class of entrepreneurs who came to control increasing amounts of land late in the Yi dynasty and who used the profits from cultivation and management skills to become upwardly mobile. In the absence of tenancy data from the colonial period, such a conclusion is plausible but impossible to substantiate.

In the villages studied here, Kwangmu-period tenants—even those cultivating large amounts of land—did not become landowners in the colonial period. Indeed, if mobility is measured as a change from tenant to landowner, little evidence of mobility appears in the data. For example, Yi Sŏng-ch'il did not own land in Kongsu-ri during the entire colonial period, and there is no evidence available to indicate that he redirected investments in urban areas.

Tenancy fees, usually around 50 percent of the harvested crop, were determined by one of two methods. In a few instances, the landlord and tenant arrived at a fixed amount of rent in advance, based upon an average of recent harvests. This type of tenancy fee gave the tenant incentive to increase production, but it provided no security in the event of an unforeseen calamity. Less-than-average rainfall could easily result in a smaller harvest and therefore in a higher percentage of rent. Thus, this type of tenancy arrangement was generally limited to those areas with ample rainfall or irrigation and ideal growing conditions.[36]

More commonly, an agent of the landlord inspected the crop immediately before or after harvest and determined the amount of produce equal to approximately half of the crop. Under this sharecropping arrangement, the agent was then responsible for sending the harvested commodity, usually rice or its cash equivalent, to Seoul or a nearby market town. In addition to determining rent levels, the agent controlled the daily operations of the landlord's estate. For services rendered, the agent—frequently also a tenant of the same landlord—was paid a salary and was often accused of graft and corruption.[37]

Tenancy contracts, mostly oral, were made for varying lengths of time. The shortest period, one year, placed the tenant at the mercy of the landlord, who decided whether to renew the tenancy contract or negotiate with someone else. Most advantageous to tenants were contracts that guaranteed them the right to cultivate land for life. These long-term tenancy arrangements were probably common in most areas of Korea at the turn of the century, but the increase in available farm labor around commercial centers undoubtedly resulted in shorter tenancy contracts in those areas. Many contracts left the length of tenancy vague, keeping the tenant insecure and dependent on the benevolence of the landlord.[38]

Summary

Throughout the last decades of the nineteenth century, reformers in and outside the Korean government had three basic goals in their policy toward land: to increase land-tax revenue, to centralize taxation authority, and to identify owners of individual parcels of land in order to tax cultivated land more equitably. These goals were part of a much larger effort to rationalize the Korean system of national finance and make the Korean government financially solvent. In order to attain these goals, the government successfully attempted to nationalize land owned by individual royal palaces and implement a nationwide cadastral survey.

The Kwangmu cadastral survey, undertaken between 1898–1903, identified owners of each land parcel in the areas surveyed and resulted in an increase in national tax revenue. Although halted before its completion, the survey produced voluminous land registers *(yang'an)* that provide valuable data on the nature of late nineteenth-century land tenure. These *yang'an* indicate that private individuals owned most land in rural Korea in these years but that royal palaces and government agencies controlled extensive landholdings in Kyŏnggi and other provinces near Seoul. Landownership was skewed. A small number of local and absentee landlords owned large amounts of tenant-cultivated land. This imbalance was most extreme in villages near commercial centers or transportation routes tying the village into a regional or even national market system. More isolated villages contained less tenancy and a more equitable distribution of landownership.

By undertaking the Kwangmu survey, the Korean government accomplished only part of its goal; landownership and taxation authority remained decentralized and in the hands of palaces and numerous government agencies, depriving the central government of needed tax revenue. Not until the establishment of the residency-general in 1906, when Japanese control over Korean affairs became virtually complete, did this authority return to the central government. After the Japanese colonial government was established, it undertook many of the same programs the Korean government had, and in some cases it simply completed ongoing operations.

The difference between the two governments' policies lay in their goals. The Korean government sought, with limited success, to establish a financially solvent independent state. The Japanese colonial administration, on the other hand, endeavored to open Korea's natural resources to development and exploitation by all citizens of the Japanese Empire, an endeavor which was aided by total colonial (including military) control.

In 1900, several years prior to Japan's occupation of Korea, Korean agriculture was ripe for exploitation by Japan. Unlike colonies of most other imperial powers, Korea, prior to colonization, had a system and tradition of private ownership and produced the precise agricultural commodities (rice and soybeans) that Japan needed. In addition, Korea possessed urban absentee landlords who owned large amounts of land in areas near commercial centers and who contracted local tenant laborers to cultivate it. Japanese rice brokers and shippers in the same urban areas needed only to deal with these Yi dynasty landlords to secure produce for the Japanese market.

In establishing colonial economic control in Korea, Japan did not need to introduce into Korea new modes of production, market distribution, or labor mobilization, such as plantations and slavery, to satisfy its domestic consumption requirements; rather, Japan simply needed to control the existing agricultural system. After several unsuccessful attempts to alter agricultural production in Korea by replacing Korean farmers with Japanese farmers, Japanese colonial administrators adopted the policy of controlling Korea's existing system. Japanese colonial landowners and developers acquired land near commercial centers and ports—often directly from Korean landlords living there—and used Korean tenants to produce rice and other commodities for the Japanese market. But this early Japanese policy toward land tenure must be examined before analyzing the acquisition process.

CHAPTER 4

JAPANESE IMPERIAL POLICIES
AND SETTLEMENT IN KOREA

IN THEIR EFFORTS to satisfy domestic
and international demand for raw materials, most colonial powers reorganized agricultural production in colonized lands to exploit natural resources. Traditional modes of production were inadequate in meeting the level of demand, and they did not insure reliable and predictable amounts of products and profit. In most instances, colonial powers mobilized indigenous peoples or imported slave laborers to develop large-scale agricultural plantations.[1] As Michael Hechtor has shown, other colonizing efforts, such as the British conquest and domination of Ireland, used large numbers of settlers from the colonial power itself to drive indigenous farmers from their lands and establish expansive agricultural operations.[2]

One of the major goals of Imperial Japan's colonial rule of Korea was to increase agricultural production on the peninsula. To achieve this goal Japanese government officials, like their predecessors in the former Korean government, saw the need to make the Korean system of landownership and registration more rational and systematic. To this end, early colonial administrators adopted two objectives: to make landownership rights legally secure and reliable for both Korean and Japanese investors; and, borrowing from the British internal colonial model, to use Japanese farmers to develop Korean agricultural land.

By attaining these two objectives, Japan hoped to gain important secondary benefits. The Japanese government hoped to resolve three critical problems: the considerable peasant unrest in Japan caused by population growth and the depressed state of the rural economy during the first decade of the twentieth century; a shortage of agricultural products to satisfy domestic Japanese demand—a demand Japan had not been able to meet since the 1890s; and growing Russian and Chinese influence and encroachments in Manchuria and Korea, which Japan hoped to stem by settling Japanese farmers on the Asian continent.

Japan's many-faceted efforts to achieve its two basic objectives toward agriculture in Korea resulted in extensive institutional developments. These efforts led to the creation of the Oriental Development Company (among others), the settlement of large numbers of Japanese citizens throughout Korea, and the nationwide cadastral survey initiated in March 1910. However, Japanese policies in Korea, like those of Great Britain in Ireland, were significantly influenced by opposition among colonized peoples. During Japanese colonial rule, some plans were postponed; others were abandoned. The transition of Japanese policy toward land and landownership in Korea between the end of the Kwangmu survey in 1902 and the completion of the colonial government's cadastral survey during the second decade of the twentieth century was marked by failures and redirection due to necessity.[3]

Pre-Protectorate Japanese Emigration and Access to Korean Land

To understand Japanese colonial policy toward Korean agriculture, one must first examine the Japanese government's plans for Japanese emigration to Korea. Indeed, emigration to Korea was part of a much larger emigration from the three main Japanese islands to Hokkaido and to numerous countries in North and South America, which started in the 1880s and continued through the first and second decades of the twentieth century.[4] Most of the emigrants were destitute farmers from northern Kyūshū and southwestern Honshū—areas that had not benefited from the industry and commerce growth of the Meiji years. Unemployed and unskilled, they faced a bleak future in Japan during the economically depressed years between the Sino-Japanese and Russo-Japanese wars.[5]

Some of Japan's leaders saw emigration as one means by which Japan could solve domestic unrest caused by population increases and rising unemployment among farmers. Inoue Kaoru, for example, noted that the overseas settlement program of the Oriental Development Company was established to "save the country from the suffering and hardships brought about by population increases."[6] Left-wing groups also saw emigration as a means of "rescuing" Japan's poor,[7] but some writers criticized the callous treatment emigrants suffered at the hands of the numerous colonization corporations.[8] Well-known figures such as the Christian leader Uchimura Kanzō also advocated sending Japanese emigrants abroad and particularly supported plans to send Japanese farmers to Korea. Uchimura felt Japanese farmers could serve as beneficial models for the Koreans, while at the same time their emigration from Japan would take pressure off Japan's surplus rural population.[9]

The Japanese government also worried about the increasing need to import foodstuffs, particularly rice and soy beans, to feed Japan's growing and increasingly urban population. Japan had become a net importer of food in the 1890s, and imports rose in importance through the next decade.[10] Taiwan, Japan's first colony, provided a certain percentage of imported food needs, but increasingly other sources were required. High Japanese government leaders regarded the settlement of Japanese farmers in Korea to be one means of solving the food shortage problem. A May 1904 cabinet-position statement on Japanese policy toward Korea included the following opinion:

> Of all occupations in Korea, the one to which Japanese aspire most is farming. Up until now, Korea, as an agricultural country, has exclusively provided Japan with food and raw materials and we have supplied it with manufactured goods. However, now the economic relationship between the two countries must develop beyond this principle. Korea can absorb large numbers of Japanese settlers easily because its population is small relative to its land area. Therefore, if many of our farmers are able to move into the Korean interior, on the one hand we can gain a colony for our surplus population and at the same time increase our scarce supply of food—in effect solve two problems with one policy.[11]

In addition to seeing Korea as an outlet for poor Japanese farmers, many public figures in Japan viewed emigration as a means of contributing to Japan's security against Chinese and Russian encroachments in Northeast Asia. During the first several years of the twentieth century, the Chinese government actively encouraged Chinese settlers to move to Manchuria.[12] China's policy, coupled with Imperial Russia's activity in Manchuria and Korea, threatened Japanese influence in the area and caused deep anxiety among Japanese military and political strategists. Korea's pro-Russia stance from 1896, when Korea's king fled to the Russian legation for protection from the Japanese, until the early 1900s heightened Japanese concerns. During these years, Russia obtained considerable concessions from the Korean government to exploit Korea's mineral and timber resources.[13]

Japanese leaders in and out of government envisioned Japanese settlers being used as a frontline defense against these Russian encroachments. By settling these farmers in Korea, Uchimura, for example, felt that, "there is no better method than this to block the incursion of Russia into Korea. . . . With 100 yen [for settlement and development expenses] Korea would in reality be Japan's."[14] Gotō Shimpei, the architect of Japanese colonial policy in Taiwan, also perceived the strategic importance of settling Japanese farmers in Korea.[15]

Determined not to lose the struggle for control of Korea and southern Manchuria, the Japanese government initiated steps to encourage settlers, particularly farmers, to emigrate to Korea. In May 1904, shortly after the outbreak of the Russo-Japanese War, the first Katsura cabinet adopted a policy of encouraging such emigration to Korea. Foreign Minister Komura Jutarō strongly supported the cabinet's policy statement, which analyzed Japanese-Korean relations in some detail and discussed the possibilities of such settlement.[16]

Concerned with the security of Japanese economic and political interests in Northeast Asia, Komura saw the advantage to Japan in settling Japanese nationals on the Asian continent. Soon after this consensus on emigration policy had been established, Komura, returning from Portsmouth in 1905, drafted an opinion paper urging that Japanese emigrants be concentrated in the Korea-Manchuria region.[17] Under the section heading "Policy Toward Settlers," he wrote:

> As a result of the Russo-Japanese War, the position of the Empire has changed radically and Japan has even become a continental country possessing territory on the Asian continent. But right next to our continental territory are the large countries of China and Russia and the future of both is uncertain. In attempting to determine a plan for the next one hundred years of our Empire, I feel we must position ourselves right next to these two extremely powerful countries and be sure that there are no chance miscalculations. . . . In this regard, in order to confront these two large countries the Empire must as much as possible concentrate our people in the East Asian region.[18]

Although the decision to concentrate settlers in East Asia was in part a result of anti-Japanese sentiment in other countries subject to Japanese emigration,[19] Komura also clearly felt that Japanese settlers in Korea and Manchuria could serve as frontline soldiers in Japan's security policy.

In 1904 approximately fifteen thousand Japanese families lived in Korea, most engaged in business in nine cities.[20] The overall Japanese presence was not felt outside these cities, although a few Japanese did live in scattered settlements in Korea's interior.[21] The Korean government required those Japanese residing in or venturing into the interior to seek permission to do so and to carry identification papers with them at all times.

In order for Japanese farmers to settle in Korea and thereby help solve Japan's domestic and security problems, they needed agricultural land. Despite a legal ban on foreign purchase of Korean land, the Japanese government sought in early 1904 to secure land and the right of Japanese to own and develop it. Shortly after the outbreak of the Russo-Japanese War, Japan and Korea signed a protocol that in effect enabled Japan to act freely in Korea while conducting the war.[22] At the same time, Hayashi Gonsuke, Japanese minister in Korea, and Yi Ha-yŏng, Korea's foreign minister, signed a secret agreement that gave broad concessions to Japan to assist in developing Korean agriculture.[23]

Article four of this secret agreement, for example, gave Japanese nationals the right to acquire de facto ownership and utilization rights to agricultural land throughout Korea through mortgages assumed (and subsequently defaulted on) by Korean landowners. That is, ownership and land utilization rights were to be used as guarantees on loans by Japanese nationals to Koreans. Default on the loan repayments would result in the transference of rights from Korean to Japanese. This de facto right for Japanese to own land in Korea circumvented the Korean ban on foreign purchase or lease of land outside of 10 Korean *ri* from the treaty ports. Numerous Japanese accounts from this period cite the "mortgage-purchase" procedure as a means of acquiring land in Korea.[24]

According to this secret agreement, Japanese capital could be used to develop nonagricultural land without interference from the Korean government. Article five, for example, stipulated that the Korean and Japanese governments would quickly determine an "appropriate management policy" toward forest and other uncultivated land under the control of Korean palaces and government agencies.[25]

The Japanese negotiator of this agreement, Minister Hayashi, became the prime moving force behind Japan's search for land on which to settle Japanese farmers. Hayashi presented his ideas on the problems faced by Japanese nationals seeking to develop Korean agriculture in a letter to Itō Hirobumi shortly after Itō's state visit to Korea in March 1904. In his letter, dated April 1, Hayashi wrote that it was imperative that Japan secure the right of Japanese nationals to purchase land beyond the 10 Korean *ri* limit. He felt that Japanese farmers had an advantage in competing with other nationals for Korean agricultural land because of farming skills gained in Japan. Hayashi did concede that there might be a problem winning the approval of the Korean government, but in his mind this was not an insurmountable obstacle. He suggested that Japan work through the Korean royal household ministry, an agency with which Itō was well connected.[26] Hayashi also noted that he favored the development of wasteland in Korea by Japanese individuals rather than through direct Japanese government sponsorship.[27]

Development of this uncultivated wasteland in Korea also received the support of the Japanese consul in Mokp'o, Wakamatsu Usaburō. On April 2 Wakamatsu cabled a secret letter to Foreign Minister Komura advocating the settlement of Japanese farmers on Korean land not currently being cultivated.[28] He proposed opening such land to Japanese settlers on the condition that they make the land productive within a set number of years. This, he felt, would result in increased tax revenue, yet would not antagonize Korean farmers by displacing them.

The Japanese government's interest in settling Japanese farmers in Korea was matched by the enthusiasm of Japanese developers to assist in the endeavor. One development scheme, hinted at in Hayashi's 1904 letter to Itō, was the infamous Nagamori proposal.[29] Early in 1904 Nagamori Tokichirō, a former official in the Japanese finance ministry, devised a comprehensive plan by which the reportedly large amounts of wasteland control led by royal palaces and government agencies—of which some land was located in the villages of this study—would be developed by Japanese corporate interests.[30] Nagamori, with the approval and assistance of Hayashi, negotiated with officials in the royal household ministry, chiefly Prince Yi Chae-sun and Minister Min Pyŏng-sŏk,[31] over how Nagamori could develop the large amount of land under palace control.

Nagamori planned to develop uncultivated land owned by the royal palaces or controlled by government institutions by leasing all such land in his name and then subleasing it to Japanese farmers.[32] Although actual ownership of the land would remain in the hands of the palaces or the Korean government, Nagamori proposed that he be able to buy any of this land when he deemed it necessary. The similar nature of the proposals by Hayashi, Wakamatsu, and Nagamori suggest a high degree of cooperation between Nagamori and Japanese consular officials in Korea. In fact, Hayashi personally endorsed Nagamori's plan and included it in a letter to Foreign Minister Komura on April 8. He also included a tentative agreement for development of Korea's uncultivated land signed by Nagamori and Minister Min Pyŏng-sŏk.[33]

Komura gave his approval to the Nagamori proposal in early May 1904 and then, in a cable to Hayashi in Seoul, ordered Nagamori back to Korea to conclude negotiations with the Korean government. Responding to this cable, Hayashi noted the necessity for the Japanese government to deny that it was directly or indirectly involved in the arrival of Japanese developers in Korea.[34] At the same time Hayashi cabled that he felt a directive *(kunrei)* from Tokyo to the Korean government would make cooperation by the various Korean ministers of state easier to obtain.

Later that same month, the Japanese government established its policy of settling Japanese farmers in Korea. That policy statement, partially quoted earlier, went on to note that there were some legal problems involved in such a settlement and development of Korean agriculture:

> . . . presently Japanese are prohibited by treaty from renting or buying land unless it is within one [Japanese] *ri* of the consular ports, and so even if in reality they own arable land in the interior, their rights are not at all secure, making capitalists unsure and reluctant to make investments. For that reason we must adopt the following two policies as means of opening the Korean interior to Japanese farmers: 1) Regarding state-owned land and

wasteland, permission or authorization to cultivate it or use it for livestock should be obtained in the name of one individual and [the land] should be managed by qualified Japanese farmers under the authority of the Imperial government; 2) Regarding privately-owned land, the ability to purchase or lease for the purpose of cultivation or grazing must be secured beyond one *ri* from the consular areas. That is, there must be no hindrance by the Korean government to recognition of the right of Japanese citizens to own, lease for long-term periods, or use land in the interior.[35]

The Japanese cabinet thus gave its approval to the Nagamori proposal. With this action, Japanese leaders not only approved Japanese emigration as a tool of domestic and foreign policy, but they also felt they had found land for Japan's settlers in Korea.

However, opposition to the proposal, first among high-ranking Korean government officials in early June 1904 and later by the public at large, impeded negotiations.[36] In late June, when the Korean public became aware of the negotiations, opposition took the form of a public outcry and demonstrations in the streets of Seoul. Opponents of the proposal reportedly also destroyed railroad and telegraph lines.[37] The Japanese minister cabled Tokyo that the "Confucian faction," a label often attached to individuals opposed to Japanese policies, demonstrated frequently against the proposal.[38] Articles in *Hwangsŏng sinmun,* Seoul's daily newspaper, and the paper's publication of the draft proposal itself on June 21, fanned public antagonism toward the proposal.[39] Faced with these displays of opposition, Hayashi submitted a new proposal to Prime Minister Yi Ha-yŏng that reduced the scope and scale of Nagamori's proposed project.[40]

Hayashi returned to Japan in early June and was replaced temporarily by Hagiwara Moriichi in Seoul. From late June Hagiwara conveyed information to the Japanese foreign ministry on the nature and scope of Korean opposition to the Nagamori proposal. For example, on June 30 he transmitted a statement from the Korean foreign ministry to Komura disavowing the Nagamori proposal.[41] On July 7 Hagiwara sent a secret letter to Komura that included a statement from the various Korean ministers of state. This statement sharply criticized Japan's plans to send large numbers of Japanese farmers to other countries to cultivate surplus land. The ministers asserted that any uncultivated land in Korea should be farmed by Koreans, not Japanese. They also felt that Japanese farmers would not be willing to stay in agriculture because they could not compete with the Korean farmer's lower wage scale, a prediction that proved to be accurate.[42]

The following week the Korean royal household ministry and agriculture-commerce-industry ministry approved an alternate Korean proposal to establish a Korean corporation to develop Korea's uncultivated land.

This corporation, called the Korean Agriculture and Mining Corporation, was to be capitalized at ten million *wŏn,* and stockholders were required to be Korean nationals.[43] The mission of the corporation was to oversee all mining operations in the country—including foreign concessions—and develop Korea's uncultivated land. Representatives of various foreign nations strongly opposed the creation of the corporation, fearing the loss of special rights to develop Korea's mineral resources granted to them five years earlier.[44] In the face of heavy foreign pressure, the Korean government withdrew its approval of the corporation in August.

Anti-Japanese demonstrations sparked by the schemes to develop Korean agricultural land continued throughout the summer in Seoul. In response Hayashi, who by then had returned from Tokyo, formally withdrew the Nagamori proposal on August 2. In Hayashi's words, the proposal was withdrawn until a "more appropriate time."[45] Due to adverse publicity over the proposal, Nagamori himself was also withdrawn temporarily to Japan.[46] The depth and intensity of Korean opposition to the development of Korean agriculture by Japanese settler-farmers as proposed by Nagamori took the Japanese government by surprise and forced it to revise its policy.

A "more appropriate time" came the following month when Hayashi submitted a new draft proposal to Komura on September 16 to develop Korea's uncultivated land through the Japan-Korea Development Corporation, Ltd.[47] This corporation was to be financed by the Korean royal household ministry, which would receive the taxes from developed land for three years from the date of cultivation. Hayashi proposed that 90 percent of the cultivators be Koreans, an apparent concession to Korean sensitivities and political realities. The royal household ministry was to entrust the establishment of the corporation to none other than Nagamori Tokichirō.[48] By submitting this proposal, Hayashi clearly indicated both his continuing interest in finding land for Japan's emigrant farmers and his belief that he could do so through the Korean royal household ministry. Although the proposal did not result in the creation of any actual corporation, it was the precursor of another proposal several years later to establish the Oriental Development Company, with which Korean court officials were also intimately involved.

Satō Torajirō, an early twentieth-century Japanese politician, raised the matter of the development of Korea's uncultivated land in the Japanese Diet in December 1904. Satō expressed concern over the Japanese government's relationship with Nagamori and possible costs to the Japanese taxpayer of the proposed land development in Korea.[49] Komura replied several months later to the Diet request by stating that it was not the time to make a public statement on the matter.[50] This apparently delayed discussion of the subject until June 1905. In a letter to Komura dated June 12, Mokp'o Consul Wakamatsu noted that the Korean government was adamant in its refusal to allow foreigners to own land in Korea and suggested that special permission to simply use uncultivated land be secured. Wakamatsu argued that in reality Japanese individuals already owned land in the Korean interior with quiet acquiescence by the Korean government. To push for outright legalization of ownership was not necessary and could even be counterproductive.[51]

Protectorate-Period Land and Settlement Policies

This low-key approach became the policy of the Japanese government until Japan assumed virtual control over Korea with the establishment of the residency-general eight months later, in February 1906. In October of that year the colonial government enacted the Agricultural and Residential Land Certification Law, giving foreigners the right to own land anywhere on the Korean peninsula.[52] This law overcame one of the major obstacles to Japan's agricultural policy in Korea. But finding land and livelihood for the planned emigrant farmers proved to be much more difficult.

During the decade following the Russo-Japanese War, the Japanese settler population in Korea swelled, largely due to Japanese government encouragement and financial subsidies paid to persons willing to emigrate. By 1915, the government-general reported a total 303,659 Japanese nationals in Korea.[53] However, contrary to the Japanese government's intentions and efforts, these emigrants continued to settle in Korean urban centers, with few engaging in agriculture.[54] Those who did were predominantly tenants who worked for Korean and Japanese landlords; few owned agricultural land in the first decades after annexation.[55]

Many of the thousands of Japanese emigrants leaving for Korea after 1904 were encouraged by Japanese government publications that described economic possibilities existing in Korea, particularly for persons interested in agriculture.[56] As part of the preparation for large-scale emigration, the Japanese foreign ministry commissioned an impressive investigation of agricultural conditions in Korea between 1904–1905. After extensive travel throughout all provinces of the peninsula, the investigative team published a report concluding that great potential existed for expanding cultivation and improving productivity by Japanese farmers in Korea.[57] According to the report, these farmers needed only to add capital improvements such as irrigation and fertilizer to succeed in farming. This multivolume report describes in great detail the farming customs, implements, and conditions in each province, and it went on to suggest areas in which Japanese farmers might settle. Other government sources even mapped out precisely where land could be reclaimed along rivers and coasts and gave glowing reports of the feasibility of such reclamation projects throughout Korea.[58]

Scholars of agriculture wrote treatises at this time on the advisability of sending Japanese farmers to Korea and bringing unskilled Korean laborers to Japan in a grand exercise in comparative advantage.[59] These authors wrote convincingly, if incorrectly, of Korea's underpopulation and of the availability of large amounts of uncultivated land throughout the peninsula. Early reports back from the Korean frontier, usually sponsored by the Japanese government, went into detail about how much Japanese settlers could expect to make in various occupations in Korea.[60] Finally, the daily war reports of Japanese successes on the continent during 1904–1905 stimulated thousands of young Japanese emigrants (mostly men) to follow the troops and try their luck in Korea. Many parallels can be drawn between this migration and the American westward movement under the protection of the frontier cavalry in the nineteenth century.[61]

Efforts to resettle large numbers of Japanese farmers in Korea did not end with the demise of the Nagamori proposal. Government and corporate leaders envisioned the realization of large-scale emigration through a new corporation founded in 1907, the Oriental Development Company.[62] The first directors of the Oriental Development Company planned to settle approximately thirty thousand Japanese farmers annually.[63] The establishment of such a company became even more urgent as Japanese emigration to the United States was all but halted due to the Gentlemen's Agreement of 1907–1908.[64] In addition, other countries either terminated or drastically reduced Japanese immigration at about this time.[65]

The proposal to establish the Oriental Development Company was drawn up in mid-1907 by members of the Tōyō kyōkai, an association of Asia-hands in Japan composed of corporate and government leaders.[66] The head of the Tōyō kyōkai, Katsura Tarō, instructed the association's chief secretary, Komatsuhara Eitarō, to examine the possibility of such a company. Komatsuhara spent more than one month traveling in Korea in May 1907 and reported back to Katsura that in order to implement colonial management of Korea, Japan needed to advance and improve agriculture in the country.[67] Komatsuhara, writing in a July issue of *Bōeki* (Foreign trade) on his trip to Korea, sharply criticized Japanese policy in Korea at that point.[68] He found that Japanese landlords (usually absentee) using Koreans as tenants were satisfied with their tenancy fees and were therefore not interested in making any improvements in Korean agriculture. Agreeing with the Nagamori proposal, Komatsuhara felt that Japanese farmers should be sent to Korea, with transportation and farm implements provided by the Japanese government.

Upon Komatsuhara's return to Japan in early June, members of the Tōyō kyōkai drafted a proposal for the development of Korea. It called for the creation of the Oriental Development Company to "settle experienced and skilled farmers [in Korea] and provide them with low interest capital. They (Koreans) will provide fertile land and cheap labor."[69] After obtaining the sanction of Itō Hirobumi and Inoue Kaoru, a revised draft was submitted to the finance ministry.[70] At that stage the proposal reportedly encountered the opposition of the finance minister, Sakatani Yoshirō, who had his own ideas on Japanese emigration. Sakatani envisioned sending fifty thousand Japanese farmers to Korea to develop Korean agriculture and as a result delayed giving his approval to the proposed company.[71]

Moving ahead on his own, Katsura personally traveled to Korea late in 1907 to secure the signatures of Korean government officials on the proposal to establish the Oriental Development Company. Meanwhile, Sakatani's opposition was overcome when he was convinced that large-scale emigration would be a major function of the new company, and the finance ministry gave final budget approval. Not surprisingly, the final proposal before the cabinet emphasized emigration of Japanese farmers and gave lower priority to the development of Korean agriculture. It was this proposal that the Diet easily passed in the spring of 1908.

Promulgation of the law establishing the Oriental Development Company was delayed until August, however, due to fear of negative public reaction in Korea and unexpected anxiety in Japan. For example, Itō Hirobumi, who had exerted a great deal of effort and prestige in combating Korean guerrillas during the preceding six months, feared that the Oriental Development Company would be greeted with violence.[72] In Japan, some politicians feared that the Oriental Development Company would monopolize economic development in Korea at the expense of smaller Japanese businesses. These critics saw the Oriental Development Company as a tool of the Japanese government and *zaibatsu*.[73]

The two governments and a public stock sale (restricted to Japanese nationals) provided financing for the Oriental Development Company, and the Korean royal household ministry donated 2,840 *chŏngbo* (about 7,000 acres) of agricultural land.[74] However, to settle up to thirty thousand farmers annually, the Oriental Development Company needed considerably more land.

To meet this need, the residency-general in Seoul initiated measures to bring all royal palace and government institutional land under central government authority. In the summer of 1907 the residency-general enacted an ordinance that established the Provisional Bureau for the

Investigation of Royal and State Property to investigate and identify all property owned by the royal household and government agencies.[75] As part of a public relations effort, the government claimed that this bureau would rectify abuses of the past that had resulted in Koreans losing ownership of land to the various palaces.[76] During the year-long investigation, all land registered in the name of a royal palace or government institution, including land found in the villages examined in this study, was identified in anticipation of awarding ownership either to the state or to private individuals.

Upon completion of the investigation, the residency-general immediately reclassified part of this land as state land—principally land that had been controlled by government institutions. This included all land previously classified as station land or used to finance local government operations.[77] The residency-general also nationalized all land that had been under the direct control of the royal household ministry and the Kyŏngsŏn-gung.[78] One month later, July 1908, the residency-general reorganized the bureau into the Provisional Property Reorganization Bureau and gave it the responsibility of deciding ownership over all other palace-owned land. This land reportedly totaled about 104,000 *chŏngbo* (about 255,000 acres), or approximately 3.5 percent of all cultivated land and somewhat less than 1 percent of all land on the peninsula.[79] The Provisional Property Reorganization Bureau was placed under the administration of the Korean finance ministry (T'akchibu) and was headed principally by Japanese bureaucrats (sixteen of the top twenty-five posts) from various agencies of the residency-general.[80] Three of the Korean officials had served in the influential Kyŏngniwŏn, the agency of the royal household ministry that had been responsible for management of palace lands. From the summer of 1908 through 1910, this bureau ruled on questions of ownership over all palace land throughout Korea.

Not surprisingly, the Provisional Property Reorganization Bureau awarded ownership over most royal lands to the state and turned over 2,433 *chŏngbo* to the Oriental Development Company as the Korean government's share of the capitalization of the corporation—per the agreement of 1908.[81] Some individuals received monetary compensation for nationalized land, including those who had formerly overseen cultivation of the land and those who were connected with the palaces or government agencies and had benefited from the land's produce.[82] The bureau's final report stated that those who received three-year compensatory grants had been *tojang,* or agents of the palaces and government agencies who oversaw cultivation. This may have been the case for some individuals, but the list also included officials of the Korean government and their relatives—individuals who clearly were not *tojang.*[83] The bureau ruled that some former palace land had been privately owned and had been taken from individuals by the palaces' agents during the Yi dynasty. This land was reportedly returned to its former and rightful owners. On the whole these individuals received small plots of land that had bordered on palace land.[84]

By stripping the palaces of their former sources of income (land) and either nationalizing it or awarding ownership to private individuals, the residency-general reduced the potential economic and political threat of the royal family to Japanese domination on the peninsula. More importantly for this study, the residency-general also obtained control over a large amount of arable land on which to settle Japanese farmers. In addition to this former palace land, some of which was eventually owned by Japanese corporate land developers, the Oriental Development Company bought a great deal of land from the general public and leased other land from the residency-general between 1908 and 1910 on which to settle these farmers. By 1910, when the first group of Oriental Development Company settlers arrived in Korea, the company had over 18,000 *chŏngbo* (44,000 acres) at its disposal.[85] However, events in Korea forced Japanese government and corporate officials to revise their original settlement plans. In the end, most of the land originally designed for Japanese farmers was eventually owned by Japanese interests but was farmed primarily by Korean tenants.

During the summer of 1907 a series of incidents in Korea caused the Korean public to once again strike out in anger against Japanese colonial administrators and Japan itself. In the midst of the furor over the secret Korean mission to The Hague in July, the residency-general, Itō Hirobumi, forced King Kojong to abdicate and concluded a new agreement with the Korean government that strengthened Japanese control over the administration of Korea's internal affairs.[86] Further, in a move to weaken Korean military capability, Itō disbanded the Korean army on August 1. These events resulted in massive armed resistance to Japanese rule by former Korean soldiers and other opponents of Japan's domination of the peninsula.[87] Guerrilla warfare initiated at this time increased in 1908 and continued into 1909, resulting in heavy casualties on both sides.[88]

The warfare threatened the safety of Japanese nationals in Korea, and from all accounts life for Japanese settlers in the interior was extremely precarious during these years. Fujii Kantarō, one of several large-scale land developers who started business in Korea immediately after the Russo-Japanese War, included the following narrative in his memoirs:

> In 1908–1909 at the time of the uprisings of the disbanded troops we were plagued by wandering soldiers, called *ŭibyŏng*, in retreat. Each farm had its own arms at ready and we at the North Chŏlla farm distributed 30 cast-off army guns with which we organized farm employees (Japanese) into a self-defense force. Every day we trained for two hours. We dug a trench around

the perimeter of the farm and were prepared for an attack of even 100 riot-
ers. At the time, the majority of our farm employees had participated in the
Russo-Japanese War and were battle-seasoned soldiers. There were even
some who had received the Order of the Golden Kite.[89]

Fujii also described the heroics of various Japanese settlers in fighting
off the "rioting hordes," sometimes with single-handed valor. These vic-
tories were later celebrated annually in Japan according to Fujii.[90] Other
areas of the interior were just as dangerous for emigrants. In the Nonsan
area of South Ch'ungch'ŏng province, Japanese settlers established a
night patrol to keep a nightly vigilance for guerrilla bands.[91]

Widely circulated periodicals also carried stories of the dangers of life
for Japanese in Korea during these years. For example, the leading Japanese-language journal on Korea, *Chōsen,* contained one article giving the
following account:

1. The situation is such that rather than gather in regional market towns,
Japanese merchants and customers are withdrawing to the major cities such
as Seoul and Taegu. Even dealing in Japanese-made goods has been sus-
pended.
2. Due to the danger, Japanese landlords living in Seoul and other cities are
not venturing into the villages and collection of tenancy fees is in jeopardy.
Moreover, merchants are no longer able to collect money due them.
3. Japanese engaged in agriculture, mining and fishing have been able to
retreat from the lands.[92]

In the summer of 1908, at the height of intensive guerrilla warfare and
anti-Japanese sentiment throughout Korea, the residency-general assembled the first Korean founding committee of the Oriental Development
Company. The colonial government appointed thirty-three leaders of the
Korean business community to serve on this committee. The government
then sent the committee members to Japan in September as part of a lobbying effort on behalf of the Oriental Development Company to "see the
real situation in Japan"; that is, to see that Japanese agriculture was far
more advanced than in Korea.[93] The officials of the Oriental Development Company and the residency-general hoped that by convincing leading members of Korea's business community of the need for development
of Korean agriculture by Japanese farmers, these men would support the
idea when they returned to Seoul. Itō addressed the committee members
in Tokyo and expressed his concern that Japan's good intentions for the
Oriental Development Company might be misunderstood by the Korean
public.[94]

That fear was based on anxiety over the guerrilla movement, which
continued in the fall of 1908 despite the residency-general's partially successful efforts to combat it. Concern arose among the organizers of the

Oriental Development Company over the advisability of settling large numbers of Japanese farmers in strife-torn Korea. This worry surfaced in December 1908 and resulted in a scaled-down estimate of the numbers of emigrants that could be sent through the company. Usagawa Kazumasa, the first president of the Oriental Development Company, addressed the emigrant issue at the company's first general meeting in December. He referred to the guerrilla warfare in a speech to the assembled officers and shareholders and suggested that the company might have no choice but to use Korean labor to develop Korean agriculture. Usagawa stated:

> Following the new Treaty of Cooperation, a group of Koreans, misunderstanding Japan, gradually succeeded in inciting riots in various places [in Korea]. Although [Korea] has generally returned to peace and quiet now, still today it is regrettable that there are a small number of outbreaks of disturbances. For that reason, in addition to managing the corporation's endeavors, the principal task of achieving harmony between our two peoples lies in promoting development in Korea and fostering productivity from the latent national (Korean) manpower.[95]

Initial emigration plans and the Oriental Development Company's budget allowance called for about ten thousand emigrants the first year, 1910–1911. Potential disturbances in Korea, however, forced the company to drastically scale down its plans. In addition, Oriental Development Company officials apparently learned at this time that earlier estimates of the availability of uncultivated wasteland were grossly exaggerated.[96] This exaggeration may also have contributed to the feeling that large-scale emigration was no longer possible. The Oriental Development Company finally announced that an experimental group of about two hundred families would make up the first emigration project.[97] In the end, only 116 families actually sailed to Korea the first year under Oriental Development Company auspices—a far cry from the thirty thousand originally estimated. Some Oriental Development Company officials even discussed terminating the program entirely after this first group.[98]

This shift in the Oriental Development Company's policy could also be seen in Japan's government position statements. The government no longer encouraged Japanese farmers to settle in Korea. For example, in a major position paper on Korea approved by the Japanese cabinet in July 1909, the government did not mention emigration of farmers at all.[99]

GETTING ACCESS TO THE LAND

After the Russo-Japanese War Japanese settlers in Korea complained to Japanese consular officials that land acquisition was made more difficult by an inadequate land registration system. Because the land register, the *yang'an,* recorded only the owner at the time of the last cadastral survey, prospective buyers found it difficult to know who was in fact the legal owner of individual pieces of land. Koreans claimed ownership rights on the basis of sets of documents (*mun'gi*—see Chapter Two) in the owner's possession. But Japanese feared Koreans forged *mun'gi* in order to sell land fraudulently to unsuspecting Japanese.[100] Settlers in the Kunsan area complained bitterly of "double sales," or the sale of a piece of land by a Korean to more than one Japanese buyer. As protection against these double sales, Japanese residents of that area formed an agricultural cooperative to record each transaction and to delineate spheres of interest so that no more than one Japanese investor would be competing for land in the same area.[101]

As noted earlier, in order to facilitate land acquisitions by Japanese settlers, the residency-general enacted the Agricultural and Residential Land Certification Law in October 1906. This law legalized foreign ownership of land in Korea. It also mandated that all land transactions, such as sales, inheritances, and grants, be approved by local government authorities and recorded in a certification register in each county office. By systematically recording the history of transactions involving a piece of land, the government enabled prospective buyers to identify ownership more accurately.[102]

Legalization of foreign ownership and establishment of the certification register ushered in a period of rapid increase in the amount of land owned by Japanese individuals and corporations. Statistics are not available for years prior to 1909, but residency-general statistics from 1909–1912 bear out this increase. Between June 1909, when 647 Japanese individuals and corporations reportedly owned over 52,000 *chŏngbo* (approximately 127,000 acres), and the fall of 1910, Japanese ownership increased by 35 percent to 70,000 *chŏngbo*.[103] By December 1912 slightly less than five thousand Japanese individuals and corporations owned over 130,000 *chŏngbo,* most of it cultivated land.[104] This total amounted to about 3 to 4 percent of the total arable land in Korea. A few (no more than eighty) large-scale landlords owned most of this land, and the vast majority of Japanese engaged in agriculture worked as tenants on land owned by Korean and Japanese landlords.

Although the 1906 certification law made Japanese ownership more secure and records of transactions more regular, it did not affect land that had changed hands prior to 1906 or land not investigated during the Kwangmu survey. Ownership of land kept off the *yang'an* in 1900 remained uncertain. The 1906 law, while improving the security of land acquisitions, did not systematize Korea's land registration system. Ownership problems continued to plague potential investors until a comprehensive reform of the registration was undertaken by the colonial government.

Since land registers were still the basis for tax assessments in Korea, the 1906 law also failed to measurably improve the government's chances of correct tax assessments on actual landowners. Therefore, the residency-general implemented various measures designed to increase tax revenue by closing registration loopholes.[105] In March 1908 the government adopted a partial amnesty policy of reducing by one-fourth the tax rate on any land reported by its owner that had been kept off the tax rolls.[106] Later that same year the government adopted an independent tax registration system designed to create accurate and up-to-date records of landowners and the value of their land. The tax register established at this time, the *kyŏlsu yŏnmyŏngbu,* became the principal source for tax assessments by the residency-general.[107] This register also became the initial bench mark for determining ownership over a particular piece of land during the cadastral survey of 1910.[108]

It became increasingly evident to the residency-general, however, that such piecemeal remedies to Korea's land registration and taxation systems were insufficient. The residency-general felt Korea needed an entirely new registration system. In early 1908 the government made the Provisional Bureau for the Investigation of Royal and State Property (and later its successor, the Property Reorganization Bureau) responsibile for preparing for a new nationwide cadastral survey and new land registers.[109] In line with its other responsibility—identifying and awarding ownership to palace-owned land—the bureau established schools staffed by Japanese advisors to train Korean surveyors.[110] The bureau increased these training efforts in 1908, and by 1910 the schools had reportedly produced 420 trained Korean surveyors.

Japanese officials tried to anticipate problems arising from a nationwide cadastral survey. In September 1908 the bureau published Korean-language books on surveying and sold them to the Korean public to convince them of the benefits of a cadastral survey. Eight thousand copies were sold the first month. The bureau also studied land surveys in India, Taiwan, and Okinawa to prepare for the cadastral survey in Korea. By the summer of 1909 the groundwork had been laid for a nationwide survey. On August 30 the resident-general, Sone Arasuke, reported to Foreign Minister Komura that preparations had been completed.[111]

Since the bureau feared the cadastral survey would spark opposition and violence among the Korean public—guerrillas were still fighting and Itō had recently been assassinated in Harbin—it undertook an experimental survey in Kyŏnggi province in November 1909 as a test of Korean public opinion. The experiment was initiated by twenty of the bureau's top Korean surveyors with the result "that the people's feelings were extremely tranquil."[112] In contrast to the public outcry at the time of the Nagamori proposal, neither Korean leaders nor the Korean public criticized the operation. Above all, the Japanese residency-general, desiring to counteract the negative press it had received from foreign missionaries and observers, wanted to avoid any widespread opposition to the survey among the Korean public. Without any obstacles to slow the time schedule, the bureau surveyed the entire experimental area by February 1910. Having trained surveyors, established a bureaucracy to undertake a cadastral survey and established that the public mood toward a survey was positive, the government reorganized the bureau into the Land Survey Bureau on March 4, 1910. Actual surveying commenced two months later.[113]

THE COLONIAL CADASTRAL SURVEY

The colonial government's survey was undertaken between 1910 and 1918 (most areas being surveyed by 1915) by highly competent surveyors and administrators. Many had been involved in surveying since the Kwangmu investigation of 1898–1902.[114] The residency-general, and later the government-general, brought Japanese technicians to Korea to assist in the operation. By 1918 surveyors had completed their survey of over nineteen million parcels of land, including agricultural, residential, urban, and forest land, at a total cost of 20.4 million yen, the approximate value of the colonial government's annual tax revenue.[115] More importantly, the Land Survey Bureau created a new land registration system using the *t'oji taejang,* which continued to the end of the Japanese administration in 1945, and which is still in use today in South Korea.

The cadastral survey had three main objectives: determination of ownership, actual surveying of each piece of land, and compilation of the *t'oji taejang.* To determine ownership, the Land Survey Bureau personnel primarily used earlier land documents. They distributed declaration of ownership forms to those individuals registered on the *kyŏlsu yŏnmyŏngbu* as paying taxes.[116] On these forms the registered owners described the land they claimed, giving names and addresses and the location and type of land in question.

These forms were the center of considerable controversy in the past. Many Korean and Japanese scholars have felt that this system, labeled as "reportism," was instituted to insure Japanese domination of Korean landownership.[117] Their argument is that the colonial government distributed these forms only to individuals it favored. In the minds of these scholars, this system enabled Japanese settlers in Korea to become large-scale landlords at the expense of former Korean owner-farmers. It is likely that some fraudulent declaration of ownership forms were submitted since most Korean farmers were unfamiliar with bureaucratic procedures and in many cases were illiterate. Analysis of land registers compiled after the cadastral survey was completed, however, show that such cases were not typical.

Throughout the survey process, the bureau sought to insure that all land in Korea was actually surveyed and registered on the *t'oji taejang*. It sought out those owners who failed to file declaration forms and compelled them to do so.[118] Through local Korean government officials, the bureau distributed additional declaration forms, and anyone not receiving a form directly from the bureau could obtain one from local authorities, who were Korean. After receiving the completed declaration forms from a particular locale, the bureau surveyed the land in each village in the area. Surveying often revealed additional undeclared land. Before recognizing claims to these lands, the bureau required an explanation for failure to report it and documentary evidence to prove ownership.

In the subsequent compilation of the *t'oji taejang* the bureau simply transferred owners' names from the declaration forms to the new register, assuming no disputes arose over ownership or boundaries. If two or more persons declared ownership over a single parcel of land, the bureau delayed making an ownership ruling *(sajŏng)* until documentary evidence supplied by each of the interested parties could be examined. This evidence consisted primarily of the *yang'an* from the Kwangmu survey and *mun'gi* in the claimants' possession. Secondary evidence included oral testimony from neighboring landowners.[119] Few instances of disputed ownership arose, suggesting that fraudulent reporting of ownership was not widespread. Of more than nineteen million parcels of land surveyed, less than one hundred thousand, or 0.5 percent, involved a dispute of any kind.[120] Multiple claimants disputed ownership in less than thirty-five thousand of these parcels; 64,449 parcels involved disputes over land that had been declared to be state-owned.

By 1916 all agricultural land in Korea had been surveyed. During the next two years, the bureau settled land disputes, compiled the land registers, and drew up detailed cadastral maps of all of Korea (on a scale of 1,200:1). Measurements recorded in the *t'oji taejang* and on the cadastral maps were of high professional quality. Some scholars may have criticized survey procedures because they may have favored Japanese landowners, but no scholars have found fault with the accuracy of the survey's statistical results. The highest tribute to the technical expertise of the surveyors, who were largely Korean, is that the same pages and maps created in the 1910–1918 survey are still in daily use today.

Summary

The decade between the Kwangmu survey at the turn of the century and the Japanese cadastral survey in 1910 was critical in our understanding of Japanese policy toward agriculture in Korea. By sending thousands of Japanese farmers to Korea, the Japanese government hoped to improve its security in Northeast Asia, provide homes and livelihoods for its surplus rural population, and further develop Korea as a source of agricultural imports. Between 1904 and 1909, the Japanese government and the residency-general in Korea attempted to secure the right of Japanese to own land in Korea and actual land on which Japanese farmers could settle. Although it successfully achieved the former in 1906, the first major effort to accomplish the latter, the Nagamori proposal, failed because of Korean public opposition. The Japanese colonial government finally secured land from the Korean royal household ministry in 1908, when the Oriental Development Company was created.

Faced with armed resistance to Japanese colonial policies by Korean guerrillas, leaders of the Oriental Development Company abandoned their effort to resettle large numbers of Japanese farmers in Korea. Instead of sending thousands of farm families to Korea, the Oriental Development Company sponsored less than a few hundred families during the first years of its settlement program. Encouraged by the Japanese government to emigrate to Korea after the Russo-Japanese War, most Japanese settlers emigrated at their own expense. In the end, the vast majority of early Japanese settlers did not engage in agriculture but became petty businesspeople in Korea's urban areas. Japanese settlers did not acquire large amounts of Korea's arable land and owned no more than 3 to 4 percent of the country's total acreage at the time of Korea's annexation in 1910. The social and economic impact of Japanese settlement and land ownership on Korea's agricultural sector would have been considerably more serious, however, if early colonial plans had been implemented. By assuming that large-scale Japanese settlement and land acquisitions occurred during this period, most historians have seriously overstated this impact.

In order to firmly establish landownership rights and facilitate land acquisition by Japanese nationals, the residency-general initiated a reorganization of the Korean land-registry system between 1906 and 1910. This effort started with several attempts to make ownership registration more systematic and culminated in the decision to conduct a nationwide cadastral survey. That survey, undertaken between 1910 and 1918, produced new and comprehensive ownership and statistical data that were then recorded on the newly compiled land registers, the *t'oji taejang*. These data reveal the nature and extent of Japanese landownership in rural Korea at the outset of the colonial period and form the basis for an analysis of landownership patterns in the following years.

CHAPTER 5

IMPLEMENTING JAPAN'S COLONIAL LAND POLICY: THE VIEW FROM THE VILLAGE CIRCA 1910

Historians of modern Korea have traditionally credited the Japanese colonial administration's cadastral survey with causing most of Korea's socioeconomic ills during the colonial period and into the post–World War II years. Han Woo-keun, for example, describes the survey as "the main instrument of depriving Koreans of their farms" and as the "legal basis for the seizure of Korean land by Japanese."[1] Professor Han's analysis typifies the conventional wisdom of Korean and Japanese scholars on the survey.[2] Clearly, the survey resulted from Japanese interest (and Korean interest dating from the Kwangmu period) in establishing a rational land-registration system that would facilitate acquisition and development by Japanese nationals and corporations. Aside from Shin Yongha's insightful study, however, the survey has been subjected to little scholarly analysis despite its alleged importance as a vital tool of Japanese imperialist policy. The genesis and role of the survey process have been examined; the next step is to examine landownership as found and recorded by colonial surveyors in the first years of the government-general.

Generally, land-distribution patterns changed very little between 1900 and 1914 in the villages studied. Villages with a sharply skewed ownership structure in the last years of the Yi dynasty—that is, villages with a small number of landlords owning large portions of village arable land—continued to exhibit that characteristic after the Japanese cadastral survey. Similarly, in villages with more equal land distribution, a large measure of continuity existed after the cadastral survey.

The names of individual landowners changed significantly between 1900 and 1914, and in some cases landownership shifted from a large Korean landlord to a Japanese one, but the overall picture of land distribution differed little before or after annexation in 1910. This finding should not be altogether unexpected. The colonial government did not intend the survey to reform Korean land tenure and redistribute land. Rather, the government sought to identify the legal owner of each parcel of land in the country based on past claims of ownership. The cadastral survey was simply one mechanism of a Japanese agricultural policy designed to create an accurate land register and to secure accessibility to landownership through changes in the Korean legal system. Therefore, one would expect a continuation of land-tenure patterns from the Yi dynasty, not a disruption or upheaval of them.

An examination of the *t'oji taejang* from the villages studied reveals this continuity. Distinct differences in land-distribution patterns from village to village paralleled differences in the *yang'an* data. The data used in analyzing these differences are, for the most part, for the years 1913 and 1914, the years in which most villages were surveyed by the new colonial administration.

Overview of Village Data

Before analyzing the individual villages in detail, a macroscopic view is helpful. Figure 5-1 depicts levels of landownership by Koreans, Japanese, and corporations in 1914 in the villages studied. As seen in this chart, Koreans owned most of all types of land in 1914, over 85 percent of all paddy land, almost 81 percent of upland, and over 90 percent of residential land. Japanese individuals and corporations owned approximately 8 percent and 7 percent, respectively, of the arable land in the villages. Thus, these villages contained a higher percentage of Japanese-owned land than the national average.[3] The central government, local governments, one clan, and one church also owned small amounts of land in the villages.[4]

Some scholars have suggested that Japanese individuals and corporations acquired the highest-quality land in Korea when they arrived in the peninsula in the early twentieth century, but data from the villages studied suggest otherwise. In general, colonial surveyors assessed Korean-owned land at a higher value than Japanese-owned land. Some may suggest Japanese-owned land was assessed at a lower rate in order to reduce taxes, but there is no evidence of this. One *p'yŏng* (about 36 square feet) of Korean-owned paddy land averaged 17.1 sen in 1914, while land owned by Japanese individuals and corporations averaged only 15.5 sen and 12.1 sen, respectively (see Table 5-1). Similarly, the assessed value of Korean-owned upland exceeded the value of upland owned by Japanese —8.8 sen per *p'yŏng* compared with 7.0 sen. Corporate-owned upland, at 10.2 sen per *p'yŏng,* averaged the highest assessed value in 1914.

FIGURE 5–1
Land Distribution in Villages in 1914 (in percent)

Paddy Land

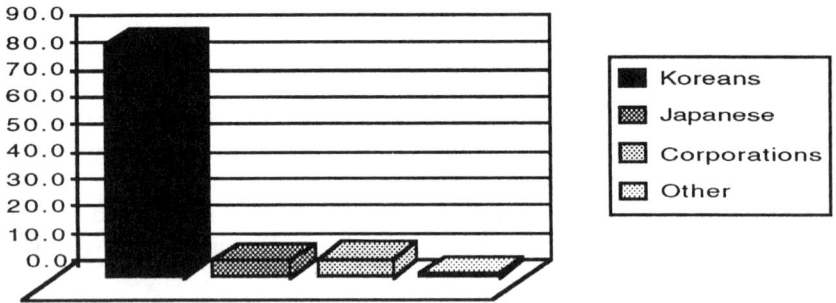

Upland

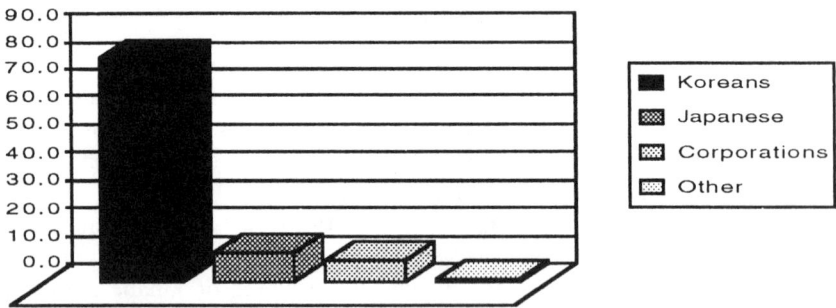

Residential Land

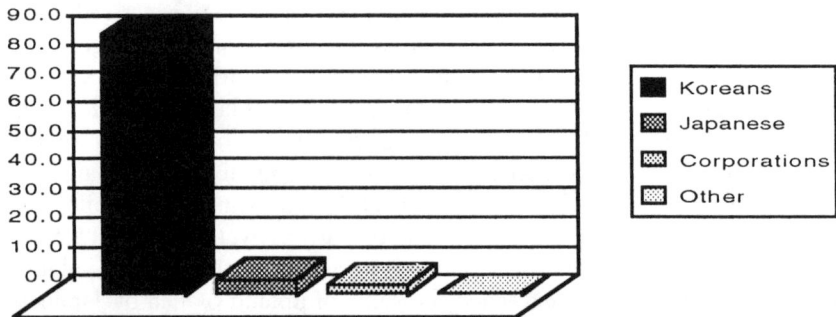

Source: *t'oji taejang*

Table 5-1　Average Assessed Value of Arable Land in the Villages
(in sen per *p'yŏng*)

| | PADDY | | | UPLAND | | |
	KOREAN	JAPANESE	CORPORATE	KOREAN	JAPANESE	CORPORATE
1914	17.1	15.5	12.1	8.8	7.0	10.2
1916	17.1	15.5	12.1	8.8	7.1	10.2
1918	17.0	15.7	12.1	8.8	7.1	10.2
1920	17.0	13.4	13.7	8.7	6.9	9.9
1922	17.0	13.4	13.6	8.7	7.0	9.8
1924	17.0	13.7	13.6	8.7	7.0	9.8
1926	17.0	13.7	13.7	8.7	7.3	9.8
1928	17.0	13.7	13.8	8.6	7.6	9.8
1930	16.5	18.4	13.7	8.7	7.3	9.8
1932	16.4	18.2	13.7	8.6	7.2	9.8
1934	16.4	18.0	15.9	8.2	7.2	11.0
1936	16.3	18.2	15.8	8.2	7.2	10.7
1938	16.3	18.2	16.0	8.2	7.0	10.5
1940	16.4	18.2	16.1	8.1	7.1	10.5
1942	16.4	18.3	16.3	8.0	7.3	10.5

SOURCE: *t'oji taejang*

Apparently, at the outset of the colonial period Japanese individuals owned lower-quality land than Korean landowners.

By the end of the colonial period, however, this situation had changed. Although Korean landowners continued to own higher-value upland than the Japanese in 1942 (the year before all land in Korea was reappraised), Japanese individuals controlled the highest-quality paddy land. During the course of the colonial period Japanese landowners raised the average assessed value of their paddy land to 18.3 sen per *p'yŏng,* while the value of Korean-owned land actually dropped below the 1914 rate.

During the colonial period an owner could legally change the average assessed value of land by improving the land or allowing it to deteriorate so that it was reclassified as a different land type and by acquiring new, higher-value plots of land. Village data for 1914 suggest that Japanese investors initially acquired relatively low-value land. They later improved the land through capital-intensive investments such as chemical fertilization and irrigation and also acquired large amounts of high-quality land from Korean landowners. This acquisition did not occur at the outset of the colonial period, as has been alleged, but rather during the worldwide depression of the early 1930s.

Owners of arable land in the villages resided throughout Japan and Korea in 1914, as shown in Table 5-2. Individuals living within the villages owned more land than any other single area. These local residents owned about 25 percent of all privately owned paddy land. Land-

Table 5-2   Residency of Landowners in 1914 (All-Village Total) by Owner Group

OWNER	WITHIN THE VILLAGE	SAME MYŎN	SAME COUNTY	SAME PROVINCE/ PROVINCE TOWN	SEOUL	JAPAN	OTHER AND UNKNOWN	TOTAL
Koreans								
Paddy	145,133	58,234	141,144	51,088	112,834	—	12,694	521,127
Upland	154,448	20,790	27,267	21,758	25,886	—	1,835	251,984
Japanese								
Paddy	—	—	1,208	11,864	1,145	25,098	—	39,315
Upland	—	418	17,686	3,924	—	18,489	—	40,517
Corporate								
Paddy	—	—	1,710	—	39,287	—	—	40,997
Upland	—	—	—	—	18,270	4,457	—	22,727
Government								
Paddy	5,929	—	—	—	3,905	—	—	9,834
Upland	3,149	—	—	—	—	—	—	3,149
Other								
Paddy	—	—	—	—	—	—	1,275	1,275
Upland	—	—	—	—	—	—	—	0
Totals*								
Paddy	151,062 (24.7)	58,234 (9.5)	144,062 (23.5)	62,952 (10.3)	157,171 (25.7)	25,098 (4.1)	13,969 (2.3)	612,548
Upland	157,597 (49.5)	21,208 (6.7)	44,953 (14.1)	25,682 (8.1)	44,156 (13.9)	22,946 (7.2)	1,835 (.6)	318,377

*Numbers in parentheses represent percentages of total
SOURCE: t'oji taejang

owners living within walking distance of the villages (within the *myŏn* in which the village was located) owned another 9 percent of total paddy land.[5] However, landowners living beyond the immediate vicinity of the villages (absentee landlords using tenants to cultivate their lands) controlled most cultivated land in 1914—approximately 56 percent of all privately held land. Landlords living in rural areas within the same *kun* (county) or province possessed much of this privately owned land, most of which was paddy land. Residents of Seoul and regional towns owned about 25 percent of the arable land in the villages, most of which was also paddy land. The farther an owner lived from the villages, the more likely this person was to own paddy land instead of upland.

Many Japanese individuals owning land in the villages in 1914 had settled in the Korean interior, but those living in Japan owned most of the Japanese-owned land. This land, predominantly paddy land, provided both a reliable supply of agricultural products to the Japanese market and capital, in the form of rents paid to absentee landlords, to the Japanese economy. According to Michael Hechtor, absentee British landlords played a similar role in colonial Ireland, withdrawing capital that could under other circumstances be used to make improvements on the land.[6] In Japan's case, one corporation headquartered in Kyūshū owned land in one of the Korean villages at the outset of the colonial period. Japanese landowners residing in Korea tended to live in small towns and communities along the Korean coast and occasionally in the interior, not in Seoul or in the the villages themselves.[7]

These data, like the aggregate data compiled by the government-general, provide a general picture of landownership in 1914. Aggregate data, however, are a composite of data from a number of Korean villages, each village having different characteristics and varied experiences during the twentieth century. Therefore, it is useful to examine the land-tenure situation in each of the villages separately.

Individual Villages

SONGSAN-NI

Songsan-ni, near Hansan, was one of the two isolated villages studied and was characterized in the waning years of the Yi dynasty by local landownership, little tenancy, and a relatively equitable distribution of arable land. Did that situation change after the colonial cadastral survey and registration of landowners on the *t'oji taejang?*

As shown in Table 5-3, Korean landowners in Songsan-ni owned most of the arable land in the village in 1914—92.1 percent of all paddy land and 96 percent of total upland. Japanese individuals and corporations owned the remainder of Songsan-ni's arable land. Korean owners con-

Table 5-3   Landownership in Songsan-ni in 1914 (in *p'yŏng*)

TYPE OF LAND	KOREAN	JAPANESE	CORPORATE	OTHER	TOTAL
Paddy	137,005	687	8,314	2,704	148,710
	(92.1)	(.5)	(5.6)	(1.8)	
Upland	34,511	1,433			35,944
	(96)	(4)			
Residential	9,644				9,644
	(100)				
Forest	4,529			3,909	8,438
	(53.7)			(46.3)	
Cemetery	402				402
	(100)				
Total land	186,091	2,120	8,314	6,613	203,138
	(91.6)	(1)	(4.1)	(3.3)	
Total arable land	171,516	2,120	8,314	2,704	184,654
	(92.9)	(1.1)	(4.5)	(1.5)	
Number of owners	121	2	1	1	125
Average holding size	1,417	1,060	8,314	2,704	1,477

Notes: Numbers in parentheses represent percentages of total
    "Other" in Songsan-ni included only the village itself
SOURCE: 1914 *t'oji taejang*

trolled all residential land in the village. The two Japanese individuals who owned land in the village in 1914—an obscure farmer in a neighboring *myŏn* and a fairly large-scale landlord living in Kunsan—owned small plots of land and made no significant contribution to the village's economy. One corporation, the Oriental Development Company, owned land in Songsan-ni. Individual Korean landowners and the village itself owned all undeveloped land.

As was the case at the turn of the century, individuals living in Songsan-ni owned about half of all village arable land in 1914 (Table 5-4). They owned over 42 percent of village paddy land, approximately 72 percent of upland, and almost 83 percent of residential land. In addition, some landowners living in neighboring villages within Hansan-myŏn undoubtedly walked across village boundary lines to cultivate fields in Songsan-ni. Thus, the percentage of local ownership by individuals living close enough to their fields to cultivate them would be even higher if their lands were included in these figures. Local landownership in Songsan-ni contrasted sharply with two of the other villages studied but had changed little from the years of the Kwangmu survey. Throughout the colonial period, Songsan-ni was characterized by a high rate of local ownership.[8]

Individuals and corporations outside the vicinity of the village owned from one-third to one-half of Songsan-ni's arable land.[9] Residents of areas of Sŏch'ŏn-gun outside of Hansan-myŏn owned much of this land.[10] Landowners—all Korean—living in Seoul owned 12 percent of all paddy land in the village but no upland or residential land. As shown in Table 5-4, individuals living elsewhere in Ch'ungch'ŏng province or in nearby provincial towns owned another 15 percent of all arable land in Songsan-ni.[11]

A direct correlation existed between the place of residence and the size of an owner's plots of land. In general, a larger plot of arable land meant the field was well situated near the floor of the valley and close to irrigation and transportation sources. Owners living in the vicinity of the village, either in Songsan-ni itself or in Hansan-myŏn, owned plots averaging under 500 *p'yŏng* each, whereas owners residing elsewhere in Sŏch'ŏn-gun and in Seoul owned plots averaging 600 *p'yŏng* and 1,000 *p'yŏng,* respectively. In general, the farther an owner lived from Songsan-ni, the more likely the land would be large rice fields rather than small upland plots situated on the outskirts of the village.

A small number of individuals, most living within Songsan-ni itself, owned a disproportionately large percentage of the village's arable land in 1914. Seven individuals, less than 6 percent of all village landowners, owned 42,435 *p'yŏng,* or approximately 23 percent of all cultivated land in the village.[12] Most of this land was paddy land. Over half of all landowners possessed less than 900 *p'yŏng* each, the amount of arable land considered necessary to support a farming family at that time. These individuals owned a total of 19,380 *p'yŏng,* or only about 11 percent of the total arable land in Songsan-ni.

Over one-quarter of the ninety individuals owning arable land in Songsan-ni owned less than 450 *p'yŏng* each. In addition to farming these small plots, they worked as wage laborers and/or tenants on land owned by others. Also, seven individuals owned residential land in the village but did not own any arable land. Some of these landowners may have owned land in neighboring villages, but they were still probably subsistence tenant farmers and represented a large percentage of the owners registered on the *t'oji taejang.*

An examination of landholding patterns among the residents of Songsan-ni also reveals unequal land distribution in 1914. As shown in Figures 5-2 and 5-2-1, six individuals possessing the largest landholdings, each over 5,000 *p'yŏng* of cultivated land, comprised 10.7 percent of Songsan-ni's resident landowners, but they owned a total of 36,626 *p'yŏng,* almost 20 percent of all arable land in the village. On the other hand, individuals owning less than 900 *p'yŏng,* or 41.1 percent of resident landowners, possessed less than 5 percent of arable village land. In addition, 12.5 percent of Songsan-ni's resident landowners possessed residential land only and worked as tenants or wage laborers on farmland owned by landlords, or they engaged in by-employment.

Table 5-4   Residency Patterns among Landowners ca. 1914

VILLAGE	LAND TYPE	IN THE VILLAGE	SAME MYŎN	SAME COUNTY
Songsan-ni	Paddy	63,005 (42.4)	31,680 (21.3)	16,133 (10.8)
	Upland	25,825 (71.8)	5,133 (14.3)	3,854 (10.7)
	Residential	7,981 (82.8)	806 (8.3)	653 (6.8)
Paeksŏng-ni	Paddy	41,975 (58.5)	9,335 (13.0)	3,044 (4.3)
	Upland	69,018 (73.6)	5,313 (5.7)	6,286 (6.7)
	Residential	9,519 (81.7)	507 (4.4)	321 (2.8)
Kongsu-ri	Paddy	36,144 (13.7)	15,976 (6.1)	41,690 (15.8)
	Upland	36,939 (26.4)	6,655 (4.8)	27,503 (19.7)
	Residential	3,531 (24.5)	—	1,744 (12.1)
P'albong-ni	Paddy	9,938 (7.8)	1,243 (1.0)	83,195 (65.6)
	Upland	25,815 (61.3)	4,107 (9.8)	7,310 (17.4)
	Residential	6,411 (90.0)	160 (2.2)	395 (5.5)
Total all villages	Paddy	151,062 (24.7)	58,234 (9.5)	144,062 (23.6)
	Upland	157,597 (50.6)	21,208 (6.8)	44,953 (14.4)
	Residential	27,442 (64.1)	1,473 (3.4)	3,113 (7.3)

Note: Numbers in parentheses represent percentages of total
SOURCE: *t'oji taejang*

As shown in the chart, this uneven land distribution worsened between 1900 and 1914. The percentage of arable village land owned by Songsan-ni's largest landowners increased significantly at the expense of individuals owning small amounts of land. However, despite the obvious imbalance in land distribution in 1914, Songsan-ni, compared to the other villages studied, had a significant percentage—almost 25 percent of total resident landowners—of middle-ranking landowners, or those owning between 1,500 and 5,000 *p'yŏng.*

The landownership data from 1914 also suggest a trend toward concentration of land in the hands of fewer village families. In 1900 members of three clans in the village—the Hansan Yi, Yongsŏng Ch'a, and

SAME PROVINCE/ PROVINCE TOWN	SEOUL	JAPAN	OTHER AND UNKNOWN	TOTAL
17,978	17,822	—	2,092	148,710
(12.1)	(12.0)		(1.4)	
1,132	—	—	—	35,944
(3.2)				
204	—	—	—	9,644
(2.1)				
278	8,415	4,396	4,329	71,772
(0.4)	(11.7)	(6.1)	(6)	
4,396	1,449	4,457	2,803	93,722
(4.7)	(1.5)	(4.8)	(3)	
510	—	351	440	11,648
(4.4)		(3.0)	(3.7)	
16,884	129,730	20.702	2,911	264,037
(6.4)	(49.1)	(7.8)	(1.1)	
17,074	42,707	9,024	—	139,902
(12.2)	(30.5)	(6.5)		
3,488	4,988	676	—	14,427
(14.2)	(34.6)	(4.7)		
27,812	1,204	—	3,362	126,754
(21.9)	(1.0)		(2.7)	
3,080	—	1,465	307	42,084
(7.3)		(3.5)	(0.7)	
162	—	—	—	7,128
(2.3)				
62,952	157,171	25,098	12,694	611,273
(10.3)	(25.7)	(4.1)	(2.1)	
25,682	44,156	14,946	3,110	311,652
(8.2)	(14.2)	(4.8)	(1.0)	
4,364	4,988	1,027	440	42,847
(10.2)	(11.6)	(2.4)	(1.0)	

Koryŏng Pak—owned 46.7 percent of all arable village land and 85 percent of land owned by Songsan-ni residents.[13] By 1914 members of the Ch'a and Pak clans had increased their landholdings in Songsan-ni at the expense of the Hansan Yi and other clans in the village. Together, members of these two clans owned over 45 percent of village arable land and almost 95 percent of all land owned by Songsan-ni residents. Other villages exhibited a similar trend toward land concentration among locally powerful clans.[14]

To what extent did the largest landowners possess the highest-quality land in the village? As was the case for the *yang'an* data from the turn of the century, no pattern emerges from the 1910–1918 cadastral survey

FIGURE 5–2
Land Distribution among Songsan-ni Residents, 1900

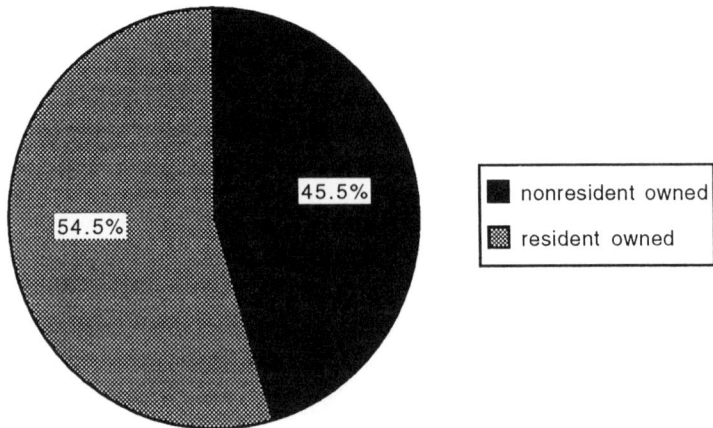

Breakdown of the 54.5% of Village Land Owned by Residents,
According to Size of Holding

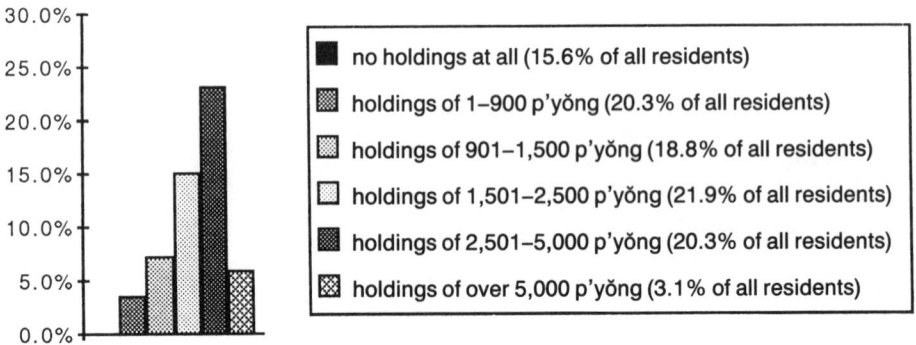

Source: Kwangmu *yang'an*

data. The Land Survey Bureau assessed paddy land in Songsan-ni at an average value of 17.2 sen per *p'yŏng,* higher than the other villages studied because paddy land in Songsan-ni was of high fertility.[15] Village paddy land owned by individuals who each possessed over 5,000 *p'yŏng* of arable land averaged a lower assessed value than the village as a

FIGURE 5–2–1
Land Distribution among Songsan-ni Residents, 1914

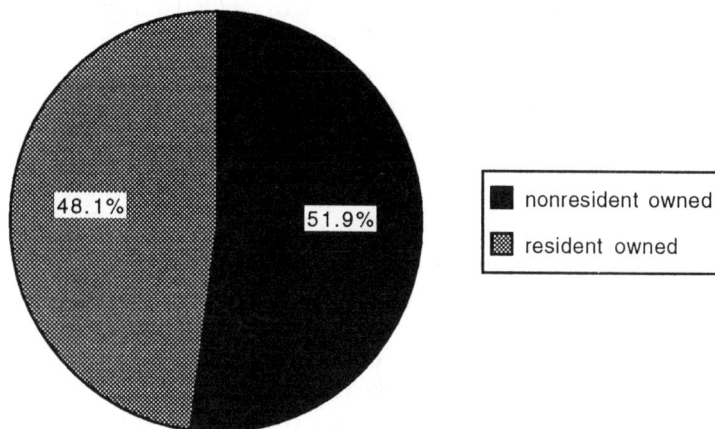

Breakdown of the 48.1% of Village Land Owned by Residents,
According to Size of Holding

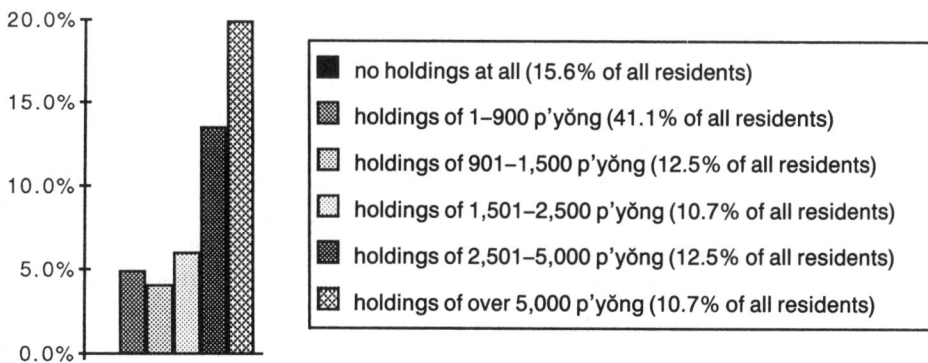

Source: *t'oji taejang*

whole. Their total holdings of paddy land, 36,395 *p'yŏng,* were assessed at 5,692 yen, or 15.6 sen per *p'yŏng.* The average assessed value of upland owned by these large-scale landowners was slightly higher than the village average.[16] The largest landowners in Songsan-ni did not own the best land in the village.[17]

A correlation between value of land owned and place of residence did exist in Songsan-ni in 1914, but it was not particularly strong. In general, the closer owners lived to Songsan-ni the lower the value of their land. Owners living within Songsan-ni owned both paddy land and upland of the lowest assessed value. Conversely, residents of Seoul and provincial towns owned land of the highest assessed value. This pattern also corresponds to the larger plot size owned by these absentee landlords.

Contrary to conventional wisdom, Japanese individuals did not own highly valuable land in Songsan-ni in 1914. The Oriental Development Company's 8,314 *p'yŏng* of paddy land, for example, averaged an assessed value of only 12.7 sen per *p'yŏng*. The company's land consisted of some of the lowest-quality land in the village. This fact is significant because it strongly suggests that Oriental Development Company officials did not seek out high-value land; rather, they acquired marginal land sight unseen, or land that was not in high demand and therefore less expensive. This practice parallels the practice of other immigrant settlement corporations that also acquired lower-quality land on which they attempted to settle unsuspecting Japanese farmers. The two Japanese individuals owning land in Songsan-ni in 1914 also owned land assessed below the village average.[18]

The *t'oji taejang* reveal a high degree of continuity in the ownership of residential land between 1900 and 1914. The Kwangmu *yang'an* indicated that most of the homes (sixty-five of sixty-eight) in Songsan-ni were owned by the people living in them. The 1914 data suggest a similar situation. In that year Songsan-ni contained sixty-four plots of residential land totaling 9,644 *p'yŏng*. These sixty-four plots were owned by fifty-four different landowners, the majority of whom owned only one residential plot. Most 1914 landowners owned a house in Songsan-ni regardless of the total amount of arable land in their possession. Even among residents owning less than 900 *p'yŏng* each, fifteen of twenty-three owned their own homes. Further, as in 1900, some individuals who did not own any arable land in the village owned houses of their own.[19] Most owners with more than one residential plot lived within the village. Individuals living outside Songsan-ni owned only ten homes in the village. In contrast to land in the less-isolated villages, residential land in Songsan-ni had not yet become a marketable item in 1914, presumably because rents were too low. This continued throughout the colonial period.[20]

Residential plots in Songsan-ni tended to be small compared to those in the other villages studied, averaging between 100 and 160 *p'yŏng* each; many plots were smaller.[21] Generally, the size of an owner's residence paralleled the size of his agricultural holdings. The largest landowner in the village, Pak Tŏk-ha, owned the largest home site, one of 286 *p'yŏng,* or about 10,300 square feet.

The most striking aspect of the *t'oji taejang* and *yang'an* data is the lack of common landowners on the two documents, although they were compiled only fourteen years apart. Although the same clans in Songsan-ni owned most village land in both 1900 and 1914, only about one-fourth of the names on the *yang'an* appear again on the *t'oji taejang*. Why this pattern existed in Sonsang-ni, and to a lesser degree in the other villages, is not clear. Land may have changed hands on a large scale during the intervening decade, having been sold or passed along through inheritance. However, it is unlikely that so much village land would have changed hands that rapidly.

Ownership may have been awarded in 1914 to individuals who had not previously owned land in the village. That is, individuals may have used the cadastral survey to fraudulently register land as their own. Indeed, several historians have alleged that this type of fraud was widespread. However, this does not explain why only the names of landowners, and not the distribution and residency patterns as well, changed so drastically between the two land surveys. Further, if fraud existed on such a scale, it would have resulted in large-scale disputes, outraged farmers protesting the injustice, or both.

Another possibility is that the Land Survey Bureau recognized long-term cultivation rights as de facto ownership and awarded legal ownership to individuals who had been tenants in 1900. Bureau documents suggest that this was not the case however, and no other evidence indicates any such recognition. In Songsan-ni, for example, no individual registered in 1900 as a pure tenant, or one renting all the land cultivated, owned land in 1914. Further, owner-tenants, while maintaining possession of land owned in 1900, did not assume ownership over any of the land they had previously rented from landlords.

Possibly, the name recorded on the *yang'an* may not have been the actual current owner in 1900. Individuals frequently went by several names and used Chinese characters interchangeably even if they were not actually homonyms.[22] Perhaps surveyors in 1900, rather than perform an actual survey and exhaustive research into the current owner, simply transcribed names of owners, some possibly already deceased, from *yang'an* of an earlier period. There are sufficient examples of this with earlier *yang'an*. This practice would account for the speed with which the survey was undertaken and for the high correlation of surnames between the *yang'an* and *t'oji taejang*. It would also help explain the infrequent repetition of given names and the absence of protest—land was registered in the same family's name. The high degree of surname continuity strongly suggests that no significant upheaval in local clan control prevailed. In some instances owners simply did not register their land in 1900, thereby avoiding taxation; thus, the introduction of "new" landowners in 1914 may have been more illusory than real.

Although most accounts of the colonial period state that Japanese acquired land from the government-general or small-scale Korean farmers, thereby forcing these farmers to migrate north to Manchuria, data from Songsan-ni and the other villages suggest otherwise. The 1914 data indicate that the Oriental Development Company acquired its land in Songsan-ni (eight plots of paddy land totaling 8,314 *p'yŏng*) from private individuals living outside the village. None of this land had been previously owned by royal palaces or government institutions.[23] In several instances, the previous owner had lived in Seoul, so it is possible that the company arranged its purchase there. The Oriental Development Company acquired its land from absentee landlords, not from small-scale farmers, a point made clearer in data from the other villages. The company presumably bought this land between 1908 and 1913 when it bought thousands of other plots throughout the peninsula.[24]

Songsan-ni changed little between 1900 and 1914. Two Japanese landowners and the Oriental Development Company acquired only a few small plots of land in the village during these years. Urban investors, some living in Seoul, owned a significant portion of Songsan-ni land, but probably no more than in the late Yi dynasty. The village remained isolated in the foothills of Hansan-myŏn, seemingly little affected by the economic changes evident in areas surrounding urban commercial centers or by political changes in Seoul. For all intents and purposes, land-tenure patterns of the late nineteenth century continued in Songsan-ni into the twentieth century, at least during the early years of the colonial period.

PAEKSŎNG-NI

Paeksŏng-ni, near Nonsan, resembled Songsan-ni in several key respects: both villages were and still are relatively isolated, landownership tended to be dominated by local individual landowners, land tended to be relatively equitably distributed, and both villages' economies were tied into a regional, rather than national, market system. Such was the case in 1900, and very little had changed by 1913, when the village was surveyed and *t'oji taejang* compiled.[25] Table 5-5 represents the land-distribution pattern in Paeksŏng-ni in 1913.

As seen in the table, Korean landowners possessed most of the land in Paeksŏng-ni in 1913, whether paddy land, upland, or residential land. Although Japanese individuals owned a minimal amount of village land —3.4 percent of all arable land—this amount exceeded the amount in Songsan-ni during the same time. Koreans owned all residential land in Songsan-ni, but in Paeksŏng-ni both Japanese individuals and corporations owned home sites.

Despite owning homes in the village, the two Japanese owning land in

Table 5-5   Landownership Distribution in Paeksŏng-ni in 1913
             (in *p'yŏng*)

TYPE OF LAND	KOREAN	JAPANESE	CORPORATE	OTHER*	TOTAL
Paddy	62,819	5,604	3,124	225	71,772
	(87.5)	(7.8)	(4.4)	(0.3)	
Upland	88,808	—	4,457	457	93,722
	(94.8)		(4.8)	(0.5)	
Forest	8,773	—	—	8,973	17,746
	(49.4)			(50.6)	
Residential	11,297	65	286	—	11,648
	(97.0)	(0.6)	(2.5)		
Cemetery	317	—	—	—	317
	(100)				
Total land owned	172,018	5,669	7,867	9,656	195,210
	(88.1)	(2.9)	(4.0)	(4.9)	
Total arable land	151,629	5,604	7,581	682	165,496
	(91.6)	(3.4)	(4.6)	(0.4)	
Number of owners	91	2	2	1	96
	(94.8)	(2.1)	(2.1)	(1.0)	

*Includes two individuals whose identities are unknown
Note: Numbers in parentheses represent percentages of total
SOURCE: *t'oji taejang*

Paeksŏng-ni lived in Japan and in the nearby market town of Nonsan. In 1914 Kodera Genkichi, a resident of Kobe, owned 4,396 *p'yŏng* of paddy land and one plot of residential land in Paeksŏng-ni. A few years later he reportedly owned almost 40 *chŏngbo* of paddy land in Korea, all of it in Nonsan-gun. He never emigrated to the peninsula. The other Japanese landowner, Kajiwara Kikuzō, owned one small plot of paddy land. Kajiwara headed a Nonsan rice-polishing business and later served as mayor of the city. Kajiwara, who emigrated to Korea from Ōita-ken, did not own large amounts of land in Korea.[26] Two corporations owned land in Paeksŏng-ni in 1913, the Oriental Development Company (3,124 *p'yŏng* of paddy land) and the huge Kunitake gōmeikaisha (4,457 *p'yŏng* of upland), headquartered in Kurume in Fukuoka-ken.[27]

Despite its close proximity to the market towns of Nonsan and Kanggyŏng, Paeksŏng-ni was characterized by local ownership and little absentee landlordism in 1913. People living within Paeksŏng-ni owned a full 66.6 percent of all arable land in the village in that year. Individuals living in neighboring villages in Yŏnsan-myŏn owned another 8.9 percent of Paeksŏng-ni's arable land. Table 5-4 reveals the extent of this local landownership. Local owners dominated ownership of all types of land, including paddy land, upland, and residential land. Similar to Songsan-ni but in contrast to the other two villages, local residents owned almost all homes in Paeksŏng-ni. Local ownership increased and the role of absentee landlords declined during later years of the colonial period, a trend also seen in Songsan-ni.

Residents of Seoul and other urban areas played only a minor role in landownership in Paeksŏng-ni in 1913. Korean individuals living in Seoul owned 6,740 *p'yŏng,* just over 4 percent of village arable land and the Seoul-based Oriental Development Company owned the remainder, 1.9 percent of Paeksŏng-ni's cultivated land. As in Songsan-ni, Seoul residents owned a higher percentage of Paeksŏng-ni's paddy land (12 percent). Residents of provincial towns such as Nonsan and Kanggyŏng at the opposite end of the Nonsan plain also owned little land in the village at the outset of the colonial period. However, Paeksŏng-ni became more closely tied to the national economy later in the colonial period with the improvement of transportation systems through the Yŏnsan area.[28]

Similar to Songsan-ni, the place of a landowner's residence corresponded to the size of the plots owned. Although average plots were generally smaller than in Songsan-ni (due to the large amount of upland fields in Paeksŏng-ni), Seoul residents owned the large and therefore well-situated plots of and in the village. Fields owned by residents of the capital averaged 400 *p'yŏng,* and those owned by Japanese residents were even larger at over 650 *p'yŏng.* Conversely, residents of Paeksŏng-ni and other villages in Yŏnsan-myŏn owned plots averaging under 400 *p'yŏng.* Local landowners tended to own small plots of arable land on the edges of the village.

Arable land in Paeksŏng-ni was unevenly distributed among the various landowners in 1913. A small percentage of individuals (7.3 percent of all landowners), each owning over 5,000 *p'yŏng* of arable land, possessed 46,170 *p'yŏng,* or 27.9 percent of all arable land in the village. At the same time, the thirty-four individuals, or 35 percent of all landowners, owning less than the subsistence level of 900 *p'yŏng* of arable land owned only 16,132 *p'yŏng* of Paeksŏng-ni's land, or 9.7 percent of the village total. Despite this imbalance, the gap in Paeksŏng-ni between large- and small-scale landowners was not great. As in Songsan-ni, no single landowner possessed over 9,000 *p'yŏng.*

Among the fifty-three individuals owning land and living within Paeksŏng-ni itself, landownership was also imbalanced in favor of a small number of large-scale landowners. This distribution pattern is shown in Figures 5-3 and 5-3-1. Six individuals, or 11 percent of all resident landowners, each owned over 5,000 *p'yŏng* of arable land, totaling 38,161 *p'yŏng*—over 23 percent of Paeksŏng-ni's arable land. Twelve resident landowners each possessing less than 900 *p'yŏng* of arable land in the village comprised 22.6 percent of all resident owners, but together they owned only 5,590 *p'yŏng,* or 3.4 percent of total village arable land.

As shown in Figure 5-3-1, middle-ranking landowners, each owning between 1,500 and 5,000 *p'yŏng,* comprised a larger percentage, almost 40 percent, of total resident landowners and owned over one-third of village arable land. Similar to Songsan-ni, the relatively large group of middle-ranking landowners was indicative of the generally equitable wealth distribution in such isolated and self-sufficient villages in rural Korea during the second decade of the twentieth century. Paeksŏng-ni landowners were not wealthy, but the division between large and small landowners was not evident in Paeksŏng-ni.

The trend toward concentration of village arable land among fewer local families, seen earlier in Songsan-ni, also appeared in Paeksŏng-ni. As Figure 5-3-1 indicates, after the cadastral survey a large percentage of resident landowners possessed medium- and large-scale landholdings, and fewer owned less than the subsistence level. In 1913, 22.6 percent of resident landowners each owned less than 901 *p'yŏng,* whereas almost half of Paeksŏng-ni owners had done so in 1900. However, this apparent improvement in land distribution masked a situation that was in reality quite the opposite. Individuals owning small amounts of land at the turn of the century apparently owned none in 1913, having been squeezed out by large-scale landowners in the village. Small-scale landowners tended to be members of less-powerful local clans. While members of the two dominant village clans, Chŏnju Yi and Ch'ŏngju Han, significantly increased their registered landholdings between 1900 and 1913, land-ownership by village members of other clans declined sharply during the same period. Members of these two clans owned approximately 60 percent of all arable land in the village in 1900, but by 1913 these two clans had increased their holdings to over 76 percent.

Colonial surveyors assessed the value of Paeksŏng-ni paddy land and upland at rates lower than those in the other villages studied, undoubtedly due to the overall lower productivity and unavailability of irrigation sources in Paeksŏng-ni. As mentioned earlier, Paeksŏng-ni is situated in the foothills above the Nonsan plain and lacks streams that could provide irrigation. Village paddy land averaged 13.6 sen per *p'yŏng* in 1913. Koreans may have owned most agricultural land in the village, but Japanese individuals owned land of a higher assessed value. The assessed value of Korean-owned paddy land averaged 13.5 sen per *p'yŏng,* slightly less than the village average, while paddy land owned by the two Japanese individuals averaged 15.8 sen per p'yŏng. Not surprisingly, the Japanese-owned land was more advantageously located near irrigation and transportation systems.

Corporate-owned land tended to be of low quality. As in the case of Songsan-ni, paddy land owned by the Oriental Development Company was assessed lower than the village average, or only 11.2 sen per *p'yŏng.*

FIGURE 5–3
Land Distribution among Paeksŏng-ni Residents, 1900

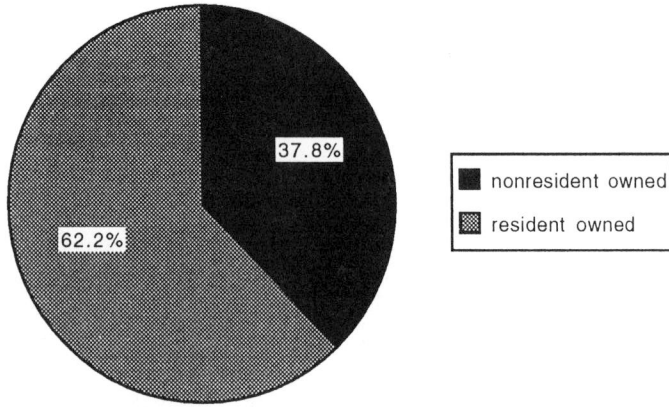

Breakdown of the 62.2% of Village Land Owned by Residents,
According to Size of Holding

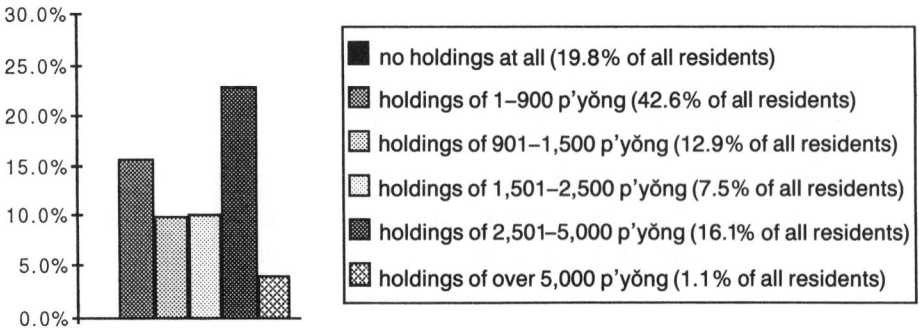

Source: Kwangmu *yang'an*

Kunitake also acquired land of relatively low quality; its upland was assessed at 7.5 sen per *p'yŏng*, compared with an average of 7.7 sen for upland owned by Koreans. These data on the value of land owned by corporations in Paeksŏng-ni suggest that the Oriental Development Company and Kunitake acquired lower quality, inexpensive land that they could subsequently develop through capital improvements.[29]

FIGURE 5–3–1
Land Distribution among Paeksŏng-ni Residents, 1914

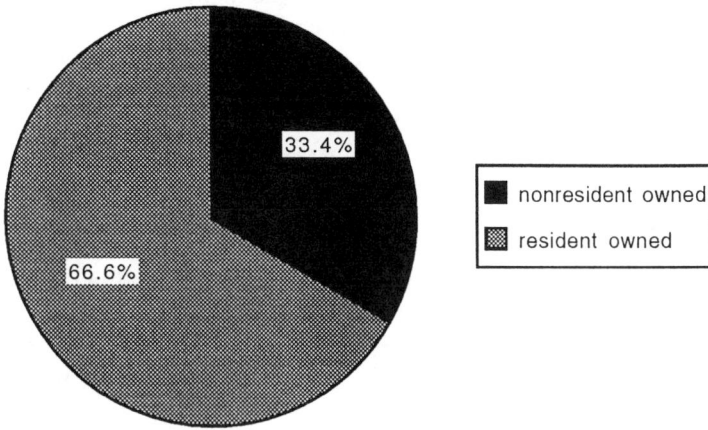

Breakdown of the 66.6% of Village Land Owned by Residents,
According to Size of Holding

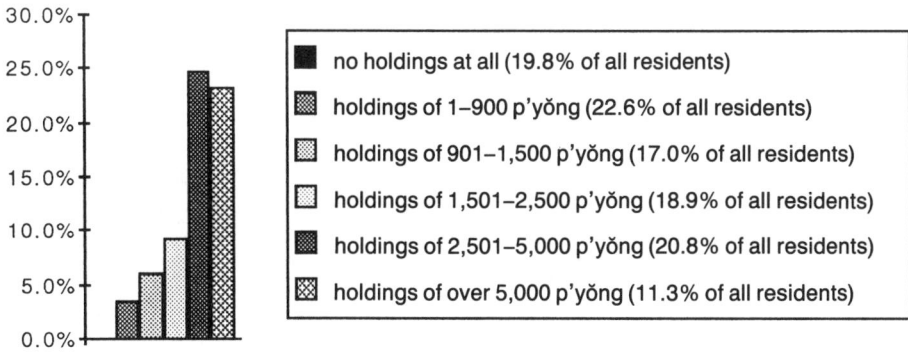

Source: *t'oji taejang*

No correlation existed between assessed land value and residence of the owner. Owners of the highest-quality paddy land lived in Japan (17.6 sen per *p'yŏng*) and in Yŏnsan-myŏn (16.0 sen). Among all landowners, those living in Seoul owned paddy land assessed at 12.1 sen, the lowest assessed value. These landowners possessed the best upland, however. Residents of Yŏnsan-myŏn owned upland assessed lowest in quality. The average value per *p'yŏng* of upland in 1913 was 7.7 sen. The upland owned by Seoul residents averaged 9.4 sen per *p'yŏng,* while upland owned by Yŏnsan-myŏn residents averaged just 7.1 sen.

Of all villages, Paeksŏng-ni exhibited the highest degree of continuity of individual landowners from the late nineteenth century into the colonial period. Landowners registered on the *yang'an* remained, on the whole, registered owners in 1913. Major local landowners retained ownership over most of their holdings and in some cases expanded them. This was particularly true for members of the Chŏnju Yi and Ch'ŏngju Han clans. Landowners belonging to clans not well represented in Paeksŏng-ni in 1900 did not continue as landowners in the colonial period. For example, neither Yi Ŭn-ch'ŏl, who owned over 6,000 *p'yŏng* of paddy land in 1900, nor his descendants owned land in the village in 1913. Most of Yi's land came into the possession of the two principal clans living within the village. In 1900 owners were replaced either by powerful local families or Japanese individuals or corporations. Whereas individuals with twenty-three different surnames owned land in Paeksŏng-ni in 1900, by 1913 this number had been reduced to sixteen. For example, the Kunitake gōmeikaisha became the registered owner of much of the land owned in 1900 by the underrepresented Chŏn and Kim families. Kodera Genkichi, one of the two Japanese landowners, acquired his land from members of the Kim and Im families who had been predominantly tenants in 1900. Unfortunately, the land registers do not describe from whom this land passed or when it passed from one owner to another between the two surveys.

Individuals registered as tenants in 1900 did not become landowners in 1913. No former tenants became registered owners of property previously rented. This is not to say that Yi dynasty owner-tenants (individuals owning part of the land they cultivated) were denied ownership of their land; in most cases they were not. In several isolated instances tenants in 1900 became registered owners of plots of land they had neither rented nor owned. For example, Yi Kwang-je, a resident of Paeksŏng-ni, owned only one small plot of arable land in 1900 and rented two larger ones from a local landlord. In 1913 Yi owned a total of five plots of arable land and two residential plots in the village. Four of the five plots were acquired from other owners in the village and did not include the two plots Yi had previously, and perhaps still, rented. A small number of former tenants acquired ownership to land, presumably by purchases, and became small-scale landowners during these years.

The lands of the Oriental Development Company came almost exclusively from one individual, Yun Cha-sam, the largest absentee landlord in Paeksŏng-ni at the turn of the century. Yun undoubtedly sold his land to the corporation when he sold other land to other absentee owners registered on the 1913 Paeksŏng-ni *taejang*. Some scholars have suggested that the Oriental Development Company acquired its land from small-scale farmers who were then forced into tenancy or into migration to other regions of Korea or to Manchuria.[30] Apparently, this was not the case in Paeksŏng-ni. Tenants working for Yun in 1900 simply switched landlords and presumably became tenants for the Oriental Development Company. A degree of uncertainty is warranted because tenants cultivating land acquired by the Oriental Development Company or any other new landlord had little security. A new landlord was not bound to honor a previous landlord-tenant contract unless it was recorded on the *t'oji tŭnggibu,* and few were. Tenancy contracts, usually oral, were generally for one year and frequently were not renewed at the same fee level due to the oversupply of available farm labor during the colonial period.[31]

KONGSU-RI

Kongsu-ri represents a colonial experience strikingly different from Songsan-ni and Paeksŏng-ni. Situated close to convenient transportation systems between Onyang and Ch'ŏn'an, Kongsu-ri was tied to and influenced by a national market dominated by Seoul and smaller commercial centers. The differentiation of Kongsu-ri's farm population into landlords, wealthy farmers, and large numbers of tenants, already visible at the time of the Kwangmu survey, continued into the colonial period. In 1900 most farmers living in Kongsu-ri had worked their land as tenants for urban landlords. A decade later, in 1913, tenants, together with wage laborers, still cultivated much of Kongsu-ri's land. This wage-labor pool existed within an hour's walk from the village—in Ch'ŏn'an, which had been transformed into a bustling commercial center by the construction of the Seoul-Pusan railroad line through the town in 1905.[32]

Although Koreans owned most land in Kongsu-ri in 1913—about 71 percent—Japanese individuals and corporations possessed a significant percentage of total village land, or over 25 percent. This was in sharp contrast to Songsan-ni and Paeksŏng-ni. As shown in Table 5-6, Japanese owned over 20 percent of paddy land, 31 percent of upland and almost one-third of all residential land, with ownership divided between ten Japanese nationals and the Oriental Development Company. Japanese landowners had a critical impact on the Kongsu-ri economy in general and on landownership in particular. The village of Kongsu-ri itself owned a small percentage of total village land consisting of cultivated and other types of land.

Although Kongsu-ri contained a large amount of arable land for local residents to cultivate, little of this land was actually owned by them. As seen in Table 5-4, residents of Kongsu-ri itself owned only 73,000 *p'yŏng* of arable land, or about 18 percent of the village total. Residents of

Table 5-6   Landownership in Kongsu-ri in 1913 (in *p'yŏng*)

TYPE OF LAND	KOREAN	JAPANESE	CORPORATE	OTHER*	TOTAL
Paddy	203,729	24,823	28,355	7,130	264,037
	(77.2)	(9.4)	(10.7)	(2.7)	
Upland	92,787	25,130	18,270	3,715	139,902
	(66.3)	(18.0)	(13.1)	(2.7)	
Residential	10,644	2,311	1,281	191	14,427
	(73.8)	(16.0)	(8.9)	(1.3)	
Forest	8,705	—	—	409	9,114
	(95.5)			(4.5)	
Cemetery	2,830	—	—	491	3,321
	(85.2)			(14.8)	
Other**	11,562	18,558	—	4,488	34,608
	(33.4)	(53.6)		(13.0)	
Total land owned	330,261	70,823	47,906	16,424	465,415
	(71.0)	(15.2)	(10.3)	(3.5)	
Total arable land	296,517	49,953	46,625	10,845	403,941
	(73.4)	(12.4)	(11.5)	(2.7)	
Number of owners	116	10	1	3	130
	(89.2)	(7.7)	(0.8)	(2.3)	

*"Other" includes Kongsu-ri itself, a neighboring village named Hoeryong-ni, and one unknown individual.
**Includes land classified as miscellaneous, roads, railroad, dikes, and streams. The bulk of this land, which had been damaged by natural calamities at the turn of the century and had yet to be re-developed, fell into the first classification.
Note: Numbers in parentheses represent percentages of total
SOURCE: *t'oji taejang*

neighboring villages in Paebang-myŏn owned an additional 6 percent of village arable land. Apparently, most residents of Kongsu-ri worked as tenants or wage laborers on land owned by others.

Indeed, absentee landowners controlled a full 80 percent of Kongsu-ri's paddy land and 68 percent of its upland. Seoul residents controlled most land owned by absentee landlords in 1913, owning half of all paddy land and about one-third of upland and residential land in the village that year. Although the Oriental Development Company owned some of this land, the bulk was owned by private individuals, all Koreans, living in the capital.

Landlords living outside of Kongsu-ri but within South Ch'ungch'ŏng province also owned a large amount of village land—about 25 percent of the total. Most of these regional landlords lived in nearby towns in Asan-gun, but many lived in Ch'ŏn'an and Onyang. Over 7 percent of arable land was owned by Japanese landlords living in Japan, and most of this was owned jointly by two Gifu-ken residents, Andō Kaneshi and Nagaya Rintarō.

Absentee landlords, regardless of their residence, owned more paddy land than upland, and in general, the farther from Kongsu-ri a landlord lived, the more likely the landlord owned paddy land. Conversely, despite the much larger amount of paddy land than upland in Kongsu-ri, residents of the village itself owned slightly more upland than paddy land.

In addition to owning arable land, absentee landlords controlled most of the homes in Kongsu-ri. This situation contrasts sharply with the two villages previously examined but parallels that found in the *yang'an* data from 1900. Of the fifty-one residential plots in Kongsu-ri in 1913, residents of the village itself owned only sixteen. The Oriental Development Company owned more homes (seven) than any other, but many individuals owned multiple residential plots. No more than ten of the homes in Kongsu-ri were owned by the individuals living in them. This fact strongly suggests that, unlike the other villages, rents were high enough in Kongsu-ri to make ownership of residential land a profitable investment. It also shows the degree to which Kongsu-ri's daily economy was determined by forces outside the village.

In 1913 a direct correlation existed between residence and average plot size of land owned: The closer an owner lived to Kongsu-ri, the smaller the plot owned. Owners living within the village owned the smallest plots of land in the village. The size of their paddy, upland, and residential holdings averaged 1,078 *p'yŏng*, 555 *p'yŏng*, and 209 *p'yŏng*, respectively. At the same time, the sizes of paddy land, upland, and residential land owned by residents of Seoul averaged 1,399 *p'yŏng*, 1,119 *p'yŏng*, and 496 *p'yŏng*, respectively. In general, this meant that the plots owned by residents of Seoul were located more advantageously in the village. Not only did absentee landlords control most village land, but it was land well-situated near transportation and water.

Landownership in Kongsu-ri in 1913 was concentrated among a small number of large-scale landlords, much more so than in Songsan-ni and Paeksŏng-ni. Some landlords resided within Kongsu-ri itself, but many others lived in urban areas. In 1913, 198,996 *p'yŏng*, or almost 51 percent of all privately owned arable land in the village, was owned by eight landlords (7 percent of all owners). Of these eight landlords, each owning over 9,000 *p'yŏng*, five were Koreans, two were Japanese, and one was the Oriental Development Company. Among these owners, two Koreans, Pak Ki-hong and Son Ch'un-je, owned a total of 90,645 *p'yŏng* of arable land—over 22 percent of the village total. At the same time, over one-third of total landowners possessed less than 900 *p'yŏng* each and together owned only 5 percent of village arable land.

This sharp division is not unexpected. A similar situation existed in Kongsu-ri at the turn of the century as well, and it presumably characterized numerous other villages close to urban centers. What is important is

FIGURE 5–4
Land Distribution among Kongsu-ri Residents, 1900

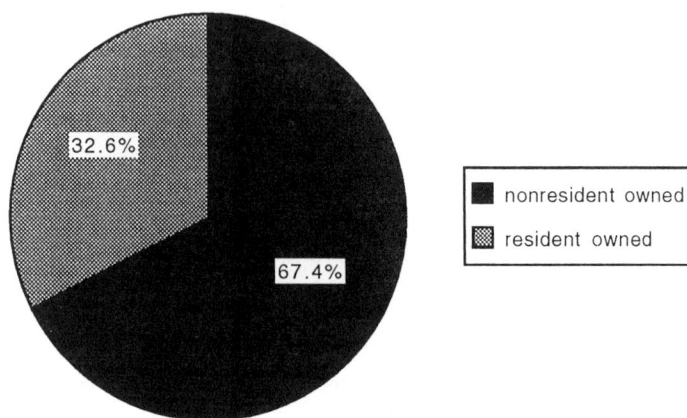

Breakdown of the 32.6% of Village Land Owned by Residents,
According to Size of Holding

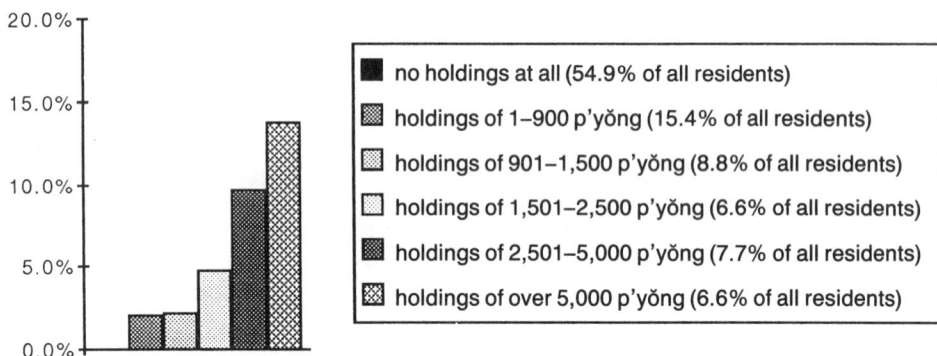

Source: Kwangmu *yang'an*

that this pattern of landownership in Kongsu-ri, like the patterns found
in the other villages, preceded the arrival of the Japanese and their colonial administration. These patterns were not the result of the cadastral
survey or even of Japanese colonial design; the survey simply confirmed
the existing late Yi dynasty landownership configuration.

A clear division also existed among residents of the village. As shown

FIGURE 5–4–1
Land Distribution among Kongsu-ri Residents, 1913

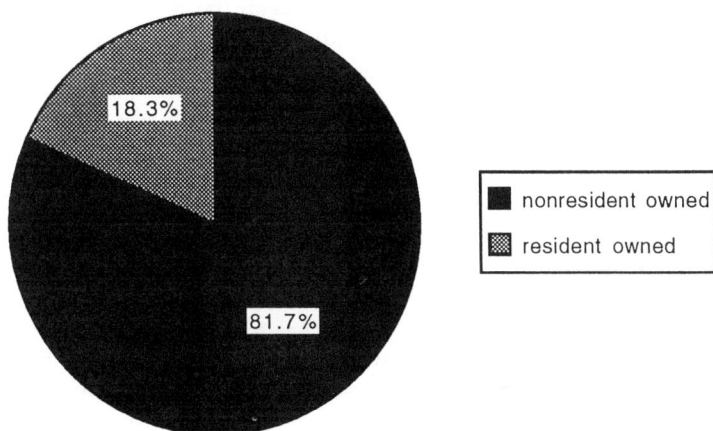

Breakdown of the 18.3% of Village Land Owned by Residents,
According to Size of Holding

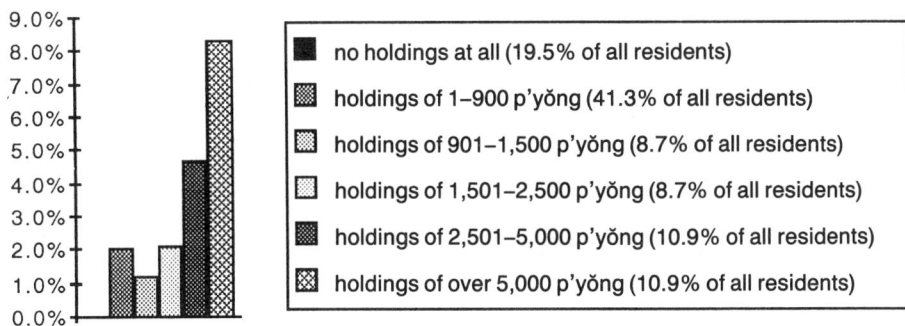

Source: *t'oji taejang*

in Figures 5-4 and 5-4-1, the thirty-seven landowners living in Kongsu-ri owned uneven shares of the small amount of locally owned land. Four residents (10.8 percent of all resident landowners), each owning over 5,000 *p'yŏng,* owned 6.0 percent of all arable land in the village, while nineteen owners (51.4 percent of resident owners) possessing less than 900 *p'yŏng* owned only 2.0 percent of village arable land. Many other residents of the village owned no land at all. Although the *t'oji taejang* recorded fifty-one home plots in 1913, only thirty-seven village residents owned any land. The small-scale landowners and the landless formed an available pool of tenants and temporary labor to cultivate the vast bulk of village land owned by absentee landlords. And, as shown in Figures 5-4 and 5-4-1, the percentage of village land controlled by these landlords increased significantly between 1900 and 1913.

Although Japanese individuals owned over 12 percent of Kongsu-ri's arable land, considerably higher than in Songsan-ni (1 percent) or Paeksŏng-ni (3 percent), Korean owners still controlled the higher-quality land. Korean-owned paddy land was assessed at an average of 16.7 sen per *p'yŏng,* whereas paddy land owned by Japanese averaged only 13.3 sen. Consistent with patterns seen in earlier villages, land owned by the Oriental Development Company was assessed at even less than that owned by Japanese individuals, averaging just over 12 sen per *p'yŏng.* As noted earlier, former Korean assessors stated that this difference was not the result of Japanese influence over the assessment process. Moreover, Japanese landowners did not maintain a low assessment throughout the colonial period as they acquired higher-value land or improved their lands through capital investments. Clearly, Japanese landowners, like some wealthy Koreans, initially acquired lower-quality land at the outset of the colonial period. Such land was in less demand by most Koreans, cheaper, and easier to improve and resell at a profit. This pattern of Japanese ownership of lower-value land also confirms stories told by early Japanese settlers of having to buy marginal-quality land when they first arrived in Korea.[33]

A similar situation existed for upland. The average assessed value of upland owned by Koreans and Japanese was 10.5 *sen* and 6.9 sen, respectively. Upland owned by the Oriental Development Company averaged 10.9 sen per *p'yŏng,* the highest of all landowner groups, but Koreans owned all of the highest-grade upland in Kongsu-ri—land that registered as grade six.[34]

Among Korean landowners, a clear correlation existed between quality of land owned and an owner's place of residence. In general, the farther an owner lived from Kongsu-ri, the higher the land was assessed. In 1913, paddy land owned by residents of Seoul averaged 16.9 sen per *p'yŏng,* while owners living in the village and within Paebang-myŏn owned paddy land of low assessed values—13.0 sen and 14.9 sen, respectively. A similar pattern existed for upland ownership. Thus, Seoul absentee landlords not only owned a large percentage of village arable land, but they controlled the best land in the village as well. This pattern also suggests that wealthy and influential landlords did not influence surveyors to undervalue their land in order to evade taxation.

As mentioned earlier, in both 1900 and 1913 Kongsu-ri's land was

concentrated among a small number of large-scale landowners. However, none of the same owners who dominated Kongsu-ri ownership in
1900 continued to own large amounts of land after the cadastral survey.
The colonial government did not, however, deprive the old landed elite
of their land in 1913 in favor of a new group of landowners. Individuals
who became the largest landowners in 1913 acquired their land from the
former landlords of the late nineteenth century. Some land transfers
involved inheritances from one family member to another. For example,
land that had been owned by the Yun family remained in the hands of
owners named Yun.[35] Likewise, some land owned by the locally powerful Yi family apparently stayed in the family's possession.[36] This type of
ownership transfer among individuals with the same surname was common among residents of the Kongsu-ri vicinity.

Land that had been owned by nonresidents of the village in 1900
(approximately two-thirds of the total arable land) came into the possession of Korean residents of Seoul and other urban areas, of Japanese individuals, and of the Oriental Development Company. The transfer pattern is unmistakable, and numerous examples can be cited. For example,
Cho No-mi, the largest landowner in Kongsu-ri in 1900, did not appear
on the land register of 1913. No individual with the surname Cho owned
land in 1913, eliminating the possibility that Cho No-mi passed his landholdings to a relative. An examination of the plots owned by Cho reveals
that ownership of his land was transferred to Marquis Yi Chae-gak, a
powerful royal family member and high-ranking official in the former
Imperial Korean government.[37] In 1913 Yi sold all of his newly acquired
land in Kongsu-ri to Pak Ki-hong, another large-scale Korean landlord
living in Seoul with court connections.[38]

As another example, Ch'oe Il-sŏk, another nonresident landlord in
1900, transferred all of his extensive landholdings to Kongju landlord U
Kye-dong. U shortly thereafter sold this land to Pak Yong-sin, a Seoul-
based moneylender.[39] In this way, the land owned by large-scale absentee
landlords at the turn of the century simply changed hands from one to
another during the first years of the colonial period. The basic landownership structure, however, remained almost unchanged.

Japanese landowners acquired their land in a similar manner. Nagaya
Rintarō and Andō Kaneshi jointly owned 20,663 *p'yŏng* of paddy land
and 4,420 *p'yŏng* of upland in 1913.[40] These men, one living in Gifu-ken
and the other from Gifu-ken but later emigrating to Ch'ŏn'an, acquired
their land almost exclusively from Yi Pok-sun and Yi Chu-sang, both
large-scale landowners in 1900 living in nearby Onyang. Neither of these
Koreans owned any land in Kongsu-ri after the cadastral survey. Similarly, the Oriental Development Company acquired its land from two
late nineteenth-century landlords.

These examples strongly suggest that Japanese landownership increased as a result of negotiations and business deals with wealthy Koreans living in Seoul or provincial towns. Japanese individuals and corporations did not enter Kongsu-ri and force small-scale owner-farmers off their land through intimidation, intrigue, or fraud. Nor did they take advantage of bureaucratic expertise to swindle individual Korean landowners. Small-scale owners were not dispossessed in great numbers. Kongsu-ri tenants, working predominantly for urban landlords in 1900, worked for new urban landlords in 1913 with an exchange of yen and the stroke of a brush. However, these tenants were likely less secure under new landlords interested in finding tenants able to pay maximum rents. As land became concentrated in fewer hands and as capital improvements were made by Japanese landowners, however, the number of cultivators needed to farm land declined. Many tenants, faced with an oversupply of rural farm labor, were forced to uproot and settle elsewhere during these years.

Undeveloped land in Kongsu-ri in 1900 either classified as wasteland or labeled as mountain and grassland not owned by anyone, was registered in the name of Kongsu-ri or the name of a Japanese land developer, Yamashita Sentarō, living in Kongju. By 1913 Yamashita had acquired over 27,000 *p'yŏng* of land in the village, almost exclusively undeveloped mountain and grassland. Because this land was not registered in any individual's name in 1900, it is impossible to know from whom, if anyone, it was acquired. Like others at this time (mainly Koreans), Yamashita may have received it as a grant from the government-general on the condition he develop it. However, Yamashita had not developed this land prior to its sale in 1913 to another Japanese land developer, Kumano Ryotarō, an Onyang bicycle manufacturer from Ishikawa-ken.[41] All land classified as wasteland in 1900 was registered in the name of the Kongsu-ri itself in 1913, and most land was still not cultivated in that year.

P'ALBONG-NI

P'albong-ni, near Iri in North Chŏlla province, resembled Kongsu-ri in many key respects, most notably in its land-distribution pattern. A small group of individuals living outside P'albong-ni owned most of the arable land within it. In contrast to Kongsu-ri, however, these absentee landlords tended to be wealthy Koreans residing in North Chŏlla province, not Seoul.

In 1914 Korean owners controlled over 90 percent of the arable land in the village. Six Japanese individuals and two corporations owned the remainder. As shown in Table 5-7, Korean landowners owned over 92 percent of village paddy land, 84 percent of upland, and all residential land. The location of P'albong-ni on the North Chŏlla plain, an area of early and large-scale Japanese land investments, makes the relatively

Table 5-7   Landownership in P'albong-ni in 1914 (in *p'yŏng*)

LAND TYPE	KOREAN	JAPANESE	CORPORATE	OTHER*	TOTAL
Paddy	117,349	8,201	1,204	0	126,754
	(92.6)	(6.5)	(0.9)		
Upland	35,421	5,954	709	0	42,084
	(84.2)	(14.1)	(1.7)		
Residential	7,128	0	0	0	7,128
	(100)				
Forest	2,905	0	0	0	2,905
	(100)				
Other**	1,485	0	0	164	1,649
	(90.1)			(9.9)	
Total land	164,293	14,155	1,913	164	180,525
	(91.0)	(7.8)	(1.1)	(0.1)	
Total arable land	152,770	14,155	1,913	0	168,838
	(90.5)	(8.4)	(1.1)		
Total number	108	6	2	1	117
of owners	(92.3)	(5.1)	(1.7)	(0.9)	

*Includes P'albong-ni
**Includes land classified as streams, roads, and uncultivated miscellaneous land
Note: Numbers in parentheses represent percentages of total
SOURCE: *t'oji taejang*

small amount of Japanese-owned land somewhat unexpected. The Oriental Development Company accumulated vast holdings in other parts of Iksan-gun and had a major branch office in Iri, only a few kilometers from P'albong-ni, but the company owned only two small plots of upland in the village in 1914.[42]

The Japanese individuals owning land in the village did not actually live in P'albong-ni. Of these six absentee landlords, five were regional entrepreneurs with business operations in various parts of North Chŏlla province. For most of them agriculture was an investment, not a livelihood. One man, Takase Heijirō, a Kunsan textile merchant with extensive landholdings in the North and South Chŏlla provinces, owned most of the Japanese-owned land. Takase, who emigrated to Kunsan from Shiga-ken in 1897 at the age of sixteen, headed the Takase nōjō, a cotton agribusiness centered near Yŏsu in South Chŏlla province. Later, he was also chief executive officer of the Yŏsu Electric Company.[43]

The other Japanese landowners were a Buddhist monk, a *sake* brewer, an innkeeper, and an agribusiness owner. Ōhashi Rōjō, Nichiren monk from Fukui-ken, emigrated in December 1910 to Iri, where he established an eclectic life, mixing ecclesiastic and commercial pursuits: managing a temple, a school, and a real estate business. Murase Akira ran a local brewery in Iri. Saeki Buntarō, whose relatives operated a large-scale agribusiness near Kimje in North Chŏlla province, lived a modest life operating an inn in Onyang. Imamura Ichijirō emigrated from Kumamoto-ken in 1906 to a small town in Iksan-gun. Although he had been an elementary school principal in Kumamoto, in Korea Imamura became a wealthy landowner and livestock producer. He reportedly owned 500 *chŏngbo* of agricultural land in the North and South Chŏlla provinces in the 1920s and 1930s.[44] The sixth Japanese landlord lived in Japan.

In the late Yi dynasty high rates of tenancy and absentee landlordism characterized much of North Chŏlla province. Although *yang'an* from the Kwangmu survey no longer exist, the data from the *t'oji taejang* suggest that P'albong-ni was typical in this regard. Landownership distribution in P'albong-ni in 1914 was severely imbalanced—more than any of the other villages studied. A very small elite owned over half the arable land in the village. Seven Koreans and one Japanese, 6.8 percent of the total landowners, each owned over 5,000 *p'yŏng* and controlled 59.2 percent of the arable land. Among these eight landowners, two Koreans owned 41.5 percent of the total arable land between them and over half of all paddy land in the village. These two men, Song T'aek-kyu and Kang Chun-yŏng, lived in small towns in Iksan-gun and were part of a late Yi dynasty landed elite living in rural areas. Although nothing is known about Song, Kang reportedly came from a *yangban* family living in a village barely two kilometers south of P'albong-ni in a neighboring *myŏn*. Several years after the survey, Kang bequeathed all of his land to his son, Kang Ki-sŏng, who was reportedly at that time part of the upper class.[45]

On the other end of the landownership spectrum, a high percentage (54 percent) of total owners possessed less than 900 *p'yŏng* each, a figure higher than any found in the other villages studied. These individuals owned a total of only 17,843 *p'yŏng*, or 10.6 percent of all arable land in the village.

An examination of the residents of P'albong-ni reveals an uneven distribution of the small percentage of locally owned land. As shown in Figure 5-5, the village contained no residents owning over 5,000 *p'yŏng*. But many owned exceedingly small amounts of arable land. Of the seventy-six resident landowners, fifty owned less than 900 *p'yŏng*. An additional fifteen residents owned homes in the village but did not own arable land to cultivate. Thus, more than 85 percent of the known residents of P'albong-ni owned too little or no arable land to support a farm family. Clearly, very little of P'albong-ni's wealth was retained within the village.

In 1913 individuals living outside the village and P'albong-myŏn owned most arable land in the village. In contrast with the other villages studied, however, these absentee landlords did not live in Seoul, but rather in other small villages and towns of North Chŏlla province. As

FIGURE 5–5
Land Distribution among P'albong-ni Residents, 1914

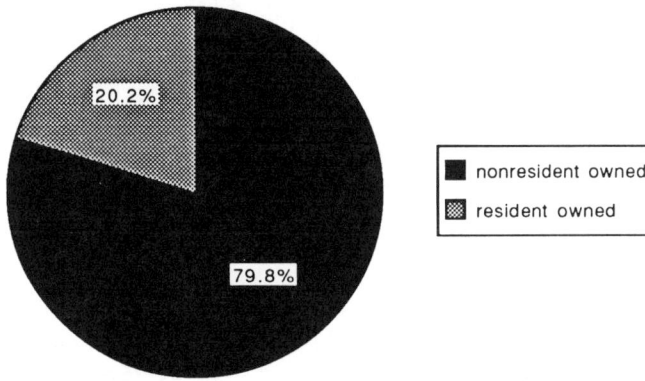

nonresident owned
resident owned

Breakdown of the 20.2% of Village Land Owned by Residents,
According to Size of Holding

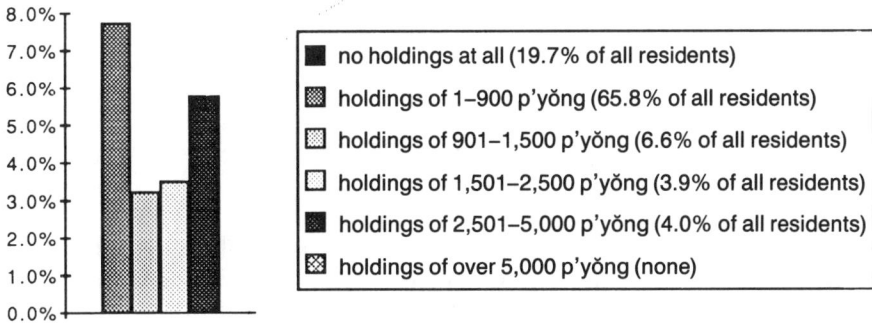

■ no holdings at all (19.7% of all residents)

▩ holdings of 1–900 p'yŏng (65.8% of all residents)

▢ holdings of 901–1,500 p'yŏng (6.6% of all residents)

□ holdings of 1,501–2,500 p'yŏng (3.9% of all residents)

■ holdings of 2,501–5,000 p'yŏng (4.0% of all residents)

▨ holdings of over 5,000 p'yŏng (none)

Source: *t'oji taejang*

shown in Table 5-4, most village paddy land (65.6 percent) was owned
by landlords living in other *myŏn* of Iksan-gun, principally in Ch'unp'o-
myŏn directly to the south. Landlords living in provincial towns, mainly
in Chŏnju, owned another 22 percent of P'albong-ni's paddy land.
Although Iri was an important commercial center during the colonial
period, it was principally a town of "new money" and Japanese influence.
North Chŏlla in general and P'albong-ni in particular were dominated by
members of "old money" groups—landlords in the traditionally more

important town of Chŏnju. Apart from the 1,204 *p'yŏng* of Oriental Development Company paddy land, no land was owned by a Seoul resident. Village residents tended to own most upland.

Regional landlords—those living within Iksan-gun but outside of P'albong-myŏn—owned most arable land in the village, and the size of their holdings was strikingly larger than the landholdings of residents of other areas. For example, in 1914 these regional landlords owned sixty-three plots of arable and residential land in P'albong-ni, totaling 90,000 *p'yŏng* and averaging 1,443 *p'yŏng* per holding. In contrast, the average size of holdings for residents of other areas amounted to 874 *p'yŏng* for residents of provincial towns, 459 *p'yŏng* for residents of P'albong-myŏn, and only 257 *p'yŏng* for residents of the village itself.

A direct correlation existed between residence and quality of land owned in P'albong-ni in 1914. Owners living within the village owned land of the lowest assessed value, while landlords living in neighboring *myŏn* owned the highest-value land. The average assessed values per *p'yŏng* of paddy land owned by residents of the village, county *(kun)*, and provincial towns were 15.1 sen, 20.6 sen and 19.4 sen, respectively. Regional landlords not only owned the largest fields of paddy land (again indicating that their fields were generally located in the most advantageous areas), but this land was of higher productive value than most other paddy fields in the village.

P'albong-ni data also reveal a clear correlation between nationality of owner and quality of land owned. Although Japanese owners possessed only 6.5 percent of village paddy land, this land was of extremely high quality, averaging almost 22 sen per *p'yŏng* in assessed value. Korean-owned paddy land, on the other hand, averaged 19.5 sen. The situation with upland was reversed, with Koreans controlling upland of a slightly higher quality than upland owned by Japanese.

The landownership data for 1914 suggest that P'albong-ni contained a land-tenure structure, relatively unchanged from the Yi dynasty, in which landlord and tenant had a strong link with each other. Subsistence farmers eked out a livelihood from small plots of fertile land rented from landlords living in the vicinity. These landlords, though living in different *myŏn,* resided three to five kilometers from P'albong-ni. They undoubtedly knew the tenants who worked for them. The purely economic relationship existing between landlord and tenants and farm laborers in Kongsu-ri was much less visible in P'albong-ni. In North Chŏlla province, landlords tended to be large-scale rural landowners, not urban entrepreneurs as in Kongsu-ri. This pattern of land distribution among regional landlords and the pattern of high tenancy rates continued throughout the colonial period not just in P'albong-ni, but in the province as a whole.[46]

SE-RI

Late in the Yi dynasty Korean government institutions and palaces owned a high percentage of land in Se-ri, a village near the town of Suwŏn, but little village land remained in Korean hands after Japan's annexation of Korea. Although actual *t'oji taejang* from Se-ri did not survive the Korean War, Table 5-8 represents a tabulation of ownership declarations from 1911.

The colonial government declared ownership of 15 percent of all paddy land in the village, which is not surprising considering the large amount of institutional land at the turn of the century. Produce from land that had been used to support local military installations and wall construction now went to government coffers in Seoul. Korean landowners claimed ownership of only 50 percent of village paddy land in 1911, the lowest percentage of all villages examined. Korean ownership of upland was approximately 74 percent, second lowest in this study. Japanese owners claimed ownership of 16.2 percent of village arable land and 19.1 percent of all residential land in the village. Two Japanese corporations, the Oriental Development Company and Kunitake gōmeikaisha, declared ownership of almost 10 percent of village paddy land and 4 percent of upland. The local school retained ownership over its land.

The proximity of Se-ri to downtown Suwŏn, Seoul, and major transportation routes brought the village under the influence of urban investors. Consequently, a few large-scale Korean landlords owned a disproportionate percentage of village land. Of the 185 Koreans owning land in Se-ri in 1911, nine individuals owned over 9,000 *p'yŏng* each, totaling 122,374 *p'yŏng*, or approximately 20 percent of all arable land in the village. Most of these landowners lived in Seoul or Suwŏn. In addition, many other residents of these two cities owned smaller amounts of village land. Residents of the village itself owned very little, perhaps as little as 10 percent, of Se-ri's arable land. Residential plots were also concentrated among a small number of landlords, and few residents owned the homes in which they lived. Although addresses for many landowners were not recorded on the *t'oji chosabu,* in all likelihood the land-distribution pattern among residents and nonresidents of Se-ri resembled the pattern of 1900.

The Se-ri data provide a clear explanation (with implications for other parts of Korea) for the approximately 12 percent of total village arable land that had been registered in the names of various royal palaces in 1900. Ownership of all this land was claimed exclusively in the name of one man, Iwasaki Hisaya, head of the Mitsubishi Corporation in Tokyo. No palace land was granted to its former overseers or to members of the royal family, as was the case in other villages.[47] In 1911, Iwasaki claimed

Table 5-8   Landownership Claims in Se-ri in 1911 (in *p'yŏng*)

TYPE OF LAND	KOREAN	JAPANESE	CORPORATE	GOVERNMENT	OTHER	TOTAL
Paddy	197,922 (50.1)	77,029 (19.5)	39,108 (9.9)	61,666 (15.6)	19,349 (4.9)	395,074
Upland	238,928 (74.1)	39,317 (12.2)	13,536 (4.2)	30,425 (9.4)	310 (0.1)	322,516
Residential	15,370 (69.6)	5,501 (24.9)		752 (3.4)	464 (2.1)	22,087
Forest	93,867 (95.3)	70 (0.1)		4,554 (4.6)		98,491
Other	1,072 (46.0)			1,257 (54.0)		2,329
Total	547,159 (65.1)	121,917 (14.5)	52,644 (6.3)	98,654 (11.7)	20,123 (2.4)	840,497

Note: Numbers in parentheses represent percentages of total
Source: *t'oji chosabu*

ownership of almost 16 percent of village paddy land and 5 percent of all upland.

During the first decade of the twentieth century, the leaders of several of Japan's *zaibatsu* acquired agricultural land in Korea in anticipation of sponsoring large-scale settlement of Japanese farmers. These leaders included Shibuzawa Eichi, Ōkura Heihachirō, and Iwasaki Hisaya, whose land in Se-ri was claimed for this purpose.

Iwasaki was no stranger to Korea, having traveled to the peninsula on several occasions between 1895 and 1906 to initiate and inspect his business endeavors in Korea and elsewhere on the Asian continent. On his last trip prior to Korea's annexation, he spent several months in late 1906 inspecting sites for his planned Korean agricultural enterprise. The following year he established a branch of his Japan-based Tōsan farm on Se-ri land that had been registered in the names of various royal palaces. Because this transaction occurred one year prior to the 1908 nationalization of much palace land, it suggests that Iwasaki bought the land directly from royal family members in Seoul. Many royal family members, Lady Ŏm for example, were disposing of their land at this time in anticipation of political and economic changes under the Japanese residency-general. By serving on the founding committee of the Oriental Development Company with many of the royal family members, Iwasaki would have had ample opportunity to conduct such negotiations.

Thus, Korea's royal elite were party to the major transfer of land from Korean to Japanese hands. If other large-scale Japanese developers acquired land in the same manner, a previously unknown link between the colonizer and ancien régime can be made. This link can also be seen in the awards of peerage and advisorships bestowed on Korean royalty by the Japanese colonial government. Iwasaki did not directly deprive Korean cultivators of their land; rather, he assumed ownership from a previous landlord.

In short, changes were made primarily at the top. When the anticipated mass migration of Japanese farmers did not occur, the Tōsan farm continued to use Korean tenants to cultivate the land. However, Koreans in supervisory positions over tenants were replaced by Japanese managers. Later, Korean tenants lost farming livelihoods as mechanization in cultivation, irrigation, and harvesting, and economies of scale resulted in fewer tenants. Also, the Korean economy as a whole was deprived of financial resources now flowing to Japan.[48]

In short, changes in Korean landownership from the Yi dynasty to the colonial period were of persons/corporations, not systems. The pattern was the same in all villages where land records exist for the full period of 1900–1918. In other words, more isolated villages characterized by relatively equitable land distribution in 1900 remained so. Similarly, villages closer to commercial centers that had marked uneven land-distribution patterns continued with little overall change. In general, the Japanese cadastral survey perpetuated the late Yi dynasty land-tenure system, not seriously altering it.

What changed, however, were the landlords themselves. In some instances descendants of late nineteenth-century landlords continued to possess large family landholdings. Elsewhere, new landlords acquired the holdings of earlier landlords. Most Japanese individuals and the Oriental Development Company acquired their holdings in this manner.

Koreans owned the largest percentage of arable land in each of the villages studied, and the land was usually of higher quality than land owned by Japanese individuals and the Oriental Development Company. Regardless of the owner's nationality, the closer the village was to Seoul and to transportation systems linking the village with Seoul, the higher the rate of absentee landlordism. Further, this absentee control extended to residential land for areas closest to Seoul, with persons owning their homes in more distant villages. This strong evidence of the economic extension of Seoul into rural villages in 1900 suggests that we need to reevaluate the level of market economy Korea had developed by the late nineteenth century.

If massive Japanese ownership did not spring from the cadastral survey in the early years of Japanese colonial control, an explanation for the patterns evident in the 1940s must be found elsewhere.

CHAPTER 6

LANDOWNERSHIP CHANGE IN AN EARLY COLONIAL ECONOMIC MILIEU (1914–1929)

Bᴇᴛᴡᴇᴇɴ 1914 ᴀɴᴅ 1929 landownership changes, many ongoing from the last decades of the nineteenth century, accelerated as the agricultural sector of the Korean economy expanded, infused with new investment capital from both public and private sources. The arrival in Korea of Japanese businesspeople and farmers—the human element in the government-general's policy of developing Korean agricultural resources—meant inevitable changes in rural Korean villages. In addition, the legal element of Japan's colonial policy, the creation of the *t'oji taejang,* facilitated land investments by making landownership accessible and secure for thousands of new investors, both Korean and Japanese.

With the government-general's encouragement and financial support, both large-scale developers and individual farmers opened new lands to agricultural production and used improved agricultural technology from abroad. The fruits of these efforts were visible by the 1920s. Total acreage under cultivation in Korea increased by approximately 5 percent between 1918 (when the survey was completed and statistics reliable) and 1929. Agricultural production increased as well, but at a much slower pace. As expected, however, these increases were accompanied by changes in landownership patterns. Absentee and local landlords concentrated greater amounts of land in fewer hands, the hands increasingly belonging to Japanese.

Much of the increased agricultural produce did not remain in Korea as colonial businesspeople exported increasing amounts of Korea's agricultural production during these years. In fact, the increase in agricultural exports, mainly rice and soy beans, actually surpassed production increases. Higher commodity prices in Japan meant that producers in colonial Korea increasingly produced for the more profitable market in the Japanese metropole. This situation was particularly apparent in areas nearest to Korea's ports and areas linked by Korea's new transportation systems. In such areas, and later elsewhere as well, Japanese individuals and corporations gained control over most facets of agricultural production, including financing and landownership. At the same time, as agricultural production in Korea became tied to the Japanese market, fluctuations in demand in Ōsaka quickly and seriously affected the economies of Korean villages that were most integrated into the colonial market economy.

Japanese Economic Policy

Political and economic conditions in Japan during 1914–1929 were instrumental in bringing about agricultural changes on the Korean peninsula—including in the villages studied. The rise in agricultural investments, expansion of cultivated land, and increased Japanese landholdings all corresponded to a Japanese colonial food policy that called for more Korean rice and other agricultural imports. Due to Japanese population increases, rapid urbanization, and a decline in cultivated land area in Japan, Korean rice imports became critically important in providing additional food and in keeping down the price of rice for the growing numbers of urban Japanese workers.

Prior to 1914 Korea provided rice for the Japanese domestic market but played a minor role compared to Taiwan, Indochina, and India. With the outset of World War I, however, ships and shipping lanes in Southeast Asian waters were preempted for the war effort, and Korea— due to its proximity and to Japanese colonial control—became Japan's largest supplier of imported rice for the first time. With the exception of 1919, a year of political unrest throughout the Korean peninsula, Korea maintained this dubious distinction through the end of the colonial period.

The decline in rice imports from South and Southeast Asia contributed to the sharp escalation in rice prices in Japan during its economic boom of the war years. Between 1914 and 1918 the cost of living rose 130 percent, with wholesale commodity prices rising even faster. The Japanese public responded in 1918 with forty days of rice riots in over thirty prefectures. The Japanese government's response to the riots was twofold: cut the price of rice in half and import more rice from Korea. As Japanese domestic rice production lagged behind population growth and as the amount of cultivated land declined in Japan, these policies continued into the 1920s. Korean rice shipments to Japan accounted for approximately 40 percent of Japan's total rice imports between 1914 and 1929. As indicated in Table 6-1, rice exports to Japan, seen from the Korean perspective, accounted for an increasing percentage of total production during this period, from approximately 8 to 15 percent in 1914 to over 40 percent in 1929. The corresponding production figures in areas of high Japanese landownership and areas near Korea's ports were much higher still.[1]

While many Japanese suffered under the inflated prices between 1914–1920, others in Japan profited from Japan's war economy. Japanese trading and manufacturing companies capitalized on rising worldwide demand for textiles, metals, and machinery at a time when the other industrialized nations were involved in the war effort. While much of the Japanese capital generated during this period was reinvested or consumed within Japan, a considerable amount of this accumulated yen was also invested in other parts of Northeast Asia. In China, this Japanese investment took the form of both government "assistance" through the infamous Nishihara loans and private corporate ventures. These ventures included plans to develop China's ports and to engage in large-scale railroad construction. The extent of Japan's interest in the Asian continent is evidenced by actual disinvestment in Taiwan by its Japanese colonial rulers during 1914–1920.[2]

Despite being a colony of Japan, Korea presented monumental legal obstacles to large-scale investment by Japanese capitalists. Early in the colonial period, the government-general enacted the corporation (or company) law prohibiting the establishment of any corporation in Korea without the permission of the colonial government. Most Korean historians successfully argue that this law severely restricted business opportunities for wealthy Koreans, but it also resulted in (and probably intended to) restrict Japanese corporate activity to a very small number of large Japanese *zaibatsu* that had begun operations on the peninsula prior to the enactment of the law. As Carter Eckert points out, the law was also designed to restrict industrial investment from Japan not related to agriculture in order to keep the peninsula a market for Japanese manufactured goods.

As a result of the restrictions, Japanese investment of World War I profits was channeled into Japanese businesses already active on the Korean peninsula, or the profits were invested in land through the actions of private entrepreneurs. As an example of the former, the Chōsen kōgyō kabushiki kaisha, founded in Korea by well-known personages such as Shibuzawa Eiichi and Sasaki Yunosuke, increased its huge capital investment in Korea by over 48 percent between 1914 and 1929. During the same period Chōsen kōgyō increased its arable landholdings in Korea by 21.9 percent while increasing its profits by 337.9 percent.[3] The experiences of thousands of private entrepreneurs, some of whom

Table 6-1 Korea's Arable Land, Rice Production, and Exports to Japan, 1910–1929

YEAR	PADDY*	UPLAND*	TOTAL ARABLE LAND*	AMOUNT OF RICE CROP**	VALUE OF RICE CROP†	RICE EXPORTED TO JAPAN**	PERCENT OF CROP EXPORTED
1910	848	1,617	2,465	10,406	92,939	487	4.7
1911	1,002	1,703	2,705	11,568	142,763	265	2.3
1912	1,024	1,823	2,847	10,865	171,450	726	6.7
1913	1,067	1,819	2,886	12,110	198,537	1,591	13.1
1914	1,089	1,870	2,959	14,131	168,330	1,143	8.1
1915	1,178	1,993	3,171	12,846	118,781	2,205	17.2
1916	1,340	2,249	3,589	13,933	156,329	1,259	9.0
1917	1,435	2,440	3,875	13,688	224,662	1,131	8.3
1918	1,544	2,952	4,496	15,294	430,194	2,062	13.5
1919	1,547	2,975	4,522	12,708	516,337	2,800	22.0
1920	1,548	2,948	4,496	14,882	549,550	1,986	13.3
1921	1,550	2,984	4,534	14,324	361,126	3,387	23.6
1922	1,552	2,968	4,520	15,014	423,428	3,138	20.9
1923	1,560	2,984	4,544	15,175	400,413	4,051	26.7
1924	1,568	3,000	4,568	13,219	436,818	4,857	36.7
1925	1,575	2,996	4,571	14,773	474,287	4,745	32.1
1926	1,586	3,017	4,603	15,301	460,163	5,776	37.7
1927	1,603	3,005	4,608	17,299	434,545	6,456	37.3
1928	1,615	2,993	4,608	13,512	341,812	7,010	51.9
1929	1,625	3,007	4,632	13,702	322,448	5,781	42.2

*in 1,000 chŏngbo (chōbu)
**in 1,000 sŏk (seki)
†in 1,000 yen
Sources: Chōsen sōtokufu, Nōgyō tōkeihyō (1936)
Chōsen sōtokufu, Chōsen no nōgyō (1939), 48–49
Chōsen sōtokufu, Bōeki nempō, cited in Kobayakawa, 116

invested in the villages studied here, paralleled corporate investments, though on a more modest scale.

Japanese Agricultural Policy

The Japanese economic boom continued after the 1919 armistice ending World War I and until the spring of 1920, when a sharp recession occurred in March. As part of a successful Japanese effort to rebound from the effects of this recession, Admiral Saitō Makoto, newly appointed governor-general of Korea, immediately repealed the restrictive corporation law on April 1. Coming partly in response to the urging of Japanese capitalists, this repeal enabled investments to flow into Korea at an accelerated rate, and it gave entrepreneurs within Korea the opportunity to establish new business enterprises. Much of this increased business activity centered on agricultural operations, including new land-development corporations. The number of land-development and agricultural corporations active in Korea jumped from thirty-five in March of 1920 to ninety-nine by the end of 1925. Most of these new corporations and branches of Japanese corporations were located in provincial towns; many were founded by individuals who had profited in the export business or were involved in commerce within Korea (see Table 6-2).

As another way of stimulating agricultural businesses operating in Korea, in August 1920 the Japanese government removed tariffs on agricultural products coming from Korea. This action had the obvious result of making Korean rice and other commodity imports cheaper in Japan and of further tying the domestic Korean rice-production industry to the Japanese market.

Aside from these measures designed to facilitate commerce between Japan and colonial Korea, the Japanese government in Tokyo granted the government-general a great deal of autonomy in formulating agricultural policy in Korea. In the minds of the Japanese government and public,

Table 6-2　Corporations Active in Korea, 1920 and 1925

	1920	1925
Number of agricultural corporations capitalized at over 10,000 yen	22	69
Agricultural corporations capitalized at less than 10,000 yen	0	10
Branches of Japanese corporations involved in Korean agriculture	13	20

Source: *Chōsen ginkō kaisha kumiai yōroku* (1933), pp. 388–395, 426–427

Korea as a policy issue ended with its annexation in 1910, and the Japanese turned their focus to other parts of the Asian continent. Other than the 1919 March First Movement, Korea rarely appeared in the Japanese media during this period. Rather, it was the growing presence of Koreans in Japan that was of more interest and concern.

In addition, Japan faced innumerable crises during this period, both domestic and foreign, leaving little time for attention to Korea. The list of crises is long: participation in World War I, Twenty-one Demands on China, the Bolshevik revolution, the Siberian expedition, the Washington conference, the Tokyo earthquake, increasing labor unrest, universal suffrage, and assassinations. A parallel can be drawn with Puerto Rico's relationship with the continental United States. Other than in times of nationalist violence in San Juan, most Americans are almost oblivious to the island's existence—but not to the growing Puerto Rican communities in U.S. cities.

As mentioned earlier, Japan's government-general had but one goal in mind in determining agricultural policy in Korea: to increase agricultural production. Early colonial measures designed to aid in reaching this goal included systematizing landownership through legal procedures and land-registration procedures and through the settlement of Japanese farmers on agricultural land in Korea. Although difficult to prove due to inadequate agricultural statistics prior to 1918, the government-general achieved only modest success in attaining its goal through these measures.

Between 1914 and 1929, the government-general took steps to further stimulate agricultural production in the private sector. The most important measures implemented during this period included maintenance of an extremely low tax rate on agricultural land, consolidation of Korea's agriculture and industry banks into the Chōsen shokusan ginkō, expansion of rural credit unions, and implementation of several ambitious (if unsuccessful) long-term agricultural plans.

Shortly after it was established, the government-general adopted a policy of taxing agricultural land at an extremely low rate—1.3 percent of assessed value. In comparison Meiji Japan taxed farm land at 3 percent of assessed value, which required about 30 percent of the yield to pay. Comparable late Yi dynasty rates averaged 11 to 40 percent of the crop.[4] A low tax rate encouraged Japanese immigrants and wealthy Koreans to invest in agricultural projects. Profits from landownership and land development were kept high, giving incentive to landowners to acquire additional holdings in order to take advantage of the regressive nature of the land tax.

During the years 1914–1929, and in fact throughout the colonial period, the government-general did not alter the rate of agricultural land taxation. Further, despite the rapid increases in land and produce prices, agricultural land was not reassessed until 1943—necessitated only by wildly inflationary price increases during World War II. In addition to continuing to steer capital into agricultural enterprises, the government-general's land taxation policy stimulated increased productivity and gave incentive to bring new land under cultivation.

Creation of Agricultural Banks and Credit Unions

As another measure to increase, control, and direct investments in Korean agriculture and land development, the government-general assumed control over one of the primary sources of rural financing by consolidating the six regional agricultural and industry banks into the Chōsen shokusan ginkō. This action in September 1918 took rural financing out of the hands of regional landowners and placed it in the control of the Seoul financial establishment. By this action, the government-general hoped to "widely accumulate capital within Korea and undertake reform of Korea's commercial financing."[5] Contemporary public statements stressed that the unified bank would have increased lending capability for agricultural development projects.

The six regional agricultural and industry banks originated from financial reforms implemented by Baron Megata Shutarō, who received a mandate from the Japanese-dominated Korean government in the fall of 1904 to completely overhaul Korea's financial system. With initial capital from Japan, the banks were established to help finance agricultural improvements by Korean farmers using additional capital obtained from provincial Korean landlords. During the early years of the banks' operation, they were modestly successful in providing Korean landowners, some living in the villages studied here, with mortgage capital.

At the outset of the colonial period all stockholder and chief executive officer positions of the agricultural and industry banks were limited to Koreans to stimulate Korean deposits—although there was at least one Japanese supervisor to direct and insure control over banking operations. With the rapid influx of Japanese farmers and businesspeople into Korea, however, Japanese individuals held most deposits in the six banks and their numerous branches throughout Korea by 1911. More importantly, as proudly asserted by Ichihara Shigehiro, first president of Kankoku ginkō, most loans made by these banks went to Japanese entrepreneurs, not Korean farmers. At the urging of Japanese businesspeople, the government-general decided that continued and expanded colonial development required a central bank, one open to and operated by Japanese and Koreans, to finance agricultural and commercial projects on a larger scale. The new bank, the Chōsen shokusan ginkō (Korea Development

Bank), lived up to government expectations and financed development projects on an unprecedented scale throughout the predepression colonial years. Included were loans of considerable size to landowners in the villages analyzed in this study.

Whereas the agricultural and industry banks and later the Chōsen shokusan ginkō provided financing primarily for large-scale development projects, the vast majority of landowners in Korea turned to local credit unions *(kŭmyung chohap* or *kinyū kumiai)* for small agricultural loans. Credit unions, for example, granted far more loans than the Chōsen shokusan ginkō during the 1920s (see Table 6-3). For a ten yen membership fee, members could borrow up to fifty yen (raised to one hundred yen in 1914 and to five hundred yen in 1918) per year at an annual interest rate of 7 percent or less. Although limited to Koreans when established in 1907, membership in local credit unions was opened to Japanese farmers in 1914 when the government-general amended the rural credit union law.

As a result of new Japanese members and the general prosperity during World War I, the number of local credit unions and their total membership swelled dramatically. Between 1912 and 1921, the number of credit unions jumped from 189 to 433, and membership increased from less than 68,000 to over 285,000. By 1930—the time of the depression—membership had doubled again. Throughout the colonial period the local credit union remained the only institutional source of small loans for farming necessities (for example, seeds, fertilizer, and oxen) available to small-scale rural landowners.

Table 6-3   Agricultural Loans Granted
(in thousands of yen)

	SHOKUSAN GINKŌ[a]	CREDIT UNIONS[b]
1918	5,724	6,601
1919	7,542	18,390
1920	12,208	26,139
1921	19,780	32,784
1922	24,958	42,148
1923	29,841	42,556
1924	22,437	46,061
1925	40,675	51,988
1926	42,248	59,748
1927	65,247	67,465
1928	—	72,368
1929	—	84,830

Sources: [a]*Chōsen shokusan ginkō jūnen-shi,* tables on pages 123, 127, 130
[b]*Chōsen kinyū kumiai no gensei,* 336–337

In addition to expanding financial institutions during 1914–1929, the government-general launched long-term agricultural plans—with great fanfare—designed to further stimulate production. The first of these was announced in December 1920. According to this thirty-year plan designed to increase rice production and improve agricultural land, the government-general hoped to increase annual rice production by 900,000 *sŏk* (a 6 percent annual increase), increase rice exports, irrigate an additional 400,000 *chŏngbo* of paddy land, convert 200,000 *chŏngbo* from upland to paddy land, and bring an additional 200,000 *chŏngbo* of wasteland under cultivation. In other words, the government-general planned to improve about one-half of Korea's total agricultural land area.

Based on its own statistics, the government-general achieved only one of its goals: increasing exports of rice and other agricultural commodities, which rose dramatically. As seen in Table 6-1, rice production and cultivated land area increased gradually over the years following the implementation of the government-general's thirty-year plan. Failure to reach the planned goals cannot be blamed on the government-general's failure to provide adequate investment capital. All of the lending institutions under the colonial government's control expanded lending in the years following announcement of the plan.

Clearly, developers seeking to engage in large-scale land improvement projects did not lack available financial capital. Apparently, the government-general overestimated the amount of land that could be improved and/or underestimated the capital needed to improve it. As happened repeatedly since the turn of the century, Japanese colonial administrators overstated development potential in Korean agriculture.

In 1926, recognizing its failure to meet the ambitious goals of the earlier agricultural plans, the government-general announced a new, more modest fourteen-year plan to improve a total of 350,000 *chŏngbo* of agricultural land and disseminate new technical information on fertilizer, seeds, and cultivation methods. To implement this plan, the government-general offered subsidies of over 65 million yen, expecting developers to provide 39 million yen of their own. In addition, the government announced the availability of grants and low-interest loans for the purchase of fertilizer, half of which were to come from the Oriental Development Company and half from the Chōsen shokusan ginkō. By implementing this plan the government sought to increase rice production by 820,000 *sŏk* over the fourteen-year period.

Following the enactment of this second agricultural plan, gradual increases in rice production and cultivated land area continued, but there was no dramatic upswing corresponding to the enormous capital investments made in the agricultural sector of the Korean economy. Rice exports to Japan, however, continued to increase rapidly. During 1926–1929, for example, rice exports to Japan shot up almost 50 percent over the preceding four years, far outstripping the rate of increase of Korea's rice crop. Whether or not the government-general would have ultimately succeeded or failed in attaining its long-term agricultural goals is unknown. Its agricultural plan was scrapped in 1934 due to the depression's economic realities.

Agricultural and Landownership Changes on the Village Level, 1914–1929

The changes that occurred in the larger colonial context paralleled those in the rural villages in Korea during the first years of Japanese colonial rule. Cultivated land area gradually increased; the percentage of land owned by absentee landlords, both Korean and Japanese, rose slightly as businesspeople in Korea invested wartime capital in agricultural land; and lending institutions made increasing amounts of financial capital available to village landowners in the form of mortgage loans for agricultural and commercial projects.

Despite these modest changes the degree of continuity on the village level is striking. Landownership patterns observed in late Yi dynasty records and in the *t'oji taejang* prevailed throughout the entire period. The changes were of degree, not structure. Given the parallelism in development, presumably this was the case on the national level as well.

Between 1914 and 1929 total cultivated land area in the villages studied rose by 6 percent, roughly the same rate of increase as for the Korean peninsula as a whole. This increase, both locally and nationally, consisted principally of additional upland brought under cultivation through reclamation projects. In the villages, for example, paddy land increased in acreage by only 1.5 percent, but acreage of upland increased by 14.2 percent, a pattern spread over all of the research villages. Significantly, most of this reclaimed land lay on the outskirts of each of the villages, strongly suggesting that, contrary to early Japanese observers' claims, very little potentially arable wasteland existed in easily accessible parts of the villages.

Most of the individuals (largely Korean) bringing this reclaimed land under cultivation lived within the vicinity of the villages. Approximately 80 percent of the 50,000 *p'yŏng* of newly cultivated land was Korean-owned, 10 percent was Japanese-owned, and the remainder was owned by the villages themselves. Most of these individuals, both Korean and Japanese, tended to be small-scale landowners who carved out small plots of upland from village hillsides, a type of reclamation requiring great amounts of labor but little capital. None of the corporations or large-scale land developers discussed earlier owned any of the reclaimed land.

The high rate of land transfers in the village during these years demonstrated how marketable land had become since the Yi dynasty and how successful colonial Japan had been in removing obstacles to the buying and selling of land. Almost one-half of all land in the villages changed hands at least once between 1914 and 1929, the vast majority of transactions being sales. This was the case regardless of nationality of the parties involved. In large part this rapid turnover resulted from the increased demand for agricultural land following the influx of Japanese settlers and from the commercial prosperity of the war years. Demand, and subsequently land prices, rose most sharply near population centers, translating into rapid ownership turnover in Kongsu-ri and P'albong-ni and a somewhat slower rate in Songsan-ni and Paeksŏng-ni.

Throughout Korea during these years, Japanese individuals invested increasingly in landownership—a trend clearly visible in each of the villages studied, though in varying degrees. A comparison of Tables 6-4 and 6-5 with Tables 5-3, 5-5, 5-6, and 5-7 reveals this trend. Although Koreans continued to own the overwhelming bulk of all types of land in each of the villages at the end of the period, their share declined after 1914. Overall, Japanese individuals and corporations increased their percentage of holdings of paddy land (up 3.5 percent) and upland (up 2.8 percent). Table 6-5 details statistics on this change.

Typical of the Japanese investors at this time were Kitaō Mannosuke and Kitagawa Shōma, who purchased land in Kongsu-ri and P'albong-ni during 1914–1929. Kitaō arrived in Korea before 1905 from Ōita-ken and worked in Onyang as head of the post office. He supplemented his income by operating a moneylending business, which became his full-time occupation by the late 1920s. In 1924 Kitaō loaned 350 yen to Yi Hyo-sŏn, a landowner of modest holdings living in a village adjacent to Kongsu-ri. To obtain the loan, Yi mortgaged his two plots of agricultural land in Kongsu-ri and agreed to repay Kitaō the following year the principal plus interest calculated at a monthly rate of 3 percent. Unfortunately for Yi, he was unable to repay the loan, so ownership of his land shifted to Kitaō in October 1926. Kitaō maintained ownership through the end of the colonial period, receiving rent income as an absentee landlord. Kitaō's occupation was registered as moneylender in 1929, a year in which he paid seventy-eight yen in taxes. In the 1930s he purchased additional land in Kongsu-ri, including the town cemetery, which he later sold to another absentee landlord.[6]

Kitagawa Shōma first sailed to Korea from his native Kōchi-ken in 1906 at the age of twenty-one. After working briefly as an accountant with a relative's business selling provisions to the Japanese army sta-

Table 6-4   Village Landownership, 1914–1929 (in p'yŏng)

	PADDY LAND					UPLAND					TOTAL CULTIVATED AREA
	KOREAN	JAPANESE	CORPORATE	OTHER	TOTAL	KOREAN	JAPANESE	CORPORATE	OTHER	TOTAL	
1914	521,124 (85.3)	39,315 (6.4)	40,997 (6.7)	9,834 (1.6)	611,273	251,984 (80.9)	32,517 (10.4)	22,727 (7.3)	4,424 (1.4)	311,652	922,925
1915	513,272 (85.1)	39,315 (6.5)	40,997 (6.8)	9,849 (1.6)	603,433	251,633 (80.7)	34,533 (10.4)	22,727 (7.3)	4,914 (1.6)	311,712	915,145
1916	511,653 (84.9)	40,001 (6.6)	40,997 (6.8)	9,849 (1.6)	602,500	248,355 (80.0)	34,533 (11.1)	22,727 (7.3)	4,914 (1.6)	310,529	913,029
1917	523,646 (85.4)	38,847 (6.3)	40,997 (6.7)	9,849 (1.6)	613,339	248,060 (74.3)	35,200 (10.5)	22,727 (6.8)	9,001 (2.4)	334,088	947,427
1918	523,297 (85.3)	39,196 (6.4)	40,997 (6.7)	9,849 (1.6)	613,339	250,993 (74.2)	36,333 (10.7)	22,727 (6.7)	26,826 (8.4)	338,154	951,493
1919	521,074 (84.5)	45,049 (7.3)	40,997 (6.6)	9,450 (1.6)	616,570	260,956 (74.8)	31,685 (9.1)	26,719 (7.7)	29,289 (8.4)	348,649	965,219
1920	521,156 (84.4)	37,942 (6.1)	48,852 (7.9)	9,450 (1.6)	617,400	260,364 (74.7)	31,685 (9.1)	26,902 (7.7)	29,712 (8.5)	348,663	966,063
1921	519,303 (83.3)	43,410 (7.0)	50,835 (8.2)	9,450 (1.5)	622,998	257,405 (74.1)	33,695 (9.7)	26,784 (7.7)	29,289 (8.5)	347,173	970,171
1922	513,201 (82.9)	44,655 (7.2)	52,058 (8.4)	9,450 (1.5)	619,364	256,138 (73.8)	33,893 (9.8)	28,337 (8.2)	28,723 (8.2)	347,091	966,455
1923	513,619 (82.7)	46,313 (7.4)	52,058 (8.4)	9,450 (1.5)	621,440	260,292 (73.6)	34,362 (9.7)	28,488 (8.1)	30,318 (8.6)	353,460	974,900
1924	510,141 (82.3)	48,471 (7.8)	52,058 (8.4)	9,450 (1.5)	620,120	260,138 (73.6)	34,314 (9.7)	28,462 (8.1)	30,318 (8.6)	353,232	973,352
1925	509,628 (82.2)	48,785 (7.9)	50,811 (8.2)	10,549 (1.7)	619,773	258,836 (73.0)	36,760 (10.4)	29,709 (8.4)	29,219 (8.2)	354,524	974,297
1926	509,720 (82.1)	49,727 (8.0)	50,613 (8.2)	10,549 (1.7)	620,609	257,849 (72.6)	38,849 (11.0)	29,220 (8.2)	29,219 (8.2)	355,137	975,746
1927	510,294 (82.2)	48,981 (7.9)	51,276 (8.2)	10,549 (1.7)	621,100	256,946 (72.4)	39,753 (11.2)	29,220 (8.2)	29,219 (8.2)	355,138	976,238
1928	509,374 (82.0)	49,771 (8.0)	51,276 (8.3)	10,549 (1.7)	620,970	255,729 (72.0)	40,935 (11.5)	29,220 (8.2)	29,219 (8.2)	355,103	976,073
1929	507,457 (81.8)	53,613 (8.6)	49,380 (8.0)	9,949 (1.6)	620,399	253,800 (71.3)	45,822 (12.9)	27,055 (7.6)	29,219 (8.2)	355,896	976,295

Note: Numbers in parentheses represent percentages of total

Table 6-5 Landownership in 1929 (in *p'yŏng*)

VILLAGE	PADDY		UPLAND		RESIDENTIAL		OTHER		TOTAL	
Songsan-ni										
Koreans	131,443	(87.6)	34,018	(96.0)	8,818	(100)	6,556	(74.2)	180,835	(89.0)
Japanese	7,568	(5.1)	1,433	(4.0)	—		—		9,001	(4.4)
Corporations	8,314	(5.5)	—		—		—		8,314	(4.1)
Others	2,704	(1.8)	—		—		2,284	(25.8)	4,988	(2.5)
Total	150,029		35,451		8,818		8,840		203,138	
Paeksŏng-ni										
Koreans	62,242	(87.4)	87,191	(75.9)	12,758	(99.5)	36,107	(85.8)	198,298	(82.3)
Japanese	5,604	(7.9)	966	(0.9)	65	(0.5)	—		6,635	(2.7)
Corporations	3,124	(4.4)	4,743	(4.1)	—		—		7,867	(3.3)
Others	225	(0.3)	21,923	(19.1)	—		5,970	(14.2)	28,118	(11.7)
Total	71,195		114,823		12,823		42,077		240,918	
Kongsu-ri										
Koreans	197,232	(73.9)	93,788	(60.0)	11,746	(73.9)	28,493	(44.5)	331,259	(65.8)
Japanese	34,122	(12.8)	39,583	(25.3)	1,374	(8.6)	10,568	(16.5)	85,647	(17.0)
Corporations	28,883	(10.8)	18,320	(11.7)	2,016	(12.7)	7,382	(11.5)	56,601	(11.2)
Others	7,163	(2.7)	4,644	(3.0)	757	(4.8)	17,565	(27.4)	30,129	(6.0)
Total	267,400		156,335		15,893		64,008		503,636	
P'albong-ni										
Koreans	116,315	(88.2)	40,067	(81.3)	6,923	(88.9)	11,745	(51.8)	175,050	(82.8)
Japanese	6,319	(4.8)	3,840	(7.8)	434	(5.6)	—		10,593	(5.0)
Corporations	9,059	(6.9)	3,992	(8.1)	—		—		13,051	(6.2)
Others	82	(0.1)	1,388	(2.8)	429	(9.5)	10,909	(48.2)	12,808	(6.0)
Total	131,775		49,287		7,786		22,654		211,502	
Total	620,399		355,896		45,320		135,295		1,156,910	

Source: *t'oji taejang*

tioned in North P'yŏng'an province, Kitagawa moved south to a small village in North Chŏlla province and opened a hospital. He soon branched out into commerce, opening a general store and providing lumber from his forest landholdings for the construction of the North Chŏlla railroad. Kitagawa's business endeavors prospered during the early colonial years, enabling him to relocate to the new bustling commercial town of Iri and to invest in large agricultural land purchases. Part of this land lay in P'albong-ni. In July 1921 he bought paddy land, upland, and the family home of Kim Tong-sik, a P'albong-ni resident who had inherited his family's land several years earlier but had fallen on hard times.[7]

In the wake of World War I corporate prosperity and new investment flexibility due to the repeal of the corporation law, external corporate investment in village landownership rose between 1915–1923. The largest corporate landowner continued to be the Oriental Development Company, which increased its net holdings very slightly through additional land purchases. Most new corporate landownership, however, came from corporations investing in village land for the first time. The activities of Moroto shokusan gōmeikaisha and Takase gōmeikaisha typify investment patterns.

In 1917 Moroto Seiroku, a twenty-nine-year-old wealthy insurance executive living in Mie-ken in Japan, established the Moroto shokusan gōmeikaisha to undertake agricultural investment projects in Korea. Hindered by the corporation law, Moroto gōmeikaisha was not incorporated in Korea itself, but it did begin purchasing agricultural land the following year. Moroto bought its land in P'albong-ni, including some of the highest quality plots, in August 1919 from an absentee Korean landlord, adding to its sizable landholdings throughout the peninsula. After the repeal of the corporation law, Moroto Seiroku expanded his agricultural investments in Korea through his newly established Mie nōjō, owning over 1,700 acres of cultivated land in 1922 and over 2,100 acres in 1928. Moroto eventually sold this land to a Korean businessperson in Seoul in May 1937.[8]

Takase Heijirō, a native of Shiga-ken, arrived in Pusan with his family in 1897 at the age of 16. After working with his adopted brother in the cotton fabric business, Takase acquired land in South Chŏlla province for cotton production, establishing the highly successful Takase nōjō in 1911. Subsequently, the Takase family expanded its agricultural landholdings throughout the Korean peninsula, acquiring paddy land in P'albong-ni in November 1914, and establishing the Takase gōmeikaisha in Pusan in 1917 to manage and develop its land throughout Korea, which in 1929 amounted to almost 2,000 acres. Much of what the Takase land produced, mostly rice and cotton, was exported to Japan. Produce from P'albong-ni undoubtedly was shipped to Japan from Kunsan, where Takase established a lucrative branch office.[9]

In light of the external capital investments made in village landowner-ship by Koreans, Japanese, and corporations during these years, one would expect a significant rise in the percentage of land owned by absen-tee landlords, but that was not so. As seen in a comparison of Tables 5-4 and 6-6, little significant difference can be found in the data on land-owner residency for 1914 and 1929. Village residents actually increased their share of village paddy land but owned a smaller percentage of upland than they had fifteen years earlier. In general, as hinted in the examples cited here, new investors acquired agricultural land from other absentee landlords, not from village residents. No major structural change took place.

For the most part, new landowners possessed less land individually than the landlords they replaced, resulting in an increase in the absolute number of landowners and a decrease in the size of the average holding. Small-scale new developers, for example, could afford to purchase only small parcels of land at rapidly inflating prices. Significantly, the number of Japanese landowners rose 33 percent between 1914 and 1929; the number of Korean landowners rose over 10 percent. These increases, which exceeded increases in cultivated land area, meant gradually smaller landholdings per individual owner. Korean farmers owning smaller farms at the outset were negatively affected by the trend toward smaller holdings. Their plight was worsened by the need to subdivide inherited land among descendants. This trend continued through the end of the colonial period and was a major factor in forcing Korean farmers to migrate to Japan and Manchuria.

Reflecting the government-general's national policy of encouraging investments in agriculture, lending institutions under its direction made mortgage capital available to village landowners at relatively low rates of interest. As shown in Table 6-7, between 1914 and 1929 these institu-tions loaned over 2.5 million yen to landowners in the villages studied— 94 percent of the total mortgage loans in these years. While it is clear that the major Seoul banks, in particular the Chōsen shokusan ginkō, and the Oriental Development Company loaned large sums to persons who hap-pened to own land in the villages, it is unclear whether this money was used for agricultural purposes. Undoubtedly, a large number of loans from local *kye* or relatives occurred "off the books" and were not regis-tered in the *tŭnggibu*. But since such loaners lacked legal recourse if the debtor defaulted, it became practice to register even personal loans if land was used as collateral.

While it is not possible to ascertain the precise use of a mortgage loan, available evidence suggests that most mortgage money loaned during these years was used for commercial endeavors. Seoul lending institu-tions did not any loan money to rural farmers in the villages studied.

Most recipients of mortgage loans from the Chōsen shokusan ginkō

Table 6-6 Residences of Cultivated Landowners, 1914–1935

	VILLAGE	MYŎN	KUN	PROVINCIAL TOWN	SEOUL	JAPAN	UNKNOWN OR OTHER	TOTAL
1914								
Koreans	299,005 (38.7)	77,765 (10.1)	168,411 (21.8)	72,824 (9.4)	138,620 (17.9)	0.0	15,804 (2.0)	772,429
Japanese	—	418 (0.6)	18,894 (26.3)	15,810 (22.0)	1,145 (1.6)	35,565 (49.5)	—	71,832
Corporations	—	—	1,710 (2.7)	—	58,266 (90.4)	4,457 (6.9)	—	64,433
Other	9,654 (67.8)	1,259 (8.8)	—	—	3,296 (23.2)	22 (0.1)	—	14,231
Total	308,659 (33.4)	79,442 (8.6)	189,015 (20.5)	88,634 (9.6)	201,327 (21.8)	40,044 (4.3)	15,804 (1.7)	922,925
1929								
Koreans	286,201 (37.5)	80,175 (10.5)	178,015 (23.4)	32,489 (4.5)	156,729 (20.6)	—	28,687 (3.8)	762,296
Japanese	8,828 (8.9)	5,099 (5.1)	10,697 (10.8)	24,944 (25.1)	8,626 (8.7)	41,241 (41.5)	—	99,435
Corporations	—	—	1,710 (2.2)	7,877 (10.3)	58,113 (76.0)	8,735 (11.4)	—	76,435
Other	2,287 (6.0)	31,351 (82.2)	601 (1.6)	—	3,181 (8.3)	709 (1.9)	—	38,129
Total	297,316 (30.5)	116,625 (11.9)	191,023 (19.6)	65,310 (6.7)	226,649 (23.2)	50,685 (5.2)	28,687 (2.9)	976,295
1935								
Koreans	297,361 (45.4)	58,300 (8.9)	175,050 (26.7)	42,415 (6.5)	70,552 (10.8)	—	10,987 (1.7)	654,665
Japanese	—	9,866 (7.0)	48,176 (34.0)	34,529 (24.4)	2,989 (2.1)	46,149 (32.6)	—	141,709
Corporations	—	—	1,292 (0.8)	—	139,629 (90.7)	13,043 (8.5)	—	153,964
Other	5,387 (11.3)	32,077 (67.4)	5,308 (11.2)	—	4,108 (8.6)	709 (1.5)	—	47,589
Total	302,748 (30.3)	100,243 (10.0)	229,826 (23.0)	76,944 (7.7)	217,278 (21.8)	59,901 (6.0)	10,987 (1.1)	997,927

Notes: Land is measured in p'yŏng
   Numbers in parentheses represent percentages of the total
Source: t'oji taejang

Table 6-7   Sources of Mortgage Loans to Landowners in the Four Villages, 1914–1929 (in yen)

VILLAGE	JAPANESE INDIVIDUALS	KOREAN INDIVIDUALS	CREDIT UNIONS	AGRICULTURE AND INDUSTRY BANKS	CHŌSEN SHOKUSAN GINKŌ (AFTER 1918)	ORIENTAL DEVELOPMENT COMPANY	SEOUL BANKS	TOTAL
Sonsang-ni								
no. of mortgages	28	9	16	7	7	4	3	74
Total mortgage value	30,510	9,370	7,610	7,178	40,050	114,000	29,500	238,218
Paeksŏng-ni								
no. of mortgages	10	12	12	—	13	—	1	48
Total mortgage value	2,580	7,176	4,270	—	15,950	—	1,700	31,656
Kongsu-ri								
no. of mortgages	2	11	16	6	5	4	1	45
Total mortgage value	1,100	69,950	4,970	7,900	78,000	21,300	36,000	219,220
P'albong-ni								
no. of mortgages	13	9	10	4	15	4	1	56
Total mortgage value	20,673	11,625	3,630	38,530	1,938,300	127,500	84,000	2,224,258
Total no. of mortgages	53	41	54	17	40	12	6	223
Total mortgage value	54,863	98,101	20,480	53,608	2,072,300	262,800	151,200	2,713,352
Average value per mortgage	1,035	2,393	379	3,153	51,808	21,900	25,200	12,167

Source: *t'oji tŭnggibu*

and other banks lived and worked in Seoul or in other Korean cities. Typically, these recipients were businesspeople or manufacturers who had sufficient landholdings for collateral on the large loans these Seoul lending institutions made. Almost all loans were made to Koreans (Japanese presumably had more personal capital and frequently did not have to use land as collateral), but rarely were these individuals engaged in agriculture as a full-time occupation. For example, in 1927 the Chōsen shokusan ginkō granted the largest mortgage loan of the period, 1.4 million yen, to Paek In-gi, a Seoul businessperson with extensive commercial enterprises in the capital as well as in North Chŏlla province. Paek (1883–1942) was the son of Paek Nam-sin, a landlord with perhaps the most land in North Chŏlla province at the end of the Yi dynasty. Paek In-gi's business endeavors were spread throughout the peninsula and included banking, electricity, insurance, and agriculture. In 1928 he reportedly owned over 5,000 acres of cultivated land in North Chŏlla province, more than any other Korean.[10] Dozens of other wealthy urban Koreans received loans of tens and hundreds of thousands of yen during 1914–1929. A direct correlation existed between the residence of the mortgage recipient and the size of the mortgage: The closer a person lived to a rural village, the smaller the mortgage received (see Table 6-8).

Small-scale landowners had the rural credit union and private individuals to provide mortgage loans for financing farming necessities. Other sources of loans existed (primarily a local *kye*) but because these landowners did not use land for collateral, the loans are not recorded in the *t'oji tŭnggibu*. As mentioned earlier, credit unions were established by the colonial government to provide small (maximum five hundred yen) loans to credit union members at low rates of interest. Each village studied was reasonably close to at least one rural credit union from which landowners could borrow capital and guarantee the loan with land. However, credit unions clearly loaned funds almost exclusively to the wealthier members of the village communities; poorer farmers could not afford the ten yen membership fee. Further, many of the credit union loans went to landowners living in the provincial towns where the unions were located, not to residents of small villages.

Between 1914 and 1929, credit unions made a total of fifty-four land-guaranteed loans to forty different landowners, averaging almost four hundred yen per loan. Less than half of these loans were made to village residents, and even these went to the largest landowners in each of the villages. Since new land acquisition was the principal use of these credit union loans, it is highly likely that these loans made it possible for individuals to further increase their holdings. For example, in P'albong-ni three of the ten credit union mortgage loans in this period went to Sŏ Chin-mun, then employed as chief of P'albong-myŏn and serving on the

Table 6-8 Residences of Mortgage Recipients, 1914–1929

VILLAGE	WITHIN THE VILLAGE	SAME MYŎN	SAME COUNTY	SAME PROVINCE/ PROVINCE TOWN	SEOUL	OTHER AND UNKNOWN	TOTAL
Sonsang-ni							
no. of mortgages	28	23	9	4	4	6	74
Total mortgage value	44,760	25,993	11,330	69,700	76,200	10,235	238,218
Paeksŏng-ni							
no. of mortgages	30	7	5	—	—	6	48
Total mortgage value	21,146	8,250	1,400	—	—	850	31,656
Kongsu-ri							
no. of mortgages	19	5	—	7	13	1	45
Total mortgage value	8,420	1,700	—	11,900	195,700	1,500	219,220
P'albong-ni							
no. of mortgages	19	5	17	10	3	2	56
Total mortgage value	11,788	10,300	96,840	243,330	1,840,000	22,000	2,224,258
Total no. of mortgages	96	40	31	21	20	15	223
Total mortgage value	86,114	46,243	109,570	324,930	2,111,900	34,585	2,713,352
Average value per mortgage	897	1,156	3,535	1,547	105,595	2,306	12,167

Note: mortgage values in yen
Source: *t'oji tŭnggibu*

North Chŏlla provincial advisory council. When he received loans from the Iksan kŭmyung chohap, Sŏ owned less than 4,000 *p'yŏng* of upland and three homes in P'albong-ni. His holdings grew annually, however, until in 1939 he owned 10,500 *p'yŏng* of paddy land, over 9,000 *p'yŏng* of upland, almost 3,000 *p'yŏng* of forest land, and eleven homes.

As another example, Pak Chae-gi, a Songsan-ni landowner of 3,000 *p'yŏng* in 1914, received a mortgage loan from the Hansan kŭmyung chohap in the summer of 1929, allowing him to expand his holdings to 4,562 *p'yŏng* by the end of the year. With another credit union loan the following year, Pak further expanded to eventually own almost 8,000 *p'yŏng* in 1935.

Moneylenders, both Japanese and Korean, provided the largest number of mortgage loans during these years, usually for short-term periods (six months to one year) at high rates of interest (up to 75 percent per annum). Many farmers were forced to borrow from these individuals. Most moneylenders were businesspersons or landlords living in provincial towns or neighboring villages who engaged in moneylending as a profitable side-employment. One such individual was Kanehira Toraichi. Kanehira emigrated to Kunsan in 1906 at the age of twenty-two from his native Hyōgō-ken. In 1907 he moved to Sŏch'ŏn, established a modest farm and "assumed command of Sŏch'ŏn's commercial world," according to one 1915 source. Although reportedly a man of high civic responsibility and benevolence (his tenants are said to have erected a stone marker in his honor), Kanehira loaned money at demanding rates. For example, in October 1924 he loaned one hundred yen to Yi Sang-gyu, a resident of a village adjacent to Songsan-ni, to be repaid April 1925 at an interest rate of 4 percent per month. Unfortunately, Yi's winter crop did not produce enough to repay the loan, so it was extended, but it was not completely repaid until December 1930, when Yi took out another loan to pay the first. He remained in debt until 1934, when he was forced to sell his land to the second moneylender.[11]

Satō Seijirō, a businessperson living in Kunsan, also provided mortgage loans to Songsan-ni landowners. Satō first visited Korea in 1903 and emigrated the next year from Ehime-ken. After serving in the Japanese army as a technical advisor to the Korean government, Satō went into fishing and farm implement manufacturing in Kunsan. As his businesses prospered, Satō began acquiring agricultural land in the North Chŏlla and South Ch'ungch'ŏng provinces, acquiring as much as 1,300 acres by the mid-1920s. Data from the Songsan-ni *tŭnggibu* suggest that Satō did not obtain this land through purchases. In November 1922 Satō provided a mortgage loan of 4,700 yen to Cho Chung-hwan, a Songsan-ni landowner living in Kunsan, who agreed to repay the loan two weeks later. Cho had still not repaid the loan two years later, when Satō initiated foreclosure procedures and assumed title to the land in September

1924. Although most mortgage loans made by private individuals did not result in foreclosures, their higher rates of interest placed the mortgagee at greater risk of default and ultimately of loss of the mortgaged property.[12]

Despite new investments in agriculture by individuals and institutions, the villages studied, viewed in terms of aggregate data, were characterized more by continuity than change between 1914 and 1929. Little new land was brought under cultivation, the percentages of Japanese and Korean landownership changed only slightly, and the ratio of local to absentee landownership remained relatively constant.

Examined separately, each of the villages carried its individual ownership and land-distribution patterns from the late nineteenth century through the first three decades of the twentieth century (see Table 6-9). In Songsan-ni at the turn of the century, landownership was shared by two groups: a relatively large number of village residents owning moderate amounts of cultivated land and a small minority with holdings of considerable size. The gap between the two groups, while clearly visible, was not as large as in the other villages studied.

This pattern, which was also observed in 1914 following the cadastral survey, remained generally intact during the first decades of the colonial period, but a slight trend toward concentration of landholdings emerged from the 1929 ownership data. The number of middle-ranking landowners and the amount of land they owned decreased during these years (Figure 6-1). At the same time, the holdings of the largest landowners (those owning over 5,000 *p'yŏng* of cultivated land) were concentrated in the hands of fewer individuals. Pak Tŏk-ha, who continued to be the largest landowner in the village, increased his landholdings by over 3,000 *p'yŏng* between 1914 and 1929, owning a total of 10,593 *p'yŏng* (approximately 6 percent of total village land).

Songsan-ni residents continued to own most homes in the village, but they owned fewer homes than fifteen years earlier. Among village residents home ownership gradually became more concentrated in the hands of fewer individuals. Almost 40 percent of village landowners rented their homes in 1929, compared to 20 percent in 1914, an increase that accelerated during later colonial years.

While Paeksŏng-ni's residents continued to own most agricultural land in that village, their share had declined markedly by 1929. Whereas two-thirds of it had been in the possession of village residents in 1914, the percentage dropped to just over 50 percent fifteen years later. Further, among village residents, cultivated land became more concentrated in fewer hands, as seen in a comparison of Figures 5-3 and 6-1. The percentage of farmers owning less arable land than needed to support a family rose sharply over 1914.

Residential land continued to be owned predominately by Paeksŏng-ni

Table 6-9   Residency of All Landowners in 1929

VILLAGE	LAND TYPE	WITHIN THE VILLAGE	SAME MYŎN	SAME COUNTY
Sonsang-ni	Paddy	60,580	29,312	22,622
		(40.4)	(19.5)	(15.1)
	Upland	23,552	4,878	2,361
		(66.4)	(13.8)	(6.7)
	Residential	6,460	834	159
		(73.3)	(9.4)	(1.8)
Paeksŏng-ni	Paddy	39,294	12,642	3,842
		(55.2)	(17.8)	(2.5)
	Upland	68,531	27,726	2,830
		(59.7)	(24.2)	(2.5)
	Residential	11,244	436	84
		(87.7)	(3.4)	(0.7)
Kongsu-ri	Paddy	49,874	18,910	32,266
		(18.6)	(7.1)	(12.1)
	Upland	28,866	12,358	21,401
		(18.5)	(7.9)	(13.7)
	Residential	3,545	517	1,633
		(22.3)	(3.3)	(10.3)
P'albong-ni	Paddy	4,675	3,225	96,842
		(3.5)	(2.4)	(73.5)
	Upland	21,944	7,574	8,859
		(44.5)	(15.4)	(18.0)
	Residential	4,513	647	1,632
		(58.0)	(8.3)	(21.0)
Total	Paddy	154,423	64,089	155,572
		(24.9)	(10.3)	(25.1)
	Upland	142,893	52,536	35,451
		(40.2)	(14.8)	(10.0)
	Residential	25,762	2,434	3,508
		(56.8)	(5.4)	(7.7)

Note: Land is measured in *p'yŏng*
      Numbers in parentheses represent percentages of total
Source: *t'oji taejang* and *t'oji tŭnggibu*

residents (forty-five of the total seventy homes), but increasingly this land also was acquired by absentee landlords. In contrast to 1914, a few village residents began to acquire a number of homes in Paeksŏng-ni and rent them to others in the village—a clear sign that residential land had become a marketable commodity for the first time. In short, by 1929 even more isolated villages such as Paeksŏng-ni and Songsan-ni exhibited some of the same land-distribution patterns seen as early as 1900 in villages closer to urban centers.

In Kongsu-ri, close to provincial market towns and situated on the main transportation route to Seoul, landownership remained grossly

SAME PROVINCE/ PROVINCE TOWN	SEOUL	JAPAN	OTHER AND UNKNOWN	TOTAL
13,243	20,958	687	2,627	150,029
(8.8)	(14.0)	(0.4)	(1.8)	
1,317	—	—	3,343	35,451
(3.7)			(9.4)	
290	—	—	1,075	8,818
(3.3)			(12.2)	
851	7,751	5,604	1,211	71,195
(1.2)	(10.9)	(7.9)	(1.7)	
1,653	491	4,743	8,849	114,823
(1.4)	(0.4)	(4.1)	(7.7)	
—	—	65	994	12,823
		(0.5)	(7.7)	
13,863	129,898	20,547	2,042	267,400
(5.2)	(48.6)	(7.7)	(0.7)	
19,922	57,366	9,544	6,878	156,335
(12.7)	(36.7)	(6.1)	(4.4)	
936	7,732	818	712	15,893
(5.9)	(48.6)	(5.1)	(4.5)	
13,129	7,355	4,348	2,201	131,775
(10.0)	(5.6)	(3.3)	(1.7)	
1,332	2,830	5,212	1,536	49,287
(2.7)	(5.7)	(10.6)	(3.1)	
162	6	—	826	7,786
(2.1)	(0.1)		(10.6)	
41,086	165,962	31,186	8,081	620,399
(6.6)	(26.8)	(5.0)	(1.3)	
24,224	60,687	19,499	20,606	355,896
(6.8)	(17.0)	(5.5)	(5.8)	
1,388	7,738	883	3,607	45,320
(3.1)	(17.1)	(1.9)	(8.0)	

imbalanced in favor of absentee landlords. In 1929 seven landlords (four Koreans, two Japanese, and the Oriental Development Company) owned a total of 230,113 *p'yŏng* of agricultural land, or 54 percent of the Kongsu-ri total, and 55 percent of all homes in the village. Table 6-10 shows the seven owners and their holdings. Only Chŏn lived in Kongsu-ri. Pak was a moneylender in Seoul. Son also lived in Seoul, in a small house in Hyŏnji-dong, but his occupation is unknown. Andō, a native of Gifu-ken, was the director of a dry goods business in Ch'ŏn'an. Kawa-mura also lived in Ch'ŏn'an, operating an iron factory and a retail gold shop.

FIGURE 6–1
Land Distribution among Village Residents in 1929

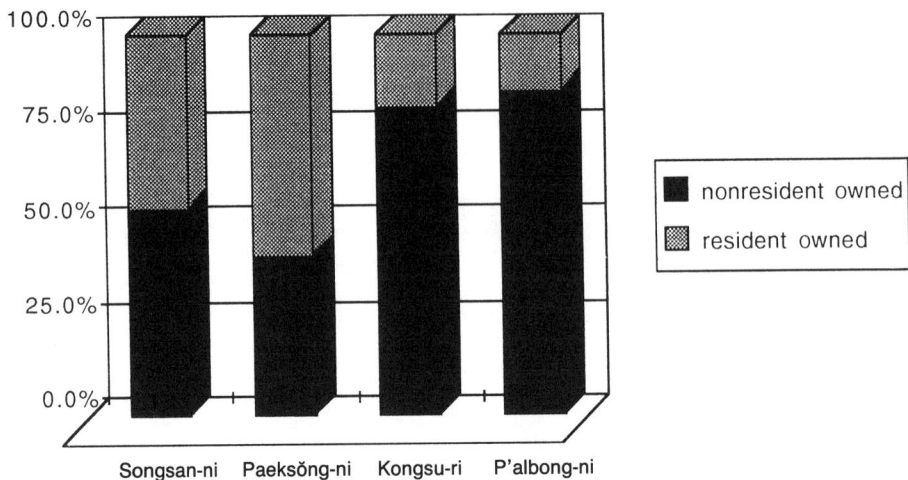

Breakdown of Village Resident Landownership

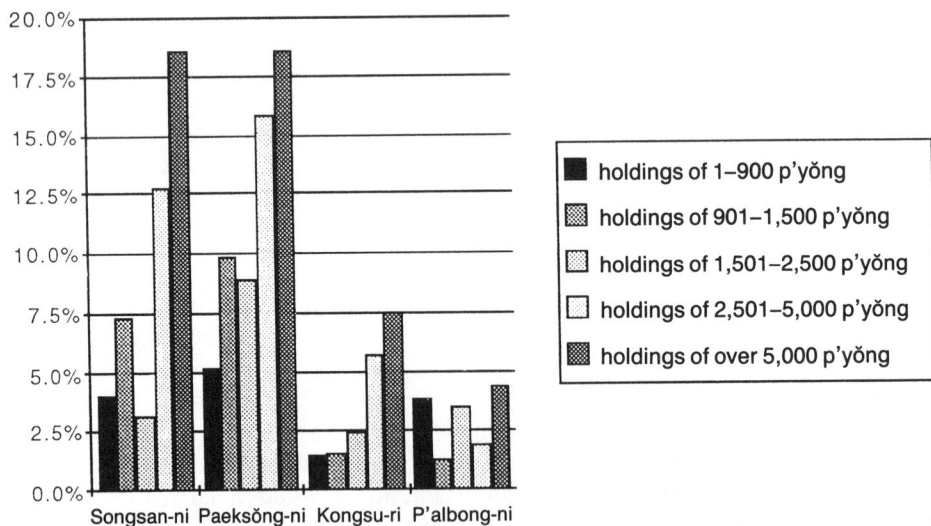

Source: *t'oji taejang*

Table 6-10   Landowners in Kongsu-ri in 1929

OWNER	PADDY (P'YŎNG)	UPLAND (P'YŎNG)	NUMBER OF HOMES
Pak Ki-hong	57,741	21,703	9
Oriental Development Company	28,883	18,298	11
Son Ch'un-je	24,929	4,856	3
Andō Kaneshi	20,003	4,208	2
Yi Kyu-sŏk	16,751	5,500	3
Kawamura Yasuichi	3,631	12,437	0
Chŏn Yŏng-yŏn	6,980	4,193	5

Kongsu-ri residents owned only 18.6 percent of the agricultural land in their village. As Table 6-9 indicates, absentee landlords living in Seoul controlled much of Kongsu-ri's agriculture. It was only in the 1930s that the role of Seoul landlords declined in Kongsu-ri as commercial and industrial endeavors became more profitable investments.

P'albong-ni in 1929 resembled Kongsu-ri in that it also continued to be dominated by a small number of absentee landlords. However, these landlords continued to live in rural areas of North Chŏlla province rather than in Seoul. For example, residents of Iksan-gun living outside of P'albong-myŏn owned almost 75 percent of all village paddy land in 1929. Among these regional landlords, P'albong-ni's land was concentrated in the hands of five individuals who together owned over 113,000 *p'yŏng* of cultivated land—63 percent of the village total—and a full 77 percent of total paddy land. Table 6-11 shows these five owners and their holdings. As seen in the table, one former Yi dynasty official, Kang Ki-hyŏng, owned almost 82,000 *p'yŏng* of village paddy land himself, or 62 percent of the total. Kang's paddy landholdings exceeded the total paddy land in the village of Paeksŏng-ni. He was born in 1874, a member of the Chinju Kang clan, and lived in a small village in a neighboring *myŏn*. He reportedly served as the official in charge of the Kyŏnggijŏn, the Chŏnju pavilion where Yi Sŏng-gye's picture is enshrined, and he could have accumulated his holdings from this source.[13] Obviously, most P'albong-ni residents owned little land of their own and had no choice but to work as tenants on land owned by absentee landlords. In P'albong-ni the alienation of the farmer from landownership was acute by 1929 and foreshadowed a similarly disastrous trend for small-scale farmers in other areas of the Korean peninsula in years to come.

The 1914–1929 period marked the maturation of the colonial relationship between Japan and Korea. Korea's role as agricultural producer had been determined by both the imperial marketplace and by colonial policy. As Japanese demand for Korean produce continued to rise and as

Table 6-11   Landowners in P'albong-ni in 1929

OWNER	PADDY (P'YŎNG)	UPLAND (P'YŎNG)	NUMBER OF HOMES
Kang Ki-hyŏng	81,745	1,814	1
So Chin-mun	468	7,496	5
Paek In-gi	5,218	2,641	0
Takase gōmeikaisha	7,855	0	0
Chu Nak-sang	6,142	0	0

colonial administrations maintained a policy assuring profits in land-ownership, entrepreneurs in Korea set about to meet that demand, in many cases by controlling the fields themselves. By 1929 even isolated villages had begun to feel the pull of strong economic forces, drawing them into the exploitative colonial system. But it was in the villages that had as early as 1900 already been brought under the influence of external investors that the signs of exploitation were most apparent. Absentee landlords, many replacing earlier landlords from the latter years of the Yi dynasty, acquired ownership over village land, extracted its produce, and left village farmers vulnerable to changes in colonial and ultimately world economics beyond their control. Farmers no longer produced for themselves but for the broker who bought and exported the crop or for the moneylender who made the crop possible. The consequences of this production pattern were tragic when, in the next period, the worldwide depression revealed the extent to which Korean agriculture in certain areas of the peninsula was tied to the Japanese economy.

CHAPTER 7

THE DEPRESSION YEARS
1929–1935: MAELSTROM
OF CHANGE

THE EARLY 1930s brought about more change in modern Korean land tenure than any other period. Never were the liabilities of Korea's colonial position more apparent, both on the national and village levels. Whereas trends had been gradual through 1929, developments during the next few years were sudden, powerful, and with ramifications lasting through the end of World War II. The devastating consequences of this period remain etched in the minds of thousands of Koreans to this day.

This maelstrom came in response to economic and political circumstances beyond Korea's control. The collapse of many of the world's trading relationships after the American stock market crash in late 1929 jolted Japan, already in a recession, into a depression. Led by the sharp decline in silk exports, foreign demand for Japanese products dropped markedly through 1930 and into 1931, resulting in a headlong plunge in Japan's industrial prices. Industrial output slackened, putting many laborers out of work and further depressing the Japanese economy.

The Japanese depression, resulting in a precipitous drop in rice and other commodity prices, "fell with crushing impact" on the agricultural sector of the Japanese economy, in the words of William Lockwood. The instability of rice prices drove thousands of Japanese farmers, faced with heavy tax and debt obligations, into bankruptcy and out of landownership. Most poor farmers found it difficult to enter the industrial work force during the depression and therefore "piled" up, as described by Shujiro Sawada, on farms as destitute tenants. Other farmers entered the military or, like many who moved to Korea twenty-five years earlier, migrated to Manchuria to start new lives.[1]

Having kept prices down using expanded rice and other agricultural imports through the late 1920s, the Japanese government found itself having to bolster the price of rice between 1930 and 1931. Part of this effort included a policy to sharply reduce rice imports from Korea during these years. The advantage of Korea as an agricultural colony was significant; the spigot of imports could be manipulated, turned on or off as the Japanese imperial economy needed, without regard for the market's actual supply and demand and the consequences in Korea.

The Korean colonial experience and its effect on farmers and landowners in the early 1930s resembled the 1846 Irish potato famine and its aftermath. Although caused by a potato shortage (rather than a rice surplus as in Korea's case), the famine created an economic catastrophe in Ireland, in large part due to British colonial control over Irish agriculture. Irish farmers, who produced principally for the British market, were victims in a controlled one-crop economy susceptible to disastrous fluctuations in that market. In the aftermath of the famine, structural changes in the use of Ireland's farmland, from cultivation to livestock pasturing, were made by absentee British landowners, and thousands of poor farmers were forced to migrate to urban areas and abroad—many to the United States.[2]

Following these years of hardships, Japan emerged from the depression much more quickly than other affected nations, able to stimulate its economy by increasing exports made more attractive by Japan's deflated prices. By 1932 the Japanese economy showed definite signs of recovery as Japan diversified its exports and the countries to which exports were sent. Asia, including Japan's colonies, played a much larger role in post-depression years as a market for Japan's products.

With the upswing in Japan's economic activity, jobs opened up in the industrial sector, releasing some of the pressure of rural unemployment. Japan's produce prices remained low (1925 price levels were not regained until 1936), but once again imported rice was needed for Japan's growing industrial labor force. By the end of 1931, there was enough improvement that rice imports from Korea were again stepped up.

The damaging effects of the depression hit all capitalist countries with great force but struck certain areas of colonial Korea like a tsunami. Tied to the Japanese consumption market through exports of rice and soy beans, Korean agriculture immediately felt the devastating impact of the sharp drop in rice prices in Japan and the reduction in rice shipments. Hardest hit were areas of the Korean peninsula most intimately integrated into the commercial and export market system—the fertile plains in North and South Chŏlla and South Kyŏngsang provinces, as well as areas around Korea's urban centers.

As pointed out earlier, many Korean landowners were deeply in debt in 1930, having assumed considerable mortgages to expand agricultural and commercial endeavors. At the height of the depression in Korea (1930–1933) many of these landowners were forced to default on mortgage loans, resulting in a significant turnover of agricultural landownership. Lending institutions, which would have normally renegotiated mortgage loans, were forced to foreclose and auction acquired land to raise capital. New landownership configurations emerged indicating an accelerated trend toward concentration of holdings in fewer hands and toward increased Japanese landownership.

Reflecting national patterns, landownership on the village level changed hands rapidly and frequently during the depression, with serious consequences for local Korean farmers. Overall, Japanese individual and corporate ownership increased dramatically during these years, particularly in P'albong-ni and Kongsu-ri—the villages most dominated by external economic forces. The landownership configuration established in the villages at this time and the countless personal sagas of hardship passed from generation to generation remain in the minds and lives of millions of Koreans today.

The Depression in Japan

The economic significance of the depression in Japan became apparent by the fall of 1930. Demand for Japanese exports dropped sharply as American and other Western buyers retrenched in the face of the 1929 stock market crash and subsequent economic panic. The tariff barriers erected by the United States at this time caused further cuts in Japanese exports to the United States. As wholesale prices in Japan fell in the ensuing crisis, hundreds of overextended businesses went bankrupt, putting thousands of workers out of work. Out of this business instability rose a trend toward greater concentration of production and commerce among a small number of *zaibatsu,* which had an increasingly important role in the Japanese economy.

Because the expansion of the Japanese economy during the 1920s had been based on increased exports, the industrial sector bore the initial brunt of the depression, but the agricultural sector was soon affected as well. The price of rice in Japan started to drop gradually beginning in 1925, due to bumper crops in Japan during the last years of the 1920s and to the rising volume of Korean imports. But this drop paled before the 33 percent decline in 1930, when the price of Japanese rice dropped to a level equal to the price in 1917. This drop occurred almost entirely during one month, October 1930, after the Japanese and Korean harvests flooded the market with surplus rice.[3] Not until December 1934 did the price of Japanese rice finally rise to its predepression level.

The drop in rice prices severely depressed rural areas in Japan, forcing former landowners into tenancy and resulted in the reduction of rice imports. The depression affected landowners more seriously than tenants because owners marketed their produce to obtain cash to pay taxes and buy farming necessities. Tenants generally paid rent, usually a fixed percentage of the crop, in kind. Landowners, deeply in debt to lending institutions, defaulted on loans and ultimately lost their land. The resulting concentration of landholdings paralleled developments in the industrial and commercial sectors. Rates of tenancy rose significantly during the depression, as did the migration rate of poor farmers to distant parts of Japan. Repeating a policy used in Korea twenty-five years earlier, these migrating farmers became critical in assuring Japanese control over Manchuria after the Manchurian Incident in 1931, when the Japanese government sought to relocate these farmers in the new "state" of Manchūkuo.[4]

Rice shipments from Korea, which had been increasing annually since its annexation in 1910, dropped off sharply in 1929—down almost 20 percent from the year before—and declined again in 1930. Korean agriculture, which had been stimulated to supply Japanese demand, now produced more than the market would or was allowed to bear. Whereas 40 to 50 percent of the Korean rice crop had been exported to Japan immediately prior to the depression, in 1930 just over one-fourth of the Korean crop was sold in Japan. The Korean economy was forced to absorb the resulting rice surplus.

The Economic Crisis in Korea

Reflecting the tightly controlled colonial relationship between Japan and Korea, Korea's rice prices more closely followed market conditions in Japan than in Korea itself. Therefore, when rice prices fell dramatically in Japan in October 1930, the prices in Korea dropped that same month. Also following the Japanese pattern, rice prices bottomed out in 1931. Between 1929 and 1931, the price of rice in Korea dropped by more than 50 percent, and pre-1929 prices were not regained until 1934.[5]

The economic effects of the depression were greater on Korea, with its one-industry economy, than on Japan. Agriculture, playing a much larger role in supporting other sectors of the economy, provided the capital with which commercial and industrial endeavors functioned. When the value of Korea's principal agricultural product declined to less than half its original value, the Korean economy was denied much-needed capital. Further, since much of Korea's commercial debt was guaranteed by agricultural produce or land, many of Korea's landowners, unable to repay debts in the depressed market, lost title to agricultural and other land through mortgage foreclosures. Others were forced to sell land at deflated prices to repay accumulated debts.

Nationally, the effects of the depression on agriculture and landowner-ship are seen in the increasing rate of tenancy among Korean farmers and the number of Koreans migrating to Japan and Manchuria. As land became concentrated in fewer hands, tenancy rates rose throughout the Korean peninsula. Landlords continued to be predominately Korean, but Japanese corporations and individuals increased their holdings signifi-cantly during the depression. Unfortunately, the exact nationwide total will never be known because the government-general stopped publishing such statistics in 1927. In the rapid turnover of ownership during these years, owners frequently became tenants for moneylenders-turned-land-lords. Between 1929 and 1932 the percentage of farmers owning no land and renting all the land they cultivated, increased to over half of all farm-ing households in Korea.[6] Correspondingly, the percentage of cultivated land area farmed by tenant labor also increased during the early 1930s. In 1931 over two-thirds of all paddy land and half of all upland was farmed by a tenant rather than an owner.[7]

In certain areas of the Korean peninsula, particularly areas near urban centers and Korea's ports, tenancy rates were even higher. For example, in the region around Ch'ŏn'an in South Ch'ungch'ŏng province, 80 per-cent of cultivated land was farmed by tenants and day laborers with no land of their own (69 percent of all farming households). Some areas of North Chŏlla province had even higher tenancy rates. Not surprisingly, in light of the higher tenancy rates, more landlords lived farther from the land they owned. In many parts of South Ch'ungch'ŏng province in 1930, for example, over half of all land owned by landlords was in the hands of individuals living outside the province.[8]

This alienation of Korean farmers from their land, which accelerated rapidly during the depression, meant that former landowners now had to pay rent to a landlord for the right to farm their own land. Moreover, during the 1930s formerly secure landowners had to compete intensely with thousands of others for this right. Tenancy contracts, predominate-ly oral, were usually for no more than one year and thus deprived tenants of long-term security. The primary grievance against landlords during these years was that landlords tried to replace one tenant with another.[9] As land became concentrated in the hands of fewer individuals and cor-porations, economies of scale and mechanization meant that less land was available for Korea's surplus tenants to cultivate.

Migration of poor farmers out of Korea, already evident on a smaller scale in the 1920s, increased rapidly. From 1931 the government-general began drafting plans to establish emigration corporations to resettle destitute Korean farmers in Manchuria and thereby resolve landlord-tenant disputes between Korean tenants and Japanese landlords. Forced off land in Korea, Korean farmers either moved to Japan to work in low-paying industrial jobs or migrated to Manchuria. Both groups were encouraged to move and were even assisted in doing so. Poor Korean farmers increased the number of Koreans in Manchuria, which rose from 600,000 in 1930 to almost 900,000 by 1936.[10]

The conditions forcing Koreans into exile were widely reported in the Korean press during the early 1930s. Articles vividly described the poverty caused by high tenancy rents and the usury that drove Koreans to flee their native villages in hopes of creating new lives elsewhere.

As the depression deepened and as Japan's priorities for colonial development changed from agriculture to industry, in part to support continental expansion, the government-general's support of agricultural expansion lagged. Financial assistance as outlined in the 1926 fifteen-year plan for agricultural development continued at a high level through 1931, but assistance dropped sharply thereafter. For example, money available in local irrigation organizations for land improvement projects dropped from 9.4 million yen in 1931 to 570,000 yen in 1935. This paralleled the drop in available mortgage capital on the national level as Seoul-based lending institutions shifted efforts to stimulate the industrial sector of the Korean economy. In 1934 flood damage in large parts of the rice-producing southern provinces further depressed Korean agriculture, forcing the government-general to abandon its 1926 plan altogether.

By the mid-1930s Korean agriculture and landownership had established structures and patterns in sharp contrast to earlier colonial years. Although further research needs to be done on the industrialization period of the late 1930s and early 1940s, landownership records suggest that these structures and patterns remained through the end of World War II. Rates of tenant-farmed land reached their highest levels and remained at approximately 60 to 70 percent of all agricultural land in Korea, and they were even higher in areas near Korea's ports and urban centers. As urban investors sought to invest in industrial and commercial enterprises, land documents indicate that absentee landlord rates also peaked in the mid-1930s. This period of suffering and destitution is ingrained in the minds of postwar scholars and almost all other Korean and Japanese observers.

The Crisis at the Village Level

Corresponding to conditions in Japan and Korea, land tenure and distribution on the village level underwent significant changes during the depression. Land transactions occurred rapidly and frequently, suggesting great instability in rural areas and resulting in new landownership configurations. The amount of land owned by Koreans dropped sharply as high-quality land shifted to Japanese individuals and corporations through large-scale purchases and mortgage foreclosures. Residency patterns also changed as new investors, frequently living long distances from the land owned, acquired village land.

The parallels between the village level and the national level are striking. Most transactions on the village level, including those resulting in land shifting from Korean to Japanese individuals, involved purchases. The timing of these purchases, most occurring in December 1930, indicates the extent to which the villages were tied into the Japanese and Korean imperial markets. As noted earlier, rice prices in Japan and Korea fell precipitously in October 1930 as demand and exports fell off drastically, and prices remained low through the mid-1930s. Confronted with year-round debts and a rice crop worth a fraction of the previous year's crop, many small-scale Korean landowners had no choice but to sell their land to repay loans and feed their families.

Mortgage foreclosures also accounted for a large number of land transactions during the depression—indeed, this was the first time under Japanese colonial rule where this was the case. Japanese lending corporations, the principal acquirers of land through mortgage foreclosures, loaned great sums of mortgage money to village landowners in the 1920s as part of the government-general's policy of encouraging the agricultural sector. These loans, most of which were from the Chōsen shokusan ginkō and land development corporations, came due during the depression and resulted in foreclosures when landowners defaulted on payments. During 1929–1933 corporations increased their landholdings in the villages studied by almost 80,000 *p'yŏng* (over 64 acres), 80 percent of which they acquired through mortgage foreclosures.

Whereas corporations increased their holdings through foreclosure proceedings, Japanese individuals acquired land during the depression through purchases (at undoubtedly dramatically reduced prices). As seen in Figure 7-1, changes in land distribution among Koreans, Japanese, and corporations between 1929 and 1934 were significant. Indeed, the change during this five-year period exceeded that of the prior fifteen years of colonial rule. In general, Japanese landowners and corporations enjoyed a net increase in all types of landownership at the expense of Korean landowners. The largest drop in Korean ownership came in paddy land, which fell from almost 82 percent of all paddy land in the villages in 1929 to approximately 68 percent in 1934. The sharp rise in Japanese landownership, however, went beyond paddy land to include upland and residential land as well. Overall, Koreans continued to own approximately two-thirds of all cultivated land at the end of the depres-

FIGURE 7–1
Changes in Land Distribution, 1929 and 1935 (in percent)

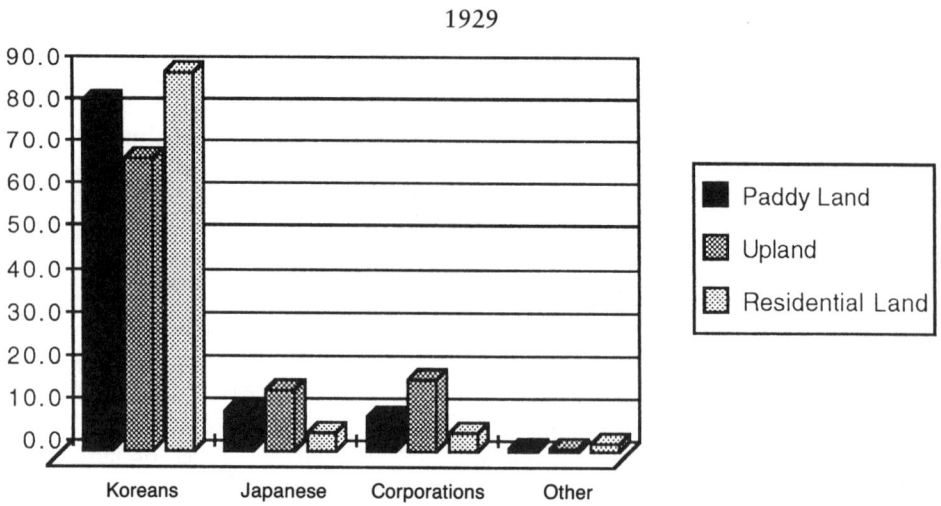

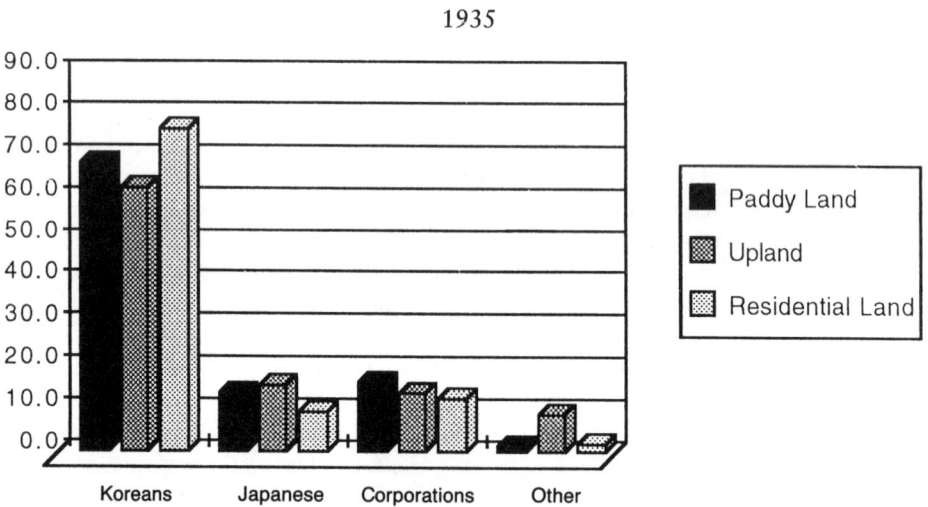

Source: *t'oji taejang*

sion, but this was significantly lower than the 75 percent owned in 1929.

Japanese individuals and corporations not only acquired a great deal of land during the early 1930s, but they also acquired some of the highest-quality land in the villages. From the outset of the colonial period through 1929 Korean landowners owned land consistently higher in assessed value. However, the land transactions of the depression altered this pattern dramatically. By 1933, following the large-scale land transfers to Japanese and corporate interests, a reversal had occurred, and these new landowners ultimately possessed the higher-quality land. Assessed land values reveal the extent of this change.

An owner increased the assessed value of land by upgrading it through capital improvements such as irrigation, by acquiring new land of a higher assessed value, or both. During the 1930s Japanese landowners improved only two plots of land in the villages studied (corporations did not improve any plots). The rise in assessed value of Japanese-owned land came about almost totally through acquisition of high-quality land from other landowners. An analysis of the land changing hands at this time supports this.

In 1930 alone, Japanese individuals bought almost 25,000 *p'yŏng* (over 20 acres) of cultivated land at an average assessed value of over 26 sen per *p'yŏng,* or approximately twice the value of land owned earlier by Japanese landowners. This average was also considerably higher than the average value of land across the villages studied.

This high quality land was not acquired by Japanese landowners by accident. The land had been owned by Korean residents of Seoul and other urban areas who had mortgaged it to finance commercial and industrial projects during the late 1920s. When the depression destroyed these endeavors, the high-quality land in the hands of absentee landlords passed to Japanese individuals and corporations. Land owned by individuals living within local villages, on the other hand, tended to be of lower quality and remained in the hands of village residents. Few local villagers mortgaged land in the 1920s, since they farmed on too small a scale to secure even a small credit union mortgage; hence, they did not stand to lose land during the depression.

Farmers producing for a local market rather than a national or Asian one were less affected by disruptions in trade and fluctuations in prices. Despite the high turnover rate in landownership, the increase in Japanese ownership, and the forced migration of destitute Korean farmers from rural southern areas, the percentage of village land under local control did not change appreciably during the 1930s. Interestingly, Korean residents of local villages not only retained holdings during the depression, but they increased them as well. This increase undoubtedly resulted from more urban landowners defaulting on mortgage loans and shifting into more lucrative industrial pursuits as Japanese expansion activity in Manchuria increased. While the rate of absentee landownership remained high, the escalation of this rate, a trend observed throughout the first twenty years of colonial rule, stopped in the 1930s.

Although absentee landownership did not increase, as new owners acquired agricultural land in local villages during the depression, the residency patterns of landowners changed over the previous period (1914–1929). Table 7-1 presents the data on the correlation between residency and landownership for Korean and Japanese owners in 1929 and 1935. As shown in the table, overall distribution of land among owners in each residency category appears to have changed very little during the six years. However, subtle yet significant changes did occur. For example, Korean landowners (frequently moneylenders loaning large amounts of mortgage funds to local landowners) living in provincial towns increased their landholdings by acquiring agricultural land during the 1930s through foreclosures and purchases at low prices.

More dramatically, landholdings of Korean residents of Seoul dropped more than 50 percent during these six years. These individuals, mostly businesspeople who had mortgaged their land to obtain capital for commercial investments in the 1920s, lost land when the crash came in the 1930s. Their mortgages, principally from Seoul lending institutions such as the Chōsen shokusan ginkō, tended to be large.

When the depression sent these individuals into bankruptcy, their land losses were staggering. Pak Ki-hong, forfeiting thousands of *p'yŏng* of agricultural land in Kongsu-ri, typified the fate of hundreds of others. Pak, a Seoul pharmacist and medical book dealer, owned 58,582 *p'yŏng* (over 47 acres) of paddy land and 20,321 *p'yŏng* (over 16 acres) of upland in Kongsu-ri in 1929. In 1926 Pak assumed an unguaranteed loan from the Chōsen shokusan ginkō worth an undetermined (but probably at least six figures) amount. In the depression Pak apparently fell upon hard times and defaulted on his loan repayments. After Pak declared bankruptcy in 1933, the Chōsen shintaku kabushiki kaisha, the real estate arm of the Chōsen shokusan ginkō, put a lien on all of Pak's land in Kongsu-ri and later that same year acquired title to all of it.[11]

Kim Hŭng-in, who lived near Tongdaemun (East Gate) in Seoul, presented a similar case. Looking for a safe investment during the uncertain years of the depression, Kim bought over 6,000 *p'yŏng* of paddy land and upland in Kongsu-ri from another Korean resident of Seoul in September 1930—one month before the price of rice plummeted. In January 1935 Kim apparently needed capital, perhaps for spring planting or a side business (of which little is known), or both; and took out a twenty-five thousand yen mortgage at 14.4 percent annual interest on his land

Table 7-1 Total Land Owned by Residents of Various Locations (in *p'yŏng*)

	OWNERS	VILLAGE (RI)	SUBCOUNTY (MYŎN)	COUNTY (KUN)	TOWNS WITHIN PROVINCE	SEOUL	JAPAN	OTHER AND UNKNOWN	TOTAL
1914	Koreans	299,005	77,765	168,411	72,824	133,620	—	15,804	772,429
	Japanese	—	418	18,894	15,810	1,145	35,565	—	71,832
	Corporations	—	—	1,710	—	58,266	4,457	—	64,433
	Other	9,654	1,159	—	—	3,296	22	—	14,231
	Total	308,659	79,442	189,015	88,634	201,327	40,044	15,804	922,925
1929	Koreans	286,201	80,175	178,015	32,489	156,729	—	28,687	762,296
	Japanese	8,828	5,099	10,697	24,944	8,626	41,241	—	99,435
	Corporations	—	—	1,710	7,877	58,113	8,735	—	76,435
	Other	2,287	31,351	601	—	3,181	709	—	38,129
	Total	297,316	116,625	191,023	65,310	226,649	50,685	28,687	976,295
1935	Koreans	297,361	58,300	175,050	42,415	70,552	—	10,987	654,665
	Japanese	—	9,866	48,176	34,529	2,986	46,149	—	141,706
	Corporations	—	—	1,292	—	139,629	13,043	—	153,964
	Other	5,387	32,077	5,308	—	4,108	709	—	47,589
	Total	302,748	100,243	229,926	76,944	217,275	59,901	10,987	997,924
1941*	Koreans	393,269	81,698	177,934	48,186	43,021	—	24,395	768,503
	Japanese	—	8,621	45,860	31,756	2,199	47,139	96	135,671
	Corporations	—	—	2,851	7,078	169,651	9,051	—	188,631
	Other	7,598	36,849	9,783	876	16,872	709	—	72,687
	Total	400,867	127,168	236,428	87,896	231,743	56,899	24,491	1,165,492

* After 1941 many Koreans were forced to adopt Japanese names, making positive identification difficult and statistics less meaningful.
Source: *t'oji taejang*

from Takahashi Masaki, a Seoul gold dealer and moneylender. On February 23, 1935, Kim took out a second mortgage of forty-two thousand yen from the Chōsen shokusan ginkō, this one to be repaid over twelve years at an annual interest rate of 7.2 percent. Two days later he took out a third mortgage, for eight thousand *yen,* again from Takahashi. Unable to meet mortgage payments, Kim defaulted in March. Although he managed to pay off the first mortgage in March, perhaps with the funds provided by the second mortgage, he had trouble meeting payments on the other two loans. His land was put into a trusteeship held by the Chōsen shintaku kabushiki kaisha until he paid off all his debts. In the summer of 1935 Kim declared bankruptcy, and the Chōsen shintaku kabushiki kaisha sold the land later the same year to another Korean resident of Seoul. Although the bank sold Kim's land in this instance, it usually kept the land it acquired through mortgage foreclosures until the end of the colonial period. As a result, it and other Seoul corporations significantly increased their holdings during the depression.[12]

As mentioned earlier, Korean landowners living in local villages actually increased their total landholdings during the depression. These individuals, owning the smallest and poorest-quality fields prior to 1930, had not assumed large mortgages and as a result did not forfeit land at a time when many others could not repay loans. Mortgages held by local landowners tended to be small, at low interest rates, and from local credit unions. When a mortgagee encountered difficulty in repaying a loan, the credit union rarely foreclosed, instead renegotiating the loan to assure continued interest payments. In addition to being less overextended when the depression began, some local landowners acquired agricultural land during the 1930s, buying it from lending institutions auctioning land gained through foreclosures. This improvement in the localization of ownership is further evidence that changes in landownership in Korea came about primarily as a result of economic forces and not from a colonial conspiracy to deprive Koreans of their land.

Japanese individuals increased their landholdings by approximately 43 percent during the depression. Gains made by Japanese moneylenders and small-scale investors living in rural provinces accounted for most of this increase. As shown in Table 7-1, Japanese individuals living in the same county *(kun)* as the land owned, but outside the local *myŏn,* acquired over 37,000 *p'yŏng* during these years. Japanese owners acquired their land primarily through private purchases, but a minority bought land auctioned by mortgage lenders after foreclosure proceedings had been completed. Between 1930 and 1935, Japanese individuals bought over 60,000 *p'yŏng* of land in the villages studied, compared to under half that amount in the six years prior to the depression, and acquired over 11,000 additional *p'yŏng* through mortgage auctions—more than twice the amount during the first twenty years of colonial rule. Japanese landowners living in provincial areas of the Korean peninsula, as well as those living in Japan itself, made the largest gains in land-ownership, led by residents of the counties and provinces in which the villages were located.

Corporations, all under Japanese control, more than doubled their landholdings between 1929 and 1935. These corporations, few in number and principally headquartered in Japan and Seoul, foreclosed on dozens of mortgages during these years and became some of the largest landlords in rural villages throughout the peninsula. Within the villages studied, the largest arable landowners in 1935 included the Chōsen shintaku kabushiki kaisha (97,278 *p'yŏng*), the Oriental Development Company (57,900 *p'yŏng*), and the Mie nōjō (4,308 *p'yŏng*).

While the vast bulk of this land consisted of cultivated land (much of it high-quality paddy land), the amount of residential land owned by various corporations rose significantly. Although the Oriental Development Company had owned a small amount of residential land since the outset of the colonial period, during the 1930s it and other corporations acquired numerous residential plots in addition to their farm land. For example, in 1935 the Chōsen shintaku kabushiki kaisha owned a total of twenty-six homes in the villages studied—more than any other single owner—followed by the Oriental Development Company with fourteen.

The depression entered each rural village, but its timing and impact differed from village to village. It affected first P'albong-ni and Kongsu-ri, the two villages producing agricultural products for urban markets and export. In these two villages landownership underwent significant changes between 1930 and 1935, accounting for much of the aggregate statistical changes mentioned above.

Landowners in many North Chŏlla province villages in the late 1920s sold their rice and other crops to merchants in Iri and Kunsan, who in turn shipped most of this produce to Japan. P'albong-ni, being relatively close to Kunsan (from which more rice was shipped than any other port during this period), was one such village. When the market for Korean rice fell in Japan in the fall of 1930, the resulting drop in the price of rice in Korea quickly affected areas like P'albong-ni. As rice prices dropped, so did land prices, attracting many new investors, both Korean and Japanese, who bought up land at deflated prices or acquired land through mortgage foreclosures. Between 1930 and 1935 approximately 50 percent of all P'albong-ni's arable land changed hands. Japanese investors increased their landholdings fourfold during these years, from about 10,000 *p'yŏng* to almost 40,000 *p'yŏng;* corporations more than doubled their holdings. These gains came at the expense of Korean landowners, who, although continuing to own most village land, gave up ownership of 15 percent of their land in the same period.

The shock waves of the depression also struck Kongsu-ri. Between the years 1930–1935, most of the village's arable land changed hands at least once, mostly by mortgage foreclosures. Because Kongsu-ri was located relatively close to Seoul, in the 1920s many of its landowners, particularly those living in the capital itself, mortgaged their land to Seoul-based lending institutions. Although a small number of individual moneylenders also foreclosed on mortgages at this time, Seoul institutional lenders acquired most land during these years. Among these institutions, the Chōsen shokusan ginkō acquired most of the land changing hands through foreclosures (as in P'albong-ni), assuming ownership of 80,000 *p'yŏng* (64.3 acres) of additional arable land in 1933 alone. This land was managed through its real estate arm, the Chōsen shintaku kabushiki kaisha, which, unlike most institutional owners acquiring land through foreclosures, held ownership over the land until Korea's liberation in 1945. In all, Korean-owned land in Kongsu-ri fell by almost 70,000 *p'yŏng* (over 56 acres) between 1930 and 1935.

Although the Chōsen shokusan ginkō's land came primarily from foreclosures on land owned by Koreans, a few Japanese individuals also lost ownership in this manner between 1930 and 1935. Indeed, total landholdings by Japanese individuals declined during the depression, a period in which corporate ownership soared by 146 percent. For example, Ogiwara Gidaichō, whose principal occupation was station master at the Kongsu-ri railroad station, took out a one thousand yen mortgage from the Chōsen shokusan ginkō in March 1929. When the depression began, Ogiwara was unable to maintain payments and eventually lost his land in 1934 to the bank, which then sold it to another Japanese individual, Nemoto Ukita, who had extensive landholdings throughout South Ch'ungch'ŏng province.[13]

In P'albong-ni and Kongsu-ri arable land became further concentrated among a few local and absentee landlords during the depression. These individuals and corporations with the largest holdings, each owning over 5,000 *p'yŏng* of arable land (a total of five in P'albong-ni and seventeen in Kongsu-ri), controlled over 75 percent of the paddy land in both villages and approximately one-half of the upland. And within this group of large-scale landlords, those owning the largest holdings greatly increased their acreage between 1929 and 1935. In P'albong-ni, for example, two individuals, one a local *myŏn* chief, owned almost 62 percent of all paddy land in the village.

Correspondingly, the number of individuals owning less than needed to support a farm family (approximately one acre) rose significantly in both villages during the depression, as did the number of residents who did not own any arable land.

As expected, the depression was less severe on the more isolated villages, Songsan-ni and Paeksŏng-ni. Like the other villages, however, mortgage foreclosures increased in frequency, and landownership changed hands more rapidly during 1929–1935 than in 1914–1929, though much less rapidly than in either Kongsu-ri or P'albong-ni.

Corporations acquiring land through mortgage foreclosures did so from both Japanese and Korean landowners. For example, in February 1932 the Oriental Development Company acquired all land owned by Anseki Chikuzaemon, a Kunsan businessperson with extensive landholdings through South Ch'ungch'ŏng province, including agricultural land in Songsan-ni and including 44 *chŏngbo* (over 107 acres) in Yesan-gun alone, for failure to repay a thirty thousand yen mortgage.[14]

In Paeksŏng-ni a landowner's mortgage debt was owed to individual moneylenders rather than corporations. For example, Ch'oe Ch'ang-gŭn, a resident of Paeksŏng-ni, assumed a mortgage of 1,300 yen from Kim Yŏng-yong, a Seoul moneylender, in January 1930. The mortgage was to be repaid in full by December 1935 at an annual interest rate of 20 percent. Unable to meet his payments, Ch'oe's land was auctioned in March 1933 to Yun Hyo-jung, an absentee landlord living in Nonsan.

The massive turnover of landownership on the village level during the depression altered residency patterns among landowners very little. No large-scale transfer of land to residents of any one location occurred. However, new trends appeared, and in this sense the 1930s were years of critical importance. As mentioned earlier, the rate of absentee landownership leveled off during this period as local residents, living in the villages themselves, significantly increased the total landholdings under their control. The only exception to this pattern was Kongsu-ri, where absentee landlords, often urban land-management corporations, actually increased their holdings. Large increases in landholdings occurred among residents of the counties *(kun)* and provinces in which the villages are situated, with the most noticeable decreases occurring among residents of Seoul and of villages located within the same *myŏn* (see Table 7-2).

When examined in conjunction with mortgage foreclosures, the significance of these land transfers becomes clear. As noted earlier, land transfers during the 1930s tended to be among residents of the same location (for example, from one villager to another or from one Seoul resident to another), whether the transfer was a purchase, foreclosure, or inheritance. Due to the large number of business failures and mortgage foreclosures when the commodity market plummeted in 1930, absentee landowners, whose agriculture tended to be more commercialized or more of a side business, were most affected. Brokers and exporters who owned

Table 7-2   Residency among All Landowners in 1935

VILLAGE	LAND TYPE	WITHIN THE VILLAGE	SAME MYŎN	SAME COUNTY
Sonsang-ni	Paddy	70,174 (46.5)	24,693 (16.3)	21,570 (14.3)
	Upland	21,840 (62.4)	5,046 (14.4)	4,246 (12.1)
	Residential	6,381 (72.7)	745 (8.5)	224 (2.5)
Paeksŏng-ni	Paddy	36,798 (50.7)	7,212 (10.0)	5,505 (7.6)
	Upland	73,188 (61.2)	26,806 (22.4)	5,078 (4.2)
	Residential	11,145 (87.7)	—	332 (2.6)
Kongsu-ri	Paddy	44,071 (16.6)	17,397 (6.5)	45,212 (17.0)
	Upland	24,950 (14.7)	10,628 (6.3)	37,796 (22.3)
	Residential	5,680 (29.6)	843 (4.4)	1,996 (10.4)
P'albong-ni	Paddy	11,338 (8.6)	2,999 (2.3)	99,766 (75.5)
	Upland	20,389 (39.3)	5,462 (10.5)	10,653 (20.5)
	Residential	5,413 (61.1)	107 (1.2)	2,132 (24.1)
Total	Paddy	162,381 (26.1)	52,301 (8.4)	172,053 (27.7)
	Upland	140,367 (37.3)	47,942 (12.8)	57,773 (15.4)
	Residential	28,619 (57.8)	1,695 (3.4)	4,684 (9.5)

Notes: Land is measured in *p'yŏng*
        Numbers in parentheses represent percentages of total
Source: *t'oji taejang*

the land producing the agricultural products they sold were particularly hard hit and were forced to sell their land to village residents or lost it to their creditors—who generally lived in the same vicinity or in towns farther from the villages. Thus, residents of the *myŏns* sold land to village residents at reduced prices or forfeited it to creditors living in provincial towns or elsewhere in the county. While Seoul residents adversely affected by the depression frequently lost land to Seoul-based institutions, many others were forced to sell land to private moneylenders to meet debts. But in the 1930s, urban investment interest centered not on agriculture, but rather on industrial and commercial endeavors to sup-

SAME PROVINCE/ PROVINCE TOWN	SEOUL	JAPAN	OTHER AND UNKNOWN	TOTAL
12,358	18,478	2,023	1,806	151,102
(8.2)	(12.2)	(1.3)	(1.2)	
714	—	—	3,189	35,035
(2.0)			(9.1)	
290	—	—	1,141	8,781
(3.3)			(13.0)	
10,077	6,920	5,604	402	72,518
(13.9)	(9.5)	(7.7)	(0.6)	
7,058	2,241	4,743	436	119,550
(5.9)	(1.9)	(4.0)	(0.4)	
518	—	65	648	12,708
(4.1)		(0.5)	(5.1)	
12,840	126,388	20,586	—	266,494
(4.8)	(47.4)	(7.7)		
25,125	53,485	12,867	4,491	169,342
(14.8)	(31.6)	(7.6)	(2.7)	
567	9,241	818	—	19,145
(3.0)	(48.3)	(4.3)		
6,424	6,936	4,558	—	132,021
(4.9)	(5.3)	(3.4)		
2,348	2,830	9,520	663	51,865
(4.5)	(5.5)	(18.4)	(1.3)	
162	6	—	1,035	8,855
(1.8)	(0.1)		(11.7)	
41,699	158,722	32,771	2,208	622,135
(6.7)	(25.5)	(5.3)	(0.3)	
35,245	58,556	27,130	8,779	375,792
(9.4)	(15.6)	(7.2)	(2.3)	
1,537	9,247	883	2,824	49,489
(3.1)	(18.7)	(1.8)	(5.7)	

port the expanding Japanese military activity in China. Seoul entrepreneurs were no longer primarily interested in landownership as an investment. As a result, land formerly owned by residents of the capital was acquired by individuals and land development/management corporations situated in smaller towns and communities closer to rural villages.

Kim Han-gyu and Im Tae-sun typify the many examples of land transfers from Seoul residents to individuals living closer to rural villages. Kim was a prominent businessperson at the outset of the colonial period, working as an executive in several banks and insurance companies. Having entered Japanese language school early (1896) and having taught Jap-

FIGURE 7–2
Land Distribution among Songsan-ni Residents, 1935

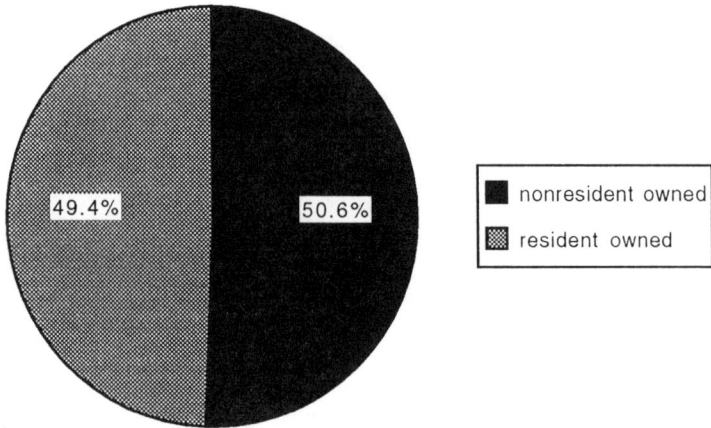

Breakdown of the 49.4% of Village Land Owned by Residents,
According to Size of Holding

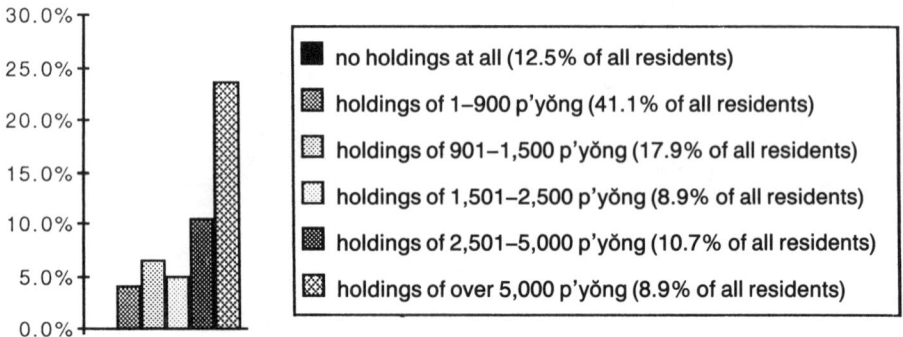

Source: *t'oji taejang*

anese language in Seoul, Kim was in a good position to succeed under Japanese rule. After his success in the banking world, Kim went into business for himself, establishing a real estate business in the late 1920s, and acquired several thousand *p'yŏng* of paddy land in Paeksŏng-ni. In the 1930s, however, his fortune changed, forcing him to leave business and return to his former profession of teaching Japanese language. His

FIGURE 7–2–1
Land Distribution among Paeksŏng-ni Residents, 1935

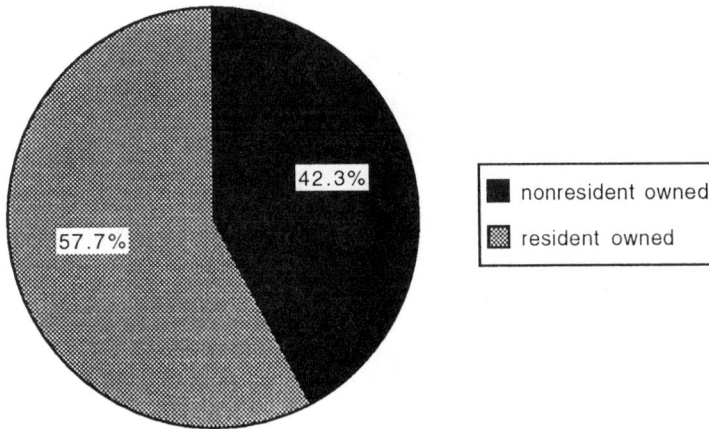

42.3%

57.7%

■ nonresident owned
▨ resident owned

Breakdown of the 57.7% of Village Land Owned by Residents,
According to Size of Holding

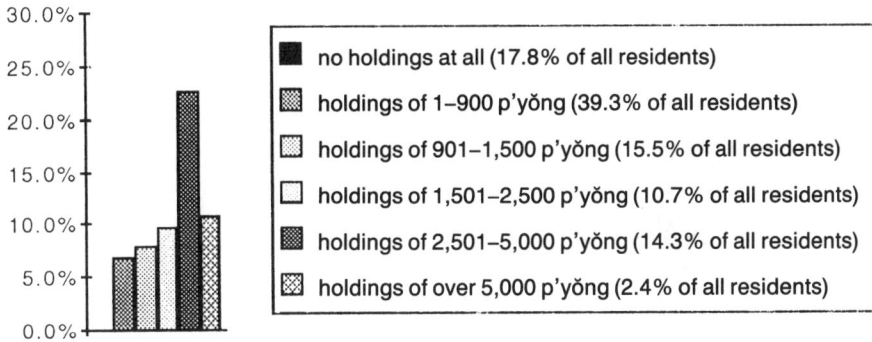

30.0%
25.0%
20.0%
15.0%
10.0%
5.0%
0.0%

■ no holdings at all (17.8% of all residents)
▨ holdings of 1–900 p'yŏng (39.3% of all residents)
▨ holdings of 901–1,500 p'yŏng (15.5% of all residents)
☐ holdings of 1,501–2,500 p'yŏng (10.7% of all residents)
▨ holdings of 2,501–5,000 p'yŏng (14.3% of all residents)
▨ holdings of over 5,000 p'yŏng (2.4% of all residents)

Source: *t'oji taejang*

land—at least his land in Paeksŏng-ni—was acquired by the Chōsen sho-kusan ginkō when Kim defaulted on his mortgage loan, and it was subsequently auctioned to a Korean resident of Nonsan.[15]

Im Tae-sun inherited his large landholdings in Songsan-ni in 1931 from his father, Im Man-je, who had served as a police officer in the Kwangmu-period Korean government. A resident of Seoul, Im ran into

FIGURE 7–2–2
Land Distribution among Kongsu-ri Residents, 1935

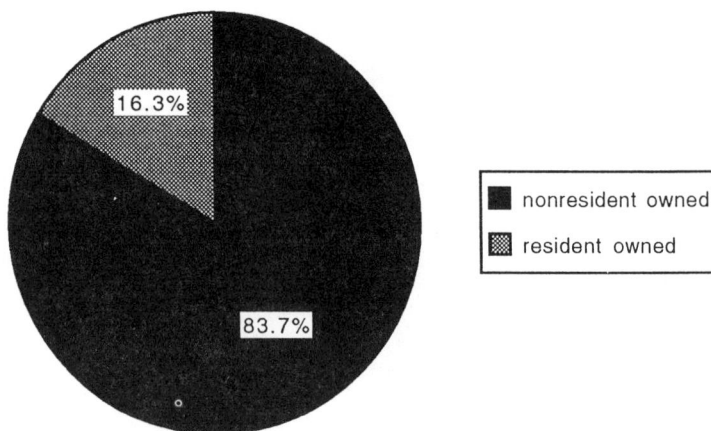

Breakdown of the 16.3% of Village Land Owned by Residents,
According to Size of Holding

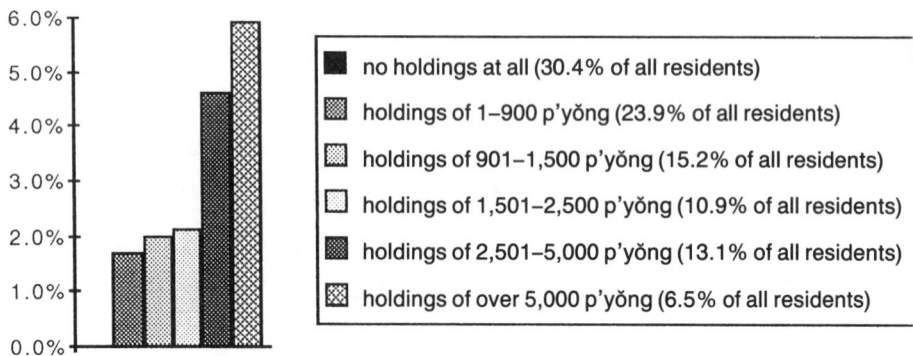

Source: *t'oji taejang*

financial difficulty in the depression due to debts, and since he had no
direct ties to the land, like so many others of his generation, he sold the
family land in Songsan-ni shortly after acquiring title. In 1934 Im sold his
land to a Pak Kyŏng-jong, a Songsan-ni landowner of moderate holdings, who kept the land through the end of the colonial period.[16]

Japanese residents of Japan continued to increase their landholdings in
the villages during the depression. As mentioned earlier, Korean agricul-

FIGURE 7–2–3
Land Distribution among P'albong-ni Residents, 1935

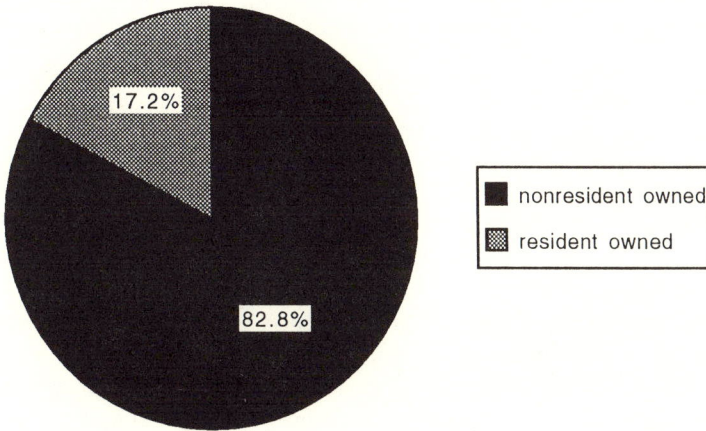

legend:
■ nonresident owned
▨ resident owned

17.2%

82.8%

Breakdown of the 17.2% of Village Land Owned by Residents,
According to Size of Holding

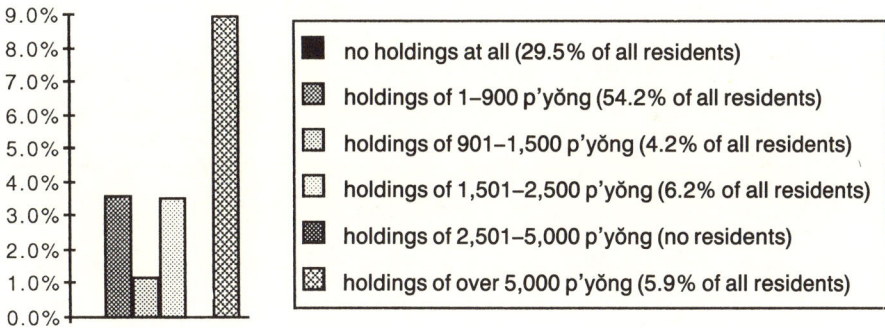

■ no holdings at all (29.5% of all residents)

▨ holdings of 1–900 p'yŏng (54.2% of all residents)

▨ holdings of 901–1,500 p'yŏng (4.2% of all residents)

☐ holdings of 1,501–2,500 p'yŏng (6.2% of all residents)

▨ holdings of 2,501–5,000 p'yŏng (no residents)

▨ holdings of over 5,000 p'yŏng (5.9% of all residents)

Source: *t'oji taejang*

tural exports to Japan, which were drastically reduced for several years, had attained their predepression level by 1932. As Korean rice again became important in Japanese food consumption and as prices of Korean agricultural land remained depressed, individuals and corporations in Japan increased their landholdings in Korea to control sources of imported Korean foodstuff. One such corporation was the Mie nōjō (Mie farm or agribusiness). This corporation, founded in Kuwana-shi in

Mie-ken in 1917, centered its agricultural operations in North Chŏlla province and acquired large amounts of both paddy land and upland. In 1925, for example, Mie nōjō owned 700 *chŏngbo* (over 1,700 acres) of cultivated land in the province. During the depression the corporation expanded its holdings significantly by reclaiming land that had fallen into disuse during the economic crisis. Over 4,000 *p'yŏng* of this land reclaimed in 1934–1935 lay in P'albong-ni.[17]

Land-distribution patterns in rural villages, inequitable to varying degrees from the turn of the century, were still imbalanced during the colony's depression. As seen in Figures 7-2 through 7-2-3, land was unevenly distributed among village residents, with a small number of individuals controlling large amounts of agricultural land while most village residents owned small fields or no land at all. This imbalance was greatest in Kongsu-ri and P'albong-ni but was clearly evident in all villages studied. In P'albong-ni, for example, almost 90 percent of all landowners living in the village owned very little land (54 percent of all resident owners possessed less than 900 *p'yŏng*) or no land at all (another 33 percent of all resident owners).

Surprisingly, despite the massive turnover in owners and ownership in each of the rural villages, residency patterns changed very little among landowners during the depression. The levels of local and absentee landownership remained fairly constant during the period, suggesting that most of the ownership changes were among residents of the same general area. A comparison of Figures 7-2 through 7-2-3 and 6-1 reveals little overall difference in land distribution among residents and nonresidents during these years. In Songsan-ni and P'albong-ni, individuals owning the most acres increased their share of village agricultural land, but the increase was modest and limited to those two villages. The percentage of villagers owning less land than needed to support a farm family (approximately 900 *p'yŏng*) remained at approximately the same level—albeit a large percentage—throughout the depression. In the majority of villages, approximately 40 to 50 percent of village residents did not own even this minimal amount of 900 *p'yŏng*.

While the upheaval in landownership during the depression was catastrophic for many individuals, the impact was greatest on landowners living some distance from rural villages. The reversal of earlier trends toward increased absentee landownership and increased concentration of land in fewer hands marked a turning point in colonial land tenure. The importance of urban landlords declined as ownership became more localized. The depression, in effect, knocked the medium-sized entrepreneur / investor out of landownership and presumably into other business endeavors, either in support of the industrial buildup for the war effort or in financial exile in Manchuria or other parts of the Japanese Empire.

CONCLUSION:
THE LEGACY OF THE DEPRESSION

STATISTICAL DATA on landownership from the last years of the Yi dynasty through the 1930s force us to rethink conventional wisdom on ownership changes. Analysis of Korea's Japanese colonial experience must include, but also move beyond, anecdotal recollections and personal stories of tragedy and hardship during the 1930s and 1940s. Life in Korea under Japanese colonial rule was harsh—even brutal—for those without economic or political power. Transfers of landownership from Korean to Japanese individuals and corporations and loss of control over the land's produce contributed to the oppressive and inequitable environment produced by Japanese imperialism.

It is no less damning of Japanese colonial control over the sovereign state of Korea to learn from the statistical data that the transfers were much less widespread than previously believed and that the transfers that did occur resulted not from official scheming but through colonial market forces. The actual acquisition process helps refocus future analysis of Japanese colonialism on what actually happened and why, instead of being diverted at the outset by incorrect assumptions.

My analysis of the available statistical data, both on a national level and in selected villages, reveals that, contrary to prior historiography, no major transfer of landownership from Korean to Japanese owners occurred at the outset of the colonial period (1910–1918). A comparison of records from the last survey of the Yi dynasty with those produced after the cadastral survey of the Japanese colonial government in 1910 reveals a clear and striking continuity of landownership patterns from the late nineteenth century. Transfers from Korean to Japanese owners primarily resulted from deals made between Yi dynasty elites and Japanese businesspeople in urban areas, not through outright expropriation, as assumed in the past. By far, most Korean land, both paddy and upland fields, remained in Korean hands after the cadastral survey. Further, after Korea was annexed by Japan, patterns of residency (local versus absentee ownership) and quality of land owned also differed little from patterns of the late 1890s.

Japanese government plans to send thousands of Japanese farmers to ease population problems in Japan and to take over Korean agriculture, which was seen as inefficient and backward, were scuttled early due to Korean opposition and Japanese settlers' failure in agriculture in Korea. Economic and agricultural development policies determined in Tokyo were often at odds with reality and colonial administration interests in Korea. Ultimately, policies lost to economic forces.

Those forces were most evident in the worldwide depression when Korean landownership patterns underwent significant restructuring in the early 1930s. Starting in 1930, a precipitous drop in agricultural commodity (principally rice) prices and the abrupt cessation of Korean rice and other agricultural shipments to Japan resulted in an impoverished colony that had been developed solely as a source of food for Japan. Large-scale agricultural land transfers occurred in these years as destitute landowners, burdened with debt from agricultural development efforts in the 1920s, were faced with no markets and sharply devalued land and produce. Forced sales and mortgage foreclosures resulted in major ownership restructuring, particularly in areas most closely connected with export markets and areas near urban areas. The images of large-scale Japanese land acquisitions, increases in tenancy rates, impoverishment, and migration to Manchuria and Japan were etched in the minds of Koreans experiencing these tragedies in the 1930s.

The rapidity of upheaval and dislocation in the Korean agricultural sector characterized in the early 1930s apparently did not continue at the same rate through the remaining ten years of colonial rule, though life remained severe. Japanese colonial interests and needs changed in the late 1930s and early 1940s, from agricultural production toward industrial development to support the war effort. As a result, trends in landownership patterns that had accelerated during the early 1930s (for example, Japanese land acquisition, concentration of ownership, and absentee ownership) seem to have leveled off in the next decade. Land distribution remained unequal.

Toward the end of the colonial years, many Japanese living in provincial towns, anticipating the end of their colonial administration, disposed of their land before the end of the war. At the same time, other Japanese living in Japan increased their holdings in Korea—apparently on the assumption that by 1943–1944 investments were safer on the Korean peninsula.

We must be cautious, however, about drawing too many conclusions from wartime data. The late 1930s and early 1940s were unlike any other previous period. Many Koreans were forced to adopt Japanese-style names after 1941, making identification of nationality frequently difficult and often impossible. Further, records are incomplete, and land registers were not changed promptly to reflect ownership and other changes, a situation that had not been rectified even three to four years after the end of the war. For example, dozens of Japanese individuals and corporations were still registered owners of thousands of acres of agricultural land in rural Korea as late as 1949–1950.

There is no indication that the U.S. military occupation had any effect on landownership in any of the villages. No Japanese-owned land, whether owned by individuals or by corporations, was registered under the administration of agencies backed by the U.S. occupation. This fact throws doubt on the effectiveness of land redistribution by the occupation's New Korea Company.

The last decade of the colonial experience, however, played a major role in shaping concepts, opinions, and scholarship on the changes in landownership that occurred in Korea during the four decades of Japanese colonial rule. The hardships of the period were fresh in postwar minds and are still vivid in the minds of millions of Koreans today. The search to explain these hardships gave rise to intense and misplaced emphasis on the cadastral survey conducted by the Japanese colonial government between 1910–1918. I hope this study will spark an equally intense look, based on new assumptions, at Korea's colonial experience using the volumes of land records available for analysis throughout the Korean peninsula.

APPENDIX

T'oji taejang for land plot no. 164 in P'albong-ni

164

Page 1 of the *t'oji tŭnggibu* for plot no. 164 in P'albong-ni

Page 2 of the *t'oji tŭnggibu* for plot no. 164

Page 3 of the *t'oji tŭnggibu* for plot no. 164

乙

順位番號	事項欄

Page 4 of the t'oji tŭnggibu for plot no. 164

T'oji chōsabu for land plots in Se-ri

Kwangmu *yang'an* for land in the vicinity of Songsan-ni, ca. 1898

NOTES

CHAPTER 1

1. John K. Fairbank and Edwin O. Reischauer, *East Asia: The Great Tradition* (Boston: Houghton Mifflin, 1960), 6–7.

2. Susan Shin, "Land Tenure and the Agrarian Economy in Yi Dynasty Korea: 1600–1800," Ph.D. dissertation, Harvard University, 1973. See also works of Kim Yong-sŏp.

3. Pak Pyŏng-ho, *Han'guk ŭi pŏp* (Seoul: Sejong taewang kinyŏm saŏphoe, 1974).

4. For copies of sample pages of these registers, see Appendix.

5. For information on wage labor at the end of the Yi dynasty, see Miyajima Hiroshi, "Chōsen kōgō kaikaku igo no shōgyōteki nōgyō: sannan chihō o chūshin ni," *Shirin* 57:6 38–77; Kim Yong-sŏp, *Han'guk kŭndae nong'ŏpsa yŏn'gu,* (Seoul: Ilchogak, 1975), 587–615.

6. Two examples of these absurd names from the Kwangmu *yang'an* in the Nonsan area are Kim Sŏng-gyo ("sexual intercourse Kim") and Yi Sŏk-tu ("stonehead Yi"). Unlike earlier *yang'an,* in which no surnames were recorded for lower classes, in 1900 everyone had a surname, blurring class distinctions.

7. The most comprehensive biographical sources for the late Yi dynasty are *Taehan cheguk kwanwŏn iryŏksŏ* (Seoul: Kuksa p'yŏnch'an wiwŏn-hoe, 1972); Ōgaki Masuo, *Chōsen shinshi daidō-fu* (Seoul: Chōsen shinshi daidō hakkō jimusho, 1913); Yi Hŭi-sŭng, *Han'guk inmyŏng taesajŏn* (Seoul: Shin'gu munhwasa, 1972).

8. For a description of the survey process, see the final report of the Survey Bureau, *Chōsen tochi chōsa jigyō hōkokusho* (Seoul: Rinji tochi chōsakyoku, 1918); or the Korean translation by Wŏn Yŏng-hŭi, *Han'guk chijŏk-sa* (Seoul: Pomun ch'ulp'ansa, 1972).

9. Very few copies of the *chōsabu* remain. Fortunately they are extant for most of the Suwŏn area, making analyses of Kwangmu *yang'an* and early colonial

land-distribution patterns possible. For a copy of one page of a *t'oji chōsabu,* see the Appendix to this study.

10. The total number of land parcels under dispute after the cadastral survey was under 100,000, most disputes involving questions of ownership. Undoubtedly, many of these parcels, involving approximately 0.5 percent of the total 19.1 million land parcels surveyed, were the subject of dispute by the same individuals. The actual number of landowners who disputed ownership decisions at the time of the survey was relatively small. See Chōsen sōtokufu, *Chōsen tochi chōsa jigyō hōkokusho,* 123–124; Wŏn Yŏng-hŭi, *Han'guk chijŏk-sa,* 231.

11. The format was based on the Japanese land register and was identical to that used earlier in Taiwan by the Japanese colonial government. See Appendix for a copy of the *t'oji taejang.* One *p'yŏng (tsubo* in Japanese) equals 35 square feet. One acre equals approximately 1,224 *p'yŏng.* One *chŏngbo* equals 3,000 *p'yŏng* or 2.45 acres.

12. As I collected data from the *t'oji taejang* in local county offices, I was told of the heroism of officials protecting these records. For example, during the Korean War, some local officials buried the *taejang* in protective plastic for the duration of the war, refusing, even at gunpoint, to reveal their location. On several occasions I was not permitted to use electric lights while filming the *taejang* in their storeroom for fear of fire.

13. South of Suwŏn the only areas that frequently do not have *t'oji taejang* dating from the cadastral survey are those that underwent "field straightening," either during the colonial period or during the 1960s and 1970s. Once the field assumes a shape different from the shape registered on the original survey, a new *taejang* must be created from that point. In addition, the Korean government is experimenting with computerization of land registers in certain areas, keeping only postwar records on file.

14. One must be extremely cautious, however, since even landowners living great distances from their land may have had members of their family farming the land. As a result, generalizations must be conditional.

15. These maps are still considered extremely accurate today, so much so that I was cautioned not to get electric light bulbs too close for fear of shrinking the paper and thereby distorting the map.

16. Although the third page of the *tŭnggibu* for land in the villages studied contained hundreds of mortgage contracts, no example of a long-term tenancy contract was ever found. They were apparently rare, or at least rarely reported.

17. I am not aware of any adjudication over the seizure of land for nonrepayment of debts from unregistered loan agreements. The absence of such a case in higher court decisions during the colonial period is evidence of this, and it is confirmed in conversations in Seoul with supreme court officials trained under Japanese colonial rule.

18. Scholars have wrestled with the process of village selection in a number of other studies. See Ramon Myers, *The Chinese Peasant Economy* (Cambridge: Harvard University Press, 1970), 4–5; Vincent S. R. Brandt, *A Korean Village* (Cambridge: Harvard University Press, 1971), 4–7; and R. P. Dore, *City Life in Japan* (Berkeley: University of California Press, 1958), 3–9.

19. For a list of Kwangmu *yang'an* available in the Kyujanggak collection at

Seoul National University, see *Kyujanggak tosŏ Han'gukpon ch'ongmongnok* (Seoul: Tong'a munhwa yŏn'guso, 1965), 199–268. See also Han U-gun, *Han'guk kyŏngje kwangye munhŏn chipsŏng* (Seoul: Tong'a munhwa yŏn'guso, 1966), 9–16.

20. See Yu Wŏn-dong, *Yijo hugi sanggong'ŏpsa yŏn'gu* (Seoul: Han'guk yŏn'guwŏn, 1968), chapter 2.

21. See *Suigen kōtō nōrin gakkō yōran,* (Seoul: Chōsen sōtokufu, 1933), vol. 1, p. 39. See also the Appendix of that publication.

CHAPTER 2

1. At that time the ministers of these three ministries were Pak Chŏng-nyang, Sim Sang-hun, and Yi To-jae, respectively. Yi's interest in such a project was first indicated fourteen years earlier when he served as a government spy sent to Kyŏngsang province to inspect the land situation. Yi reported that a new survey was needed and suggested that it be financed through increased revenues generated by putting new land on the tax registers. See *Pibyŏnsa tŭngnok,* Kojong vol. 1884.9.23, vol. 27, p. 756.

2. Yi Ki (1848–1909) was a late Yi dynasty advocate of reform in government financial matters. He was also an advocate of Korean independence from Japanese control, attempting to travel to Portsmouth, New Hampshire in 1905 to argue Korea's case at the negotiations concluding the Russo-Japanese War. In the latter years of the Yi dynasty, Yi was active in organizing politically minded intellectuals in his various endeavors to further Korean independence and domestic reform.

3. Krumm (1873–1949) was apparently chosen by Horace Allen, U. S. ambassador to Korea, but their true relationship is unclear. Very little is known about Krumm aside from what appears in his will. In addition to bequeathing a substantial amount of money to Ohio State University for Korean student fellowships, Krumm immortalized some of his Korean experiences. Krumm saw himself as one of Korea's first lobbyists in Washington, D.C., and wrote in his will: "My first assignment by the Koreans was to bring about an investigation of the malfeasance in office of the State Department's agent in Seoul, Korea. In pursuing this work my first efforts were directly with the Department itself in Washington. Continued efforts here availed nothing. Later, a call on the Department of State by the Foreign Relations Committee of the "House" for the facts, as the Department had them, was met by refusal. Finally the Department quashed and buried the whole matter by accepting Japan's control over Korea. Thus my efforts were thwarted and failure complete. However, any authorized commission probing the causes of war or seeking elements of weakness in our international negotiations, would not be denied these truths of American-Korean history." Feeling he had failed in his mission to "bring about our government's recognition of its obligations to them (the Korean people) and make corrections," Krumm left his money to Ohio State University for the education of Korean students. No mention is made of any assignment to assist in the Kwangmu land survey.

4. Kim Yong-sŏp, *Han'guk kŭndae,* 522.

5. For a copy of the implementation order, *Ch'ingnyŏng* no. 25, promulgated on July 8, 1898, see the *Kwanwŏn* of the same date.

6. The Kabo Reforms were a series of administrative, economic, and social reforms implemented by a reform government in power in Korea during 1894–1895. These reforms affected almost all aspects of Korean society and included establishment of a cabinet form of government, centralization of taxation authority, abolition of slavery, and replacement of the traditional Confucian civil service examination with one testing actual bureaucratic skills. Many of these reforms, generally associated with persons in the Korean government labeled "pro-Japanese," did not outlive the reform government itself.

7. The interests and activities of Yi Ki were not limited to matters of land reform. He took a personal role in the 1894 Tonghak rebellion, seeking out Chŏn Pong-jun and offering to lead Tonghak troops against the government forces, which he later did. Yi saw himself as a reformer in the mold of Chŏng Yag-yong and expanded on many of Chŏng's ideas on land tenure. Yi, whose pen name was Haehak, wrote numerous treatises, most of which have been collected in Yi Ki, *Haehak yusŏ* (Seoul: Kuksa p'yŏnch'an wiwŏn-hoe, 1974).

8. James Palais, *Politics and Policy in Traditional Korea* (Cambridge: Harvard University Press, 1975), 71–74.

9. Prior to the Kwangmu survey of 1898–1902, the last major survey had been conducted in 1720. In response to calls for reform in the late eighteenth century, however, the Korean government undertook a small-scale survey of part of Korea's land in 1820.

10. See, for example, Kang Man-gil, "Sirhak Thought and Its Reflection in Politics," *Korea Journal* 14:1 (May 1974): 5–7; and Ch'ŏn Kwan-u, "P'angye Yu Hyŏng-wŏn yŏn'gu sang," *Yŏksa hakpo* 3 (January 1953): 87–139 for the reforms advocated by Yu Hyŏng-wŏn.

11. See Palais, *Politics and Policy,* 68; and Kim Yong-sŏp, *Han'guk kŭndae,* 176–200, for discussions of Chŏng Yag-yong's proposals.

12. In 1789 when Chŏngjo requested ideas on how Korea's landownership system could be improved, many scholar-officials responded with memorials advocating implementation of the Chinese equal-field or well-field systems. See Kim Yong-sŏp, *Chosŏn hugi nong'ŏpsa yŏn'gu,* vol. 1 (Seoul: Ilchogak, 1971), 2–25.

13. Kim Yong-sŏp, *Han'guk kŭndae,* 437–444.

14. The fish scale land-registration system dates from the Southern Sung dynasty (1127–1279) in China. See Yi Hŭi-sŭng, *Kugŏ taesajŏn,* 1974.

15. Reformers in and out of government during the second half of the Yi dynasty criticized the practice of *ŭn'gyŏl,* or "hiding *kyŏl.* " Japanese reformers in the twentieth century cited the Korean government's failure to recover unregistered land as one of the main reasons for undertaking the 1910–1918 cadastral survey.

16. According to official government-general statistics, the total area of registered cultivated land in 1910 was about 2.4 million *chŏngbo* (approximately 5.9 million acres). By 1919, after the Japanese cadastral survey, registered arable land totaled 4.3 million *chŏngbo*—an 80 percent increase. See Wada Ichirō, *Chōsen tochi chizei seido chōsa hōkokusho* (Keijō: Chōsen sōtokufu, 1920), 756; and *Chōsen chishi shiryō* (Seoul: Chōsen sōtokufu, 1919), 438.

17. This system, the *kyŏl-bu-sŏk* system, was based on the assessed quality

and productivity of the land. Each plot was assigned a grade, from one to six, that determined the amount of tax to be collected from the owner of that plot. The *kyŏl* was a measurement of land needed to produce a certain volume of grain. Therefore, the area of a *kyŏl* varied with the quality of the land being measured. For an explanation of the *kyŏl* measurement, see Shin, "Land Tenure and the Agrarian Economy," 43–44, and Appendix of Shin's work.

18. This *chinjŏn* comprised approximately 30 percent of all arable land in Korea at the outset of the nineteenth century. See Palais, *Politics and Policy,* 77. Much of this land remained classified as *chinjŏn* from the years of the Hideyoshi and Manchu invasions in the late sixteenth and early seventeenth centuries, when much of Korea's agricultural land was destroyed, abandoned, or both.

19. Actually, this land was registered in the name of a palace with which a royal family member was associated, a common method of referring to specific individuals without using their names.

20. Kim Chin-bong, "Imsul millan ŭi sahoe hyŏngch'ejŏk paegyŏng," *Sahak yŏn'gu* (April 1967): 19, 33; Kim Yong-sŏp, *Chosŏn hugi,* 42–45.

21. For a discussion of the Taewŏn'gun's efforts to limit palace-owned land, see Palais, *Politics and Policy,* 70–85.

22. Kim Yong-sŏp, *Han'guk kŭndae,* 444–451.

23. Wada Ichirō, *Chōsen tochi chizei,* 182–184; Arai Kentarō, *Rinji zaisan seiri-kyoku jimu yōkan* (Seoul: Chōsen sōtokufu, 1911), 26.

24. *Pibyŏnsa tŭngnok,* Kojong vol. 15.7.19, vol. 27, 199–205.

25. *Ilsŏngnok,* 1890, 12th month, 30th day. See also Kim Yong-sŏp, "Kojong si ŭi kyunjŏn sudo munje," *Tong'a munhwa* (August 1968): 45.

26. Yu Kil-jun, *Yu Kil-jun chŏnsŏ,* vol. 4, 135–172.

27. *Kojong sillok,* vol. 31, 1894, 4th month, 24th day.

28. Kim Yong-sŏp, *Han'guk kŭndae,* 462–474.

29. See article 56 of the Ministry of the Interior decrees *(Naemun amun hunsi)* promulgated on March 1, 1895, and published in the *Kwanbo* of March 11, 1895. This decree also appears in the *Kojong sillok,* 1895, 3rd month, 10th day.

30. See Yi Ki, *Haehak yusŏ,* vol. 5, 89.

31. For Yi Ki's memorial, see *Haehak yusŏ,* vol. 1, 1–19. The "well-field" system was a legendary Chinese land-tenure system in which land was divided into blocks of nine equal plots—as in the Chinese character for "well." The eight outside plots were to be cultivated by individual farmers, while the interior plot was to be farmed collectively, producing for village or community operations.

32. *Turak* is a measurement of area based on the amount of seed required to sow a field. With one *mal* of seed a farmer can sow one *tu* of land, usually paddy land. Depending on the fertility of the land, this measurement varied from place to place. For pictures and a description of the differences in the size of a *mal* and *tu,* see Tokunaga Isami, *Kankoku sōran,* 1181–1196. The corresponding traditional measurement for upland has always been the *ilgyŏng,* or the number of days required for one ox to plow a field. The ox plowed slowly or quickly depending on soil conditions and terrain; thus, this measurement also varied in size. In everyday speech, one *tu* and one *ilgyŏng* are each referred to as one *majigi.*

33. By recording subsequent changes in owner and tenant and by attaching

these records to the *yang'an*, Yi hoped to keep the *yang'an* from going out of date. Earlier Yi dynasty *yang'an* lacked such records, so even one inheritance or sale transaction made an entry for a plot of land on the *yang'an* obsolete until the next survey, which may not happen for a number of decades.

34. At that time, the Japanese minister was Ōtori Keisuke. See Hilary Conroy, *The Japanese Seizure of Korea: 1868–1910* (Philadelphia: University of Pennsylvania Press, 1960) for a discussion of Ōtori's activities.

35. Several high-ranking Korean government officials, including King Kojong himself, cut off their topknots at this time as an example for Korean men. This order, in addition to being associated with a pro-Japanese political clique and following the queen's death, contradicted basic tenets of Confucian teachings of filial piety: One should not cut off what one's parents have given. Therefore, most Korean men deeply resented the order. Later, during the colonial period, keeping one's topknot took on anti-Japanese nationalist significance and was a source of pride after World War II.

36. For example, the cabinet system of the government, established by reformers in 1894, was abolished in favor of the traditional *Ŭijŏngbu,* or council of state.

37. Ironically, innovations in technology occurred rapidly in Korea during 1896–1898. Railroads were begun. Two new ports, Mokp'o and Chinnamp'o, were opened, bringing the total to five. The first telephone line was installed, running between the tomb of the late Queen Min and the royal palace.

38. For a discussion of these concessions, announcements of which appeared almost daily in the *Kwanbo* during 1897–1898, see Sin Yong-ha, *Tongnip hyŏpphoe yŏn'gu* (Seoul: Ilchogak, 1976), 277–302.

39. For examples of these proposals, see *P'ilsŏwŏn ilgi,* March 28, 1898, cited in Kim Yong-sŏp, *Han'guk kŭndae,* 513.

40. See Shin Yong-ha, *Tongnip hyŏpphoe yŏn'gu,* 579, for an excellent account of the life and death of the *Tongnip sinmun.*

41. Ibid., 222.

42. Since the British commercial treaty with Korea in 1883, foreigners were barred from purchasing agricultural or residential land located more than 10 Korean *ri* from the treaty ports. Although Japanese officials and investors frequently tried to change this law, it remained in force until 1906 when the Japanese residency-general forcibly and unilaterally abolished it (see Chapter 4). Kim Yong-sŏp cites evidence indicating that some Korean officials awarded deeds to Korean landowners during the Kwangmu cadastral survey as a means of bolstering their claims to ownership over claims by Japanese, who might have purchased land illegally. On the back of each deed, the government printed a stern warning that any land sold or granted to a foreigner would be confiscated. See Kim Yong-sŏp, *Han'guk kŭndae,* 572–582.

43. See *Korea Review* 1:3 (March 1901): 122–124.

44. *Korea Review* 1:11 (November 1901): 509.

45. *Korea Review* 2:3 (March 1902): 120–122.

46. See *Ch'ingnyŏng* number 13, promulgated on April 24, 1899, and published in the *Kwanbo* of April 26, 1899. It is impossible to know precisely how much of the Kwangmu survey costs were borne by local governments; local

records no longer exist. However, judging from the local opposition to continuing the survey after the drought of 1901, local governments must have paid a considerable share of the survey expenses.

47. See the *Kwanbo* of August 17, 1901. The harvest was so bad and the rice shortage the following spring so acute that the government reportedly issued government ranks to individuals donating rice to poor farmers. See *Korea Review* 2:4 (April 1902): 171. Other government measures to deal with the rice shortage included a ban on rice shipments to Japan (August 26, 1901) and importing rice from Southeast Asia (September 1901). Neither step was effective since Japanese pressure forced Korea to renew rice shipments in November 1901 and only part of the negotiated Vietnamese rice arrived. See *Korea Review,* August through December 1901.

48. The 1902 national budget allocated $22,000 for this project according to *Korea Review* 2:3 (March 1902): 120–122.

49. One exception was the Suwŏn area, parts of which were surveyed as late as 1903. One village examined in this study, Se-ri, was surveyed that year.

50. For a list of the counties for which Kwangmu *yang'an* exist—which differs from the number actually surveyed at the outset of this century—see Han U-gun, *Han'guk kyŏngje kwan'gye,* 9–16; and *Kyujanggak tosŏ Han'gukbon ch'ongmongnok,* 199–268. In 1914 the government-general reduced the number of counties, or *kun,* as part of an effort to centralize administrative control.

51. A note on Kwangmu survey techniques: It is likely that no actual measurements were taken during the course of this survey. The Yangji amun lacked sufficient personnel and technology to complete a full-scale survey within thirty months. Though little evidence exists one way or the other, the *yang'an* data were probably derived from discussions held in the homes of village leaders, who provided information on type of field, size, owner, and cultivator. An article in the *Korea Review* supports this supposition. Hulbert wrote that "They do not actually measure it but they call witnesses who declare how many days it takes to plow that particular field with a bullock and how many measures of seed grain it requires to plant it. These things, together with all the other conditions, help the judges to decide the grade of the field and the number of kyul (sic)." See *Korea Review* 2:11 (November 1902): 482. The collection process is questionable, not the general accuracy of the *yang'an* data. I believe the *yang'an* contain an accurate description of landownership patterns at the turn of the century. The similarity between *yang'an* data and data from the colonial period for the villages studied supports my belief.

52. Most notable in this regard are the valuable studies done by Susan Shin and Kim Yong-sŏp of eighteenth and nineteenth century Yi dynasty *yang'an,* and Pak Pyŏng-ho's pioneering work on premodern legal concepts of landownership. See Susan Shin, "Land Tenure and the Agrarian Economy"; Kim Yong-sŏp, *Chosŏn hugi,* 1 and 2, and *Han'guk kŭndae;* and Pak Pyŏng-ho, *Han'guk pŏbche sago* (Seoul: Pŏmmunsa, 1974).

53. Yi Sŏng-gye implemented the *kwajŏnbŏp,* or rank-land system, to deprive the Koryŏ dynasty's landed elite of their source of independent wealth and power. According to traditional historiography, Yi nationalized most land in Korea through this reform and used the produce from individual fields to support par-

ticular government agencies. To insure that powerful individuals did not accumulate large amounts of land, Yi, in this traditional interpretation, prohibited the sale of land. Recently, scholars have suggested that Yi carried out his land reform only in the province surrounding the Koryŏ capital of Kaesŏng in Kyŏnggi province. See Pak Pyŏng-ho, *Han'guk pŏbche sago*, 123–137.

54. Pak Pyŏng-ho, *Han'guk pŏbche sago*, 13–14.

55. Ibid., 14, 39–41. Although landowners did not receive these certificates of sale *(iban)* on a systematic basis, they used them as proof of ownership throughout the Yi dynasty and particularly at the time of the 1910 Japanese cadastral survey. See *Chōsen tochi chōsa jigyō hōkokusho* (Keijō: Chōsen sōtokufu, 1919), 127–128.

56. Many earlier historians, including Wada Ichirō, considered the individual receiving (not paying) the *cho* as the owner. Pak Pyŏng-ho has shown, however, that at the outset of the Yi dynasty, *sujogwŏn* holders had little if any control over the land itself; they simply received part of its produce. See Wada Ichirō, *Chōsen tochi chizei*, 60–118.

57. From the time of the Hideyoshi invasions, *sujogwŏn* holders increasingly assumed control over production and disposition rights on the land from which they received *cho*. Institutions used agents, or *tojang*, to directly manage their holdings and negotiate tenancy contracts with farmers who, in many cases, had previously owned the land. For a discussion of the *tojang* on palace estates, see Kim Yong-sŏp, *Chosŏn hugi*, 295–345; and Wada Ichirō, *Chōsen tochi chizei*, 134–145.

58. Although I have seen no explanation of why a twenty-year period was chosen, I assume this period corresponded roughly to the length of one generation. Since the government awarded *sujogwŏn* rights for periods of time defined in terms of generations, it would logically desire to resurvey its land every generation because it wanted to inhibit individuals from permanently holding onto land.

59. Pak Pyŏng-ho, "The Legal Nature of Land Ownership in the Yi Dynasty," *Korea Journal* 15:10 (October 1975): 7. Unlike the recording system in the United States, the Korean cadastre, both the Yi dynasty *yang'an* and the Japanese-period *taejang*, were the final word on landownership if kept up-to-date. The government numbered each plot of land in the country and accounted for each plot in the cadastre. There could not (and there cannot today) be multiple listings of owners for the same piece of land, as in the U.S. system. To locate the legally recognized owner of a plot of land, one simply had to examine the cadastre. During my research in Korea, on several occasions Korean officials commented that the American system of recording ownership worked in the United States because Americans are honest, but such a system would never work in Korea. The officials were not swayed from this conviction despite explanations of the complex legal battles that occur in the United States over questions of title.

60. For examples of *mun'gi*, see Pak Pyŏng-ho, *Han'guk pŏbche sago*, 55–69. Occasionally Yi dynasty *mun'gi*, made unnecessary by the Japanese-period *t'oji taejang*, are sold in used-book stores in Seoul; a number are in my possession.

61. Pak Pyŏng-ho, *Han'guk pŏbche sago*, 249–291.

62. Kim Yong-sŏp, *Chosŏn hugi*, 88–112.

63. See Palais, *Politics and Policy,* 77; and Shin, "Land Tenure and the Agrarian Economy."

64. Palais, *Politics and Policy,* 58–85.

65. Although concentrated in these three provinces, *kungbangjŏn* was not limited to them. Nationwide, *kungbangjŏn* amounted to about 3 to 4 percent of all cultivated land. See James Palais, *Politics and Policy,* 76–78; Arai Kentarō, *Rinji zaisan,* 75–77. Arai headed a colonial government agency that determined ownership over all palace land between 1908–1910.

66. Following these invasions, the Korean government offered tax-exempt status to any land brought back into cultivation. Reclaiming land that had lain idle for five to ten years required such high levels of capital and manpower mobilization that it was nearly monopolized by wealthy individuals and institutions. Developers with sufficient resources, including the royal palaces, gained title to large amounts of arable land that had fallen into disuse. Most of this land remained in palace hands through the end of the Yi dynasty.

67. Palais, *Politics and Policy,* 74–82.

68. For information on the Kunaichō, see *Seijigaku jiten* (Tokyo: Heibonsha, 1970), 295.

69. See Wada Ichirō, *Chōsen tochi chizei,* 150–184, 466–492 for a discussion of each palace. The seven palaces included the Myŏngnye-gung (or Tŏksu-gung), Yongdong-gung, Ŏüi-gung, Sujin-gung, Sŏnhi-gung, Kyŏng'u-gung, and the Yuksang-gung. Two other large palaces established late in the Yi dynasty were the Kyŏngsŏn-gung and Yŏnch'inwang-gung.

70. For a list of the many government agencies for which produce from particular plots of land was set aside, see Wada Ichirō, *Chōsen tochi chizei,* 278–414.

71. According to an 1899 survey, the Kyujanggak received *cho* from 400 *sŏngnak* of paddy land and 70 *ilgyŏng* of upland, or roughly a total of 440–500 *chŏngbo.* See Wada Ichirō, *Chōsen tochi chizei* 321–323. One *sŏngnak* equaled about 3,000 *p'yŏng,* and one *ilgyŏng* equaled approximately 1,500–2,000 *p'yŏng,* depending on the fertility of the land.

72. See *Ch'ingnyŏng* number 40, published in the *Kwanbo* of June 25, 1908, and *T'akchiburyŏng* numbers 27, 28, and 43, published in the *Kwanbo* of August 12 and October 23, 1908. The T'akchibu was the Korean Ministry of Finance.

CHAPTER 3

1. The three villages in South Ch'ungch'ŏng province were surveyed during 1900–1901, but Se-ri was not surveyed until 1903. See Chapter 2 for the location and description of each of these villages.

2. Kim Yong-sŏp found that other villages in Kyŏnggi province contained even lower percentages of land owned by individuals due to large amounts of government and palace land. Some contained no individually owned land. Kim also found that in some areas of Hwanghae province, palaces owned 75 percent of all arable land. See Kim Yong-sŏp, *Chosŏn hugi,* 349.

3. An examination of the *yang'an* for neighboring villages revealed residences for few of the absentee landowners. Unfortunately, few local gazetteers exist to identify these individuals. The biographical sources that do exist contain data on

a few of these landowners, who are almost exclusively residents of Seoul. Most helpful are Ōgaki Masuo, *Chōsen shinshi daidōfu,* and *Taehan cheguk kwanwŏn iryŏksŏ.*

4. Kim Yong-sŏp, *Han'guk kŭndae,* 600–604.

5. Thomas C. Smith, *The Agrarian Origins of Modern Japan* (Stanford: Stanford University Press, 1959), 124–179.

6. In light of the high rates of tenancy in the other villages and the conventional wisdom about tenancy in nineteenth-century Korea, the tenancy statistics of Songsan-ni seem difficult to believe. The statistics could be understated; however, landlords had no incentive to omit the names of their tenants. Further, differences in survey and registration practices, which could also account for differences in tenancy levels in different geographic areas, did not occur to any significant degree. Neighboring villages within the same *yang'an* had somewhat higher rates of tenancy, but in general the agricultural land in the entire Hansan region appears to have been owner-cultivated. Kim Yong-sŏp found similarly low rates of tenancy in one isolated village. See Kim Yong-sŏp, *Han'guk kŭndae,* tables 29 and 30, 604–605.

7. Neither of these men lived in Kongsu-ri or in a neighboring village. I have been unable to locate biographical data on either, which suggests that they did not hold government positions at the end of the dynasty. Neither man owned sizable amounts of land in Kongsu-ri after the colonial cadastral survey.

8. Kim Yong-sŏp has estimated that in the late nineteenth century an owner-farmer required about 1,000 to 2,000 *p'yŏng* of arable land of average fertility to support a family. See Kim Yong-sŏp, *Han'guk kŭndae,* 594. Palais and Shin have suggested about 900 *p'yŏng.* Based on estimates of the early twentieth century, I am inclined to agree with the latter. See Kambe Masao, *Chōsen nōgyō iminron,* (Tokyo: Yūhikaku shobō, 1910), 64–77.

9. Members of these three clans, who together owned 91,575 *p'yŏng* of arable land, belonged to the Hansan Yi clan (14,749 *p'yŏng*), Koryang Pak clan (55,432 *p'yŏng*), and Yongsŏng Ch'a clan (21,394 *p'yŏng*).

10. Smith, *Agrarian Origins,* 163–166.

11. The northward migration of destitute Korean farmers started in the 1890s and continued into the twentieth century. Most farmers initially moved to the Chientao region of Manchuria. By November 1907, 72,076 Koreans reportedly lived in the Chientao region, and this total increased to almost 83,000 by April 1909. See Kim Chŏng-ju, *Chōsen tochi shiryō,* vol. 1 (Tokyo: Kankoku shiryō kenkyūjō, 1970), 128–129, 146. This volume was later published in Seoul as *Ilche t'ongch'i saryo.* The rapid influx of Korean farmers touched off numerous conflicts between Koreans and Chinese in the region.

12. Unlike earlier *yang'an,* those compiled in the Kwangmu period contained a one-character designation of the type of roof a dwelling had. Tile roofs, while common in provincial towns throughout the countryside, were extremely rare in isolated villages.

13. Kim Yong-sŏp also found such a correlation. See *Han'guk kŭndae,* table 32, p. 616.

14. For example, Yi Pong-hoe, who owned no arable land and who rented a

total of 4,811 p'yŏng of paddy land from two large-scale absentee landlords, lived in the second-largest home in Kongsu-ri. He rented this house, over 550 p'yŏng (over 19,000 square feet), from Sim Wŏn-jin, one of the same landlords who owned the paddy land he cultivated. Kim Yong-sŏp also found such cases. One resident in Kim's sample did not own any land at all, yet he resided in a thirteen-room house. Some individuals in late nineteenth-century Korea may have accumulated enough resources through means other than landownership to acquire large residences. Another possibility is that these individuals were simply house-sitting for absentee owners. Some scholars of British history have found that in preindustrial England, a head tenant lived in the landowner's home while the owner was away in London, giving the impression that the tenant was better off than he was. See Peter Laslett, *The World We Have Lost* (New York: Scribners, 1965), 80–81.

15. A number of others also owned multiple dwellings, including Yi Kap-tŭk (eight homes), Yun Il-tan (seven homes), and Yi Chae-hŭi (seven homes).

16. Smith, *Agrarian Origins,* chapters 9 and 11.

17. Wada Ichirō, *Chōsen tochi chizei,* 167.

18. The Kyujanggak collection at Seoul National University contains numerous land records from each of the palaces, recording location of land plots and the names of tenants cultivating them. For a list of these documents, see Han U-gun, *Han'guk kyŏngje kwan'gye,* 17–51.

19. After annexation in 1910 Yi Hae-sŭng received the title of marquis and grants of land from the Japanese colonial government. See the *Kwanbo* of July 1, 1914, for one such grant. For biographical data on Yi Hae-sŭng, see Ōmura Tomonosuke, *Chōsen kizoku retten,* (Seoul: Chōsen sōtokufu, 1910), 42–43.

20. Wada Ichirō, *Chōsen tochi chizei,* 179–180; Yi Ch'ŏl-wŏn, *Wanggungsa* (Seoul: Tongguk munhwasa, 1954), 108.

21. Wada Ichirō, *Chōsen tochi chizei,* 180.

22. In 1896 Prince Sado, the second son of Yŏngjo, was posthumously elevated to king, and as a result the Sŏnhi-gung, which had been officially abolished in 1871, was restored.

23. In 1902 the Sŏnhi-gung, which, like all palaces, became identified with particular royal family members (not buildings), was located in the northern part of Seoul, west of Kyŏngbok-gung. See the 1902 map of Seoul, reprinted in Allen Clark and Donald Clark, *Seoul Past and Present* (Seoul: Hollym Publishing Co., 1969), 19.

24. From the reign of Yŏngjo (1724–1776), the Korean government gave each school from 5–7 kyŏl of arable land, but schools increased this allotment during the Yi dynasty. According to a 1915 investigation, during the Japanese cadastral survey some schools owned as much as 29 kyŏl. See Wada Ichirō, *Chōsen tochi chizei,* 515–518. One kyŏl of land of average fertility equaled about 2.5–3 acres.

25. Wada Ichirō, *Chōsen tochi chizei,* 393. For a discussion of the granary system in the late Yi dynasty, see Choe Ching Young, *The Rule of The Taewŏn'gun* (Cambridge: Harvard University Press, 1972), chapters 1 and 2; Palais, *Politics and Policy,* 132–159.

26. Yi Hong-jik, *Kuksa taesajŏn* (Seoul: Chimungak, 1971), 787.

27. The rest of government land in Kongsu-ri in 1900 (4,884 p'yŏng) belonged to the village itself as common land. This land remained in village hands after the 1910 cadastral survey.

28. Wada Ichirō, Chōsen tochi chizei, 349. See Ch'ingnyŏng number 32, published in the Kwanbo of July 30, 1906.

29. Chōsen no kōsaku kanshū (Seoul: Chōsen sōtokufu, 1929), 63–91; Tokunaga Isami, Kankoku sōran, 648–653; Palais, Politics and Policy, 66.

30. Kim Yong-sŏp, Han'guk kŭndae, 599–615.

31. For example, Kim Yong-sŏp found one tenant registered as cultivating about 25 chŏngbo, or over 61 acres. Ibid., 612.

32. Villages in the vicinity of Songsan-ni but closer to the small market town of Hansan had higher rates of tenancy than Songsan-ni. However, these rates were still lower than for the other three villages. These higher tenancy rates would seem to indicate that tenants were in fact registered.

33. See Hisama Kenichi, "Chūsei nandō ni okeru kōsaku seido no kenkyū," Kinen ronbunshū (Seoul: Chōsen sōtokufu suigen kōtō nōrin gakkō, 1932), tables 6–7, pp. 60–61.

34. Ibid.

35. Other tenants in the villages were registered as farming large amounts of land; seven individuals cultivated over 7,500 p'yŏng (6 acres).

36. Chōsen no kōsaku kanshū, 67–68; Kobayashi Fusajirō, Kankoku tochi nōsan chōsa hōkoku, vol. 2 (1905), 501–508.

37. For a discussion of these agents (tojang or marŭm), see Wada Ichirō, Chōsen tochi chizei, 134–145; Kim Yong-sŏp, Chosŏn hugi, 295–345; and Chosŏn munje sajŏn (Seoul: Sinhaksa, 1948), 117–118.

38. Very little has been written on late Yi dynasty tenancy. See Shin Yong-ha, "Landlordism in Late Yi Dynasty," Korea Journal 18:6, 7 (June, July 1978): 22–29; Palais, Politics and Policy, 66; Im Pyŏng-yun, Shokuminchi ni okeru shōgyōteki nōgyō no tenkai (Tokyo: Tokyo University Press, 1971), 11–106.

CHAPTER 4

1. For example, the Portuguese and Spanish, using slave labor, established sugar plantations in the Caribbean region and in Latin America. The British created large estates in Sri Lanka to produce tea and coffee for export throughout the British Empire. In Vietnam and Cambodia, French colonialists mobilized thousands of Indochinese laborers and carved out large rubber and banana plantations. See Celso Furtado, Economic Development of Latin America (Cambridge: Cambridge University Press, 1976), chapter 2; Stanley Stein and Barbara Stein, The Colonial Heritage of Latin America (New York: Oxford University Press, 1970), 39–44; Thomas B. Birnberg, Colonial Development (New Haven: Yale University Press, 1975), chapter 1.

2. Michael Hechtor, Internal Colonialism (Berkeley: University of California Press, 1975), 72–76.

3. The cadastral survey undertaken by the Japanese colonial administration was completed in 1918, but actual surveying was completed by 1916. In the villages studied surveying was finished by 1914, just over one decade after the Kwangmu survey.

4. For a good study of Japanese emigration, both prewar and postwar, see Wakatsuki Yasuo, *Kaigai ijū seisaku shiron* (Tokyo: Fukumusa shuppansha, 1975). See also the sections on emigration in Gaimushō's *Nihon gaikō bunsho* series for every year from 1896 to 1910.

5. For a discussion of the state of the Japanese economy during the interwar years, see Hugh Borton, *Japan's Modern Century* (New York: Ronald, 1970), 299–304.

6. *Segai Inoue-kō den*, vol. 5 (Tokyo: Inoue Kaoru-kō denki hensankai, 1968), 169. See also *Nitobe Inazō zenshū* (Tokyo: Nitobe Inazō zenshū henshū-iinkai, 1970), 24–28. Itō Hirobumi once acknowledged that the settlers sent to Korea were "lower class" and that due to Japan's rapid rate of population growth "it is natural that its increment should overflow into Korea." See interview with Itō printed after his assassination in the *Imperial and Asiatic Quarterly Review* 29:5 (January/April 1910): 308–337. The government-general itself noted that the settlers sent to Korea through the Oriental Development Company were at best social marginals. During the interwar years numerous corporations were established to settle Japanese emigrants in foreign countries, many with prefectural government support. For documents relating to the activities of these colonization corporations, see *Nihon gaikō bunsho* 37:2 and 42:2 (1961). One article in the *Heimin shimbun* (edited by Hattori Shisō) chided the Japanese government for thinking unemployment and other social problems could be solved by encouraging the poor and unemployed to emigrate. See *Heimin shimbun* 35 (July 10, 1904), 5.

7. See articles in *Heimin shimbun* 5 (December 13, 1903) and 49 (October 16, 1904).

8. *Heimin shimbun* 42 (August 28, 1904), 43 (September 4, 1904) 44 (September 11, 1904), and 47 (October 2, 1904). There were attempts to amend the emigration law, making the individual or corporation under whose auspices settlers emigrated responsible for the welfare of the emigrants for ten years from the date of departure. One article in a proposed amendment stipulated that the individual engaging in the emigration business had to secure government approval of the business prior to receiving any payment from potential emigrants. This amendment was defeated. See the Diet deliberations in *Dainihon teikoku gikaishi*, vol. 5, 15th session (Tokyo: Dainihon teikoku gikaishi kanbokai, 1901), 831–836.

9. Takazaki Sōshi, "Uchimura Kanzō to Chōsen," *Shisō* 9:639 (September 1977): 83. Takazaki cites an article written by Uchimura in September 1903.

10. For a discussion of Japan's need for imported foodstuff, see William Lockwood, *The Economic Development of Japan* (Princeton: Princeton University Press, 1968), 378–389, 354–355.

11. *Nihon gaikō bunsho* 37:1 (1961): 355. Also appears in Kim Chŏng-ju, *Chōsen tochi shiryō*, 639.

12. For an anonymous article critical of China's policy, see "Imin shuchusugi," *Chūō kōron* 25:3 (March 1910): 177–178.

13. For a discussion of exploitation rights granted to Russia, Japan, and other foreign powers, see Sin Yong-ha, *Tongnip hyŏphoe yŏn'gu*, 288–302, 325–331.

14. Takazaki, "Uchimura Kanzō to Chōsen," 83.

15. Tsurumi Yūsuke, Gotō shimpei den, vol. 3 (Tokyo: Taikeiyō kyōkai, 1943), 32–33. Gotō was deeply concerned about the possibility of war with Imperial Russia and advocated settling Japanese citizens in Korea to reduce the likelihood of such a war.

16. Nihon gaikō bunshō 37:1, 351–357.

17. Komura was sharply criticized in the Japanese press for not protesting the anti-Japanese discrimination in the United States at this time. His policy of concentrating Japanese settlers in East Asia was taken as a concession to the United States, in effect conceding Japan's second-class position in the world. See "Imin shuchusugi," 177–178.

18. Kuroki Yukichi, Komura Jutarō (Tokyo: Kōdansha, 1968), 802–803. See also Tani Toshio, Kimitsu nichiro sensō-shi (Tokyo: Genshōbō, 1966), 682–683.

19. Kuroki, Komura Jutarō, 802–803.

20. Japanese residents of Korea were concentrated in the following cities: Pusan, Inch'ŏn, Seoul, Wŏnsan, Mokp'o, Chinnamp'o, Kunsan, P'yŏngyang and Masan. See Sin Yong-ha, Tongnip hyŏphoe yŏn'gu, 543; Katō Masanosuke, Kankoku keiei (Tokyo: Shitsugyo no nihonsha, 1905), 140–142; Shikata Hiroshi, Chōsen shakai keizaishi kenkyū (Tokyo: Kokusho kankōkai, 1976), 187.

21. The existence of Japanese-language schools in the Korean interior as early as 1900 indicates that by that year Japanese settlers lived in inland cities. See Hwangsŏng sinmun (edited by Namgung Ŏk) of February 5, 1900. Japanese observers noted settlements in inland Korea prior to the Russo-Japanese War. See Kobayashi Fusajirō, Kankoku tochi nōsan hōkokusho vol. 2 (Tokyo: 1905), 728–735; Katō Masanosuke, Kankoku keiei, 140–165.

22. Kojong sidae-sa, vol. 6 (Seoul: Kuksa p'yŏnch'an wiwŏnhoe, 1971) 19–20; Nihon gaikō bunshō 37:1 (1961): 345–346.

23. Kojong sidae-sa, 60–64.

24. For example, see Tomimura Rokurō, Chūnan ronsan hatten-shi (Tokyo, 1913), 62; Kobayashi Fusajirō, Kankoku tochi nōsan, 728; Yamamoto Kotarō, Chōsen ijū annai (Tokyo: Minyūsha, 1904), 205–206.

25. Kojong sidae-sa, 61.

26. Nihon gaikō bunsho 37:1, 282–286. While Itō Hirobumi was in Korea in March, he had extensive meetings with numerous members of the royal household and royal household ministry. He transmitted grants of cash to several members of the royal family from the Japanese emperor. Ibid., 297–298.

27. Ibid., 284.

28. Ibid., 569.

29. For an excellent article on the Nagamori proposal, see Yun Pyŏng-sŏk, "Ilbonin ŭi hwangmuji kaech'ok yogu e taehayŏ—1904 nyŏn Nagamori myŏng-g'ŭi ui wiim kyeyak kidorŭl chungsimuro," Yŏksa hakpo 22 (January 1964): 25–72.

30. For an official copy of the Nagamori proposal, see Nihon gaikō bunsho 37:1, 573–575. See chapter 3 of this book for a discussion of palace-owned land, or kungbangjŏn, that was classified as wasteland at the turn of the century.

31. Nagamori first raised his proposal with Prince Yi Chae-sun in January 1904. Yi was an influential member of the royal family (sixth-generation descen-

dent of Yŏngjo and nephew of Ch'ŏlchong) and overseer of the extensive land-holdings of the Sŏnhi-gung. During the course of negotiations with Nagamori, Yi died unexpectedly of an illness. Nagamori then turned to the royal household minister, Min P'yŏng-sŏk. Min (1858–1940) was a powerful member of the Yŏhŭng Min clan. He reportedly opposed the reform efforts of Kim Ok-kyun and conspired to have Kim assassinated after the coup attempt in 1884. Although associated with the conservative forces against Japan's efforts to reform Korea during the last years of the nineteenth century, Min allied himself with the Japanese colonial government and was rewarded with a peerage in 1910. He owned a small amount of land in one of the villages studied here.

32. *Nihon gaikō bunsho* 37:1, 575–576.

33. Ibid., 571–572, 576–577.

34. Ibid., 578–579. See cable numbers 213 (May 6, 1904) and 454 (May 7, 1904).

35. *Nihon gaikō bunsho* 37:1, 351–356.

36. This opposition is described in a secret letter from Hayashi to Komura, dated June 8, 1904. Ibid., 580–581.

37. See cable from Minister Pro Tem Hagiwara Moriichi to Komura dated June 20, 1904. Ibid., 583–584.

38. Ibid., 583–584, 591.

39. For example, see articles in the *Hwangsŏng sinmun* (edited by Namgung Ŏk) of June 18, 21, 22, and 23. See also cables between Hagiwara and Komura in *Nihon gaikō bunsho* 37:1, 583–584.

40. For Hayashi's new proposal, see *Nihon gaikō bunsho* 37:1, 582–583. Nagamori's original proposal included plans to establish a monopoly on tobacco and other commodities. Hayashi's proposal eliminated everything not related to the development of Korean agriculture.

41. Ibid., 587. By this time the Nagamori proposal had been publicized in Japan as well. Ministry of Agriculture and Commerce officials had to quell the fears of Diet members that the Japanese government was giving special treatment to Nagamori at the expense of other capitalists. See *Hwangsŏng sinmun* of June 22, 1904.

42. *Nihon gaikō bunsho* 37:1, 588–590.

43. See the series of cables between Seoul and Tokyo contained in Ibid., 592–596.

44. Ibid., 597–601.

45. Ibid., 601–602.

46. Ibid., 604.

47. Ibid., 604–606. This proposal was included in a secret letter from Hayashi to Komura dated September 16, 1904.

48. Nagamori's role was specified in article six of this new proposal. See Ibid., 606.

49. Satō, Ōmi Hamagorō, and thirty other Diet members submitted a formal request to the Japanese government on December 28, 1904, for information on the proposal to develop uncultivated land in Korea. Satō may have had more than just the Japanese taxpayers' interest at heart, however, when he criticized

Nagamori's monopolistic position in agricultural development in Korea. Satō had economic interests himself in Korean agriculture. By 1921 he was no longer in the Diet, but he lived in Seoul and headed the Chōsen nōrin kabushiki kaisha, one of the largest agricultural development corporations in colonial Korea. See Kusakabe Kagekatsu, *Keijō shimin meikan* (Seoul: Chōsen chūō keizaikai, 1921), 295.

50. *Nihon gaikō bunsho* 37:1, 608–609.

51. Ibid., 609–610.

52. For a text of this law, appropriately printed on Halloween, see the *Kwanbo* of October 31, 1906.

53. *Tōkei nempō* (Seoul: Chōsen sōtokufu, 1920), p. 36, Table 3.

54. According to government-general statistics, approximately 4 percent of Japanese settlers in 1910 were engaged in agriculture. By 1915 farmers comprised about 12 percent of all Japanese residents in Korea—the highest level throughout the entire colonial period. See *Tōkei nempō*, table 80; Kajikawa Hansaburō, *Gendai no chōsen* (Tokyo: Rokugokan, 1927), 255–257.

55. Of the two thousand Japanese settlers engaged in agriculture in Korea at the time of the annexation, approximately 650–700 owned land. The remaining two-thirds worked as tenants. See Yamaguchi Sei, *Chōsen sangyō-shi* (Seoul: 1910), 10. The majority of Japanese landowners were small-scale farmers, while a few owned most of the Japanese-owned land. The forty largest agricultural land investors (6 percent of all Japanese landowners) owned almost 60 percent of all Japanese-owned land in Korea in 1910.

56. One such publication was the *Kankoku sangyō shisatsu hōkokusho* (Ōsaka: Ōsaka Chamber of Commerce, 1904). Another was by Yokoyama Ippei, *Kankoku shisatsu-roku,* (Tokyo: Fukuoka shoten, 1904). See also Katō Masanosuke, *Kankoku keiei*; and *Chōsen nōgyō gaisetsu* (Tokyo: Japanese Ministry of Agriculture and Commerce, 1910).

57. The report of this investigative team, the *Kankoku tochi nōsan hōkokusho,* is voluminous. Each province is examined in detail. Particularly interesting are the team's accounts of Japanese settlers in various parts of Korea. Their report depicts a rather harsh life for settlers already engaged in agriculture in Korea in 1904, but it optimistically encourages others to emigrate to the peninsula.

58. One such government publication, *Kankoku sōran,* gave precise information on reclamation possibilities, including topographical maps showing where land could be supposedly reclaimed. The Japanese government tried to depict Korea as a land of endless agricultural possibilities. These particular reclamation projects lacked real potential, however, and judging from postwar topographical maps, they were never undertaken. The projects undoubtedly were unfeasible from the outset. See Tokunaga Isami, *Kankoku sōran,* 440.

59. See, for example, Kambe Masao, *Chōsen nōgyō imin-ron.* Kambe, a noted scholar of agricultural economics, wrote that "Koreans in general are a people accustomed to cold, so [the government] ought to adopt a policy of moving them to Hokkaido or to the Tohoku region." Kambe proposed replacing five hundred thousand to one million Koreans with Japanese farmers he described as much more efficient agricultural producers. See also Itō Seizō, *Kankoku sho-*

kumin kanken (Tokyo: Zenkoku nojikai, 1907); and Togo Minoru, *Nihon sho-kumin-ron*.

60. For example, see Yamamoto Kotarō, *Chōsen ijū annai*. Yamamoto suggested that Japanese emigrants interested in business should settle in Korea's cities or along the new railroad line where other Japanese had settled. Yamamoto gave detailed information on the price of agricultural land in various places on the peninsula and suggested that the least expensive land could be acquired in Hwanghae province. Another book, Ugaya Ramon's *Chōsen e yuku hito ni* (Tokyo: 1914), described for prospective emigrants how much they could make in various professions. Innkeepers supplementing their incomes by selling *yakiimo* on the street, for example, could earn 20–30 sen per day.

61. One obvious parallel was the low socioeconomic background of settlers on the North American and Asian continents. The early settlers in Korea were, to use Nitobe Inazō's words, "marginal humanity." See *Nitobe Inazō zenshū*, 28.

62. For a good analysis of the establishment of the Oriental Development Company, see Karl Moskowitz, "The Creation of the Oriental Development Company: Japanese Illusions Meet Korean Reality," *Occasional Papers on Korea* 2 (March 1974), 73–121; and Kimishima Masahiko, "Tōyō takushoku kabushiki kaisha no setsuritsu katei," *Rekishi hyōron* 282, 285 (November 1973 and January 1974).

63. See *Jigyō gaikyō*, published by the Oriental Development Company, page 3. See also Kim Hyun Kil, "Land Use Policy in Korea: With Special Reference to the Oriental Development Company," Ph.D. dissertation, University of Washington, 1971, 61.

64. For a discussion of the Gentlemen's Agreement, see William Peterson, *Japanese Americans* (New York: Random House, 1971), 39–44. Relevant documents surrounding the negotiations between the United States and Japan over limitation of Japanese immigration into the United States can be found in *Nihon gaikō bunsho* 37:1.

65. For example, the governments of Australia, New Zealand, and Canada were under great pressure at this time to limit the number of Japanese entering their countries. One Australian proposal involved establishment of an English-language examination for all immigrants. See *Nihon gaikō bunsho* 38:2, 247–249. One Australian newspaper suggested that "a stipulation that immigrants from Japan must be married men with families would sufficiently bar the door . . . It is the young single men who come here to save money from wages and go back to Japan that the Australian dreads." Ibid., 253–254.

66. The Tōyō kyōkai was established in 1898 as the Taiwan kyōkai and was renamed in 1907 when Japanese colonial expectations were expanded beyond Taiwan. The association served as a conservative think tank that lobbied for Japanese colonial expansion throughout the first several decades of the twentieth century. The kyōkai established a school to train colonial administrators in 1900, and this school later became the Takushoku daigaku. Many of its graduates served in the government-general in Korea. The head of the school, called the Tōyō kyōkai senmon gakkō, was Katsura Tarō. See Kimishima Masahiko, "Tōyō takushoku kabushiki kaisha," no. 282, 35–38.

67. Ibid., p. 42.

68. See *Bōeki* 8:7 (July 1907): 14.

69. Kimishima Masahiko, "Tōyō takushoku kabushiki kaisha," no. 282, 42.

70. Itō's approval was necessary because of his position as resident-general. Because funding for the new corporation was partially from Mitsui and the Daiichi ginkō, with which Inoue had close ties, the Tōyō kyōkai needed to include him in any development plans for Korea. At that time Mitsui and Daiichi were the leading investors in commercial and banking activities on the Korean peninsula. See *Segai Inoue-kō den,* 170.

71. *Hara Kei nikki,* vol. 3, 182.

72. Kimishima Masahiko, "Tōyō takushoku kabushiki kaisha," no. 285, 50–51.

73. See *Tōyō keizai zasshi* 1432 (March 1908): 1–2; *Gaikō shihō* 126 (June 1909): 17.

74. Yamaguchi Sei, *Chōsen sangyō-shi,* 711–712.

75. The official version of this ordinance appears in the *Kwanbo* of July 8, 1907. A very useful handbook on laws and ordinances enacted between 1895 and August 1910 is *Kuhan'guk pŏmnyŏng mongnok* (Seoul: Pŏmmubu, 1970). Song Pyŏng-jun headed the bureau. It is extremely difficult to ascertain who was appointed to this bureau without examining every page of the *Kwanbo*. Song Pyŏng-jun had been active in Japanese-sponsored reforms in Korea in the past and on one occasion had fled to Japan. He was an early organizer of the Ilchinhoe, the early twentieth-century group of Koreans advocating Japanese-led reforms. At the time of his appointment as head of the bureau, Song was the minister of agriculture-commerce-industry in the Yi Wan-yong cabinet. Song has been branded a traitor to the country for his pro-Japanese political activities at the time of annexation. Another member of the bureau was Yu Song-jun.

76. See the notice in the *Kwanbo* of January 24, 1908. It reads in part, "The investigation into royal and state property in the Provisional Bureau for the Investigation of Royal and State Property and the separation of land into public and private ownership, is to rescue common people who have had landownership rights taken away in the past."

77. This was done through Ordinance 40, promulgated on June 25, 1908. For the text of this ordinance, see the *Kwanbo* of June 29, 1908.

78. Ordinance 39 of June 25, 1908, can be found in the *Kwanbo* of June 29, 1908. The Kyŏngsŏn-gung was established in 1896, and its land was owned by the family of Lady Ŏm, a consort of King Kojong. Wada Ichirō notes that some of this palace land had already been given to relatives prior to the promulgation of this law. A small part of the Kyŏngsŏn-gung land was reportedly returned to the previous owners, from whom it had been taken in 1896. See Wada Ichirō, *Chōsen tochi chizei,* 182–184. For a list of individuals receiving Kyŏngsŏn-gung land, see Arai Kentarō, *Rinji zaisan,* 75–77. The residency-general may have moved first against the Kyŏngsŏn-gung because Lady Ŏm was Kojong's concubine—not eligible to become queen—and did not have relatives in politically influential positions. According to the *Rinji zaisan* the Kyŏngsŏn-gung owned about 2,000 *chŏngbo* in 1907. Although about one-third of this land was declared state-owned, all of this reclassified land was given back to the Ŏm family in 1910.

79. Arai Kentarō, *Rinji zaisan,* 8–10. For a copy of the law establishing this bureau, see the *Kwanbo* of July 28, 1908. See also Yamaguchi Sei, *Chōsen sangyō-shi,* 327–328 and 388–389. The bureau had over 350 employees, 320 of whom were technicians used for surveying the palace and state property. The total area of arable and residential land in Korea was approximately 3 million *chŏngbo* in 1918. See Kobayakawa Kurō, *Chōsen nōgyō hattatsu-shi,* vol. 3 (Tokyo: Yūhōkyōkai, 1960), 97. Wada Ichirō cites government-general statistics in his estimate that the area of arable land in 1910 was approximately 2.4 million *chŏngbo.* See *Chōsen tochi chizei,* 755–756. However, this figure is simply an estimate because of the absence of accurate land registers until about 1916. Not only was land kept off the Yi dynasty land registers, but the 1910 government-general had a definite interest in underreporting cultivated-land area prior to its establishment, thereby demonstrating it had increased the area registered and under cultivation. The total area of cultivated land probably did not increase substantially during the years 1910–1918. In the villages studied, little increase occurred. The bureau report asserts that about one-third of palace land had not been reported but was found at the time of the 1908 survey.

80. Most of the technicians were Koreans. For a list of their superiors, the top twenty-five administrators in the bureau, see Arai Kentarō, *Rinji zaisan,* 31–35 of the Appendix. Many of these officials became high-ranking administrators of the Land Survey Bureau in 1910.

81. Takahashi Tomozō, *Tōyō takushoku kabushiki kaisha nijūnen-shi* (Tokyo: Tōyō takushoku kabushiki kaisha jūnenshi, 1928), 36–37. This total was less than the original agreement, but the Oriental Development Company reduced the area and chose more paddy land. The total value of the land selected by the Oriental Development Company could not exceed sixty thousand yen, the Korean government's share of the capitalization. See also Yamaguchi Sei, *Chōsen sangyō-shi,* 711.

82. Arai Kentarō, *Rinji zaisan,* 77–94.

83. For example, the list includes a large grant (over twelve thousand yen) to the mother of Min Yŏng-ik. Min Yŏng-ch'ŏl reportedly received 352 yen, and Yi Pong-nae, a high-ranking government official, was granted 1,395 yen. Bibliographical information on some individuals who received large grants remains unknown: Ch'ŏn Kyŏng-sik (over ten thousand yen) and Ha Kung-il (over four thousand yen). The majority of these *tojang* lived in Seoul. One recipient of about three thousand yen was Paek Si-yong. Paek served in the royal household ministry from 1901 and had held high positions in the ministry. In November 1906 he was appointed interpreter in the Provisional Bureau for the Investigation of Royal and State Property. In this position he may have been able to secure favorable rulings by the Provisional Property Reorganization Bureau. See *Taehan cheguk kwanwŏn iryŏksŏ,* 440, 748.

84. Two exceptions deserve mention. Yi Chae-myŏn, King Kojong's older brother, and Yi Chae-gŭk, Kojong's cousin, were both awarded ownership to relatively large amounts of land near Kimhae and outside Seoul. Yi Chae-gŭk was the royal household minister at the time. See Arai Kentarō, *Rinji zaisan,* 135.

85. This figure is computed from government-general statistics and included 13,879 *chŏngbo* of paddy land and 4,467 *chŏngbo* of upland. Most of this land

was purchased. The Oriental Development Company continued to purchase agricultural land during the next few years, and by 1913 the company had bought over 43,000 *chŏngbo* of cultivated land. See Takahashi Tomozō, *Tōyō takushoku kabushiki kaisha,* 35–36.

86. Eugene Kim and Han-kyo Kim, *Korea and the Politics of Imperialism 1876–1910* (Berkeley: University of California Press, 1968), 143–151. For the text of this new agreement, announced July 24, see the *Kwanbo* of July 25, 1907. This agreement strengthened the power of the residency-general by stipulating that more Japanese advisors were to be hired by the Korean government and that the vice-minister of each Korean ministry had to be a Japanese national.

87. Conroy, *Japanese Seizure of Korea,* 364–369; and Kim and Kim, *Korea and the Politics of Imperialism,* 198–206.

88. Estimates of the number of casualties in the fighting between 1907 and 1910 vary. Official Japanese military records state that about twenty-five thousand Koreans and Japanese were either killed or wounded. See Kim and Kim, *Korea and the Politics of Imperialism,* 205.

89. Memoirs of Fujii Kantarō, "Tōsen yori nōjō," 13 (in my possession).

90. Fujii cites the example of the Hosokawa farm near Samnye in North Chŏlla province. The attackers stormed the farm like "crazy men," and the farm's defenders had only pistols to fight them off. We are told that only through the heroics of the defenders was the farm "saved," and the victory was celebrated annually at the Hosokawa family grave site at the Suisenji in Japan. See ibid., 14–15.

91. Tomimura Rokurō, *Chūnan ronsan hattatsu-shi,* 11.

92. Yamaguchi Atsumizu, "Yonjūichinen ni okeru kankoku keizaikei," *Chōsen* 2:5 (January 1909): 102–103.

93. Kim Chŏng, *Nikkan gaikō shiryō shūsei,* vol. 6, 991. The committee was made up of representatives of each province. For a list of the thirty-three committee members, see Takahashi Tomozō, *Tōyō takushoku kabushiki kaisha nijūnen-shi,* 8–9. This committee included several individuals who later owned land in the villages studied here, the most prominent being Paek Nam-sin. Paek probably owned the most land in Chŏlla province at that time.

94. Kimishima, "Tōyō takushoku kabushiki kaisha," no. 285, 53.

95. Usagawa's speech was printed in the Tōyō kyōkai publication, *Tōyō shihō* 124 (January 1909): 72.

96. See Hayashi Ichizō, "Chōsen no nōgyō imin," *Tōyō shihō,* 151 (April 1911): 22–30.

97. Aoyagi Tsunatarō, *Chōsen tōchi-ron* (Seoul: Chōsen kenkyūkai, 1923), 664–665. See also *Tōyō takushoku kabushiki kaisha nijūnen-shi,* 81–82.

98. Hayashi Ichizō, "Chōsen no nōgyō imin," 22–30.

99. See *Nihon gaikō bunsho* 42:1, 179–180.

100. Kambe Masao, *Chōsen nōgyō imin-ron,* 140–141.

101. Fujii Kantarō, "Tōsen yori nōjō," 9–10. These "spheres of interest" had the effect—perhaps anticipated by the Kunsan area residents—of freezing the status quo ownership situation among Japanese residents, and at the same time it kept land prices down. When Kiuchi Juyojiro, representing Mitsubishi, arrived in

Kunsan in 1908 to select land to develop, he was forced to establish the Mitsubishi Tōsan farm at the foot of hills in an area that had not already been claimed. Understandably, Kiuchi was quite upset. Ibid., 10–11.

102. For a text of this law, promulgated on October 26, 1906, see the *Kwanbo* of October 31, 1906.

103. The statistics for 1909 come from Yamaguchi Sei, *Chōsen sangyō-shi,* 696–710. Similar statistics appear in *Kankoku chūō nōkaihō* 4:4 (April 1910): 10–16. 1910 figures are from the government-general's 1910 *Tōkei nempō,* Table 99.

104. Government-general statistics recorded in the *Kampō* of February 7, 1914. See also *Ilche ch'imnyakha Han'guk samsimnyungnyŏnsa,* vol. 1 (Seoul: Kuksa p'yŏnch'an wiwŏnhoe, 1971) p. 1000.

105. Mizuta Naomasa, *Tōkanfu jidai no zaisei* (Tokyo: Yūhōkyōkai, 1974), 162–163.

106. Ibid., 161.

107. For a discussion of the importance of the *kyŏlsu yŏnmyŏngbu,* see Tanaka Shinichi, "Kankoku zaisei seiri ni okeru 'chōsei daichō' seibi ni tsuite," *Tochi seido shigaku* 63 (April 1974): 1–20. To my knowledge, none of these records exist, since they were destroyed after being made obsolete by the *t'oji taejang* after 1918.

108. *Chōsen tochi chōsa,* 63.

109. Arai Kentarō, *Rinji zaisan,* 159.

110. Ibid., 160. These schools were established in Taegu, Chŏnju, and P'yŏngyang. This report claims that the students trained in these schools were *yangban* sons. The trainees practiced their new surveying skills by surveying the land granted to the Oriental Development Company by the Korean royal household ministry.

111. *Nihon gaikō bunsho,* vol. 42:1, 186.

112. Arai Kentarō, *Rinji zaisan,* 163.

113. For a historical account of the 1910–1918 survey and detailed description of survey procedures, see *Chōsen tochi chōsa.* See Wŏn Yŏng-hŭi, *Han'guk chijŏksa,* for an edited Korean-language version of this report.

114. For a list of the Land Survey Bureau employees, see *Chōsen tochi chōsa,* 513–522.

115. Sang-Chul Suh, *Growth and Structural Changes in the Korean Economy, 1910–1940* (Cambridge: Harvard University Press, 1978), 16.

116. *Chōsen tochi chōsa,* 63; Tanaka Shinichi, "Kankoku zaisei," 16–19.

117. One of the first scholars to advance this opinion was Pak Mun-gyu in "Nōson shakai bunka no kiten toshite no tochi chōsa jigyō ni tsuite," *Chōsen shakai keizaishi kenkyū* (Seoul: Seoul University, 1933). Almost all subsequent historians have followed this tradition: In Chŏng-sik, *Chōsen no nōgyō kikō* (Tokyo: Hakuyosha, 1939), 58; Yi Chae-mu, "Chōsen ni okeru 'tochi chōsa jigyō' no jittai," *Shakaikagaku kenkyū* 7:5 (1956): 22–58; Hatada Takashi, *A History of Korea* (Santa Barbara: ABC Clio, 1969), 113; Kim Yong-sŏp, "Sut'alŭl uihan ch'ŭngnyang: t'oji chosa," in *Han'guk hyŏndae-sa,* vol. 4, edited by Sin Sŏk-ho (Seoul: Sin'gu munhwasa, 1971), 115–116. It is significant that such

treatments critical of the cadastral survey began during the depression. No work written prior to 1933, either Japanese or Korean, is critical of the survey's methods or outcome.

118. *Chōsen tochi chōsa,* 63. Hoping to avoid taxation, some landowners did not register their land initially. In 1913 the bureau stopped questioning individuals who did not report land but registered the land as state-owned.

119. Ibid., 127–129.

120. Ibid., 123–124. See also Wŏn Yŏng-hüi, *Han'guk chijŏksa,* 214.

CHAPTER 5

1. Han Woo-keun, *The History of Korea* (Seoul: Eul-yoo Publishing Company, 1970), 467–568.

2. See also Hatada Takeshi, *A History of Korea,* 113–114, in which Takeshi states that the cadastral survey established modern landownership rights for the first time in Korean history.

3. According to Hoon K. Lee, Japanese individuals owned less than 5 percent of arable land in 1921; by 1927 the percentage had risen to 6.8 percent. Hoon K. Lee, *Land Utilization and Rural Economy in Korea* (Chicago: University of Chicago Press, 1936), 146–147.

4. In the cases of clan and church ownership, the total amount of land was quite small—less than one *chŏngbo* during the early years of the colonial period. After liberation in 1945 a large amount of former corporation land in the villages was acquired by Tan'guk University.

5. I have chosen to include residents of the villages and residents of the *myŏn* in which the villages were located as "local residents." These individuals lived within an hour's walk of the land they owned and were in a position to play an active personal role in its management. Some of these individuals may not have actually cultivated the land themselves, instead renting it out to local tenants. Nonetheless, the produce and profit (if any) from its sale remained on the local level and were not sent to an urban or distant landlord in the form of rent. There may have been others who lived across a *myŏn* boundary line yet tilled their land themselves. Thus, use of statistics drawn from residency data must be limited to providing only a general picture of residency patterns among landowners in Korea.

6. Michael Hechter, *Internal Colonialism,* 85–86. This is significant because it indicates that Japanese investors living in Japan found long-term investments in Korean agriculture to be economically feasible. Whereas Japanese landowners living in Korea can be identified from biographical works published during the colonial period, individuals living in Japan remain unidentified for the most part. These individuals may well have been engaged in food processing and bought land in Korea in order to obtain a secure source of agricultural products.

7. Whereas many Korean landowners lived in Seoul and owned land throughout the peninsula (a holdover pattern from Yi dynasty days), Japanese tended to limit their land acquisitions to the area immediately surrounding their place of residence.

8. There were two Japanese landowners in Songsan-ni in 1914. Tanabe Kanetsuchi lived in a small village in neighboring Masan-myŏn. He does not appear in

any biographical work known to me, suggesting that he was a man of rather modest means. Tamuki Tsuneyoshi was born in Nara-ken and emigrated to Kunsan. Little is known about him, but later in the colonial period he did own a considerable amount of paddy land in other parts of Sŏch'ŏn-gun, totaling 49 *chŏngbo* (120 acres) in 1932. See Ansai Kado, *Chūsei nandō hatten-shi* (Taejŏn: Hōnan nippōsha, 1932), 296.

9. Without a search of the land records for all neighboring areas, it is impossible to know how many of Hansan-myŏn's residents lived in the immediate vicinity of Songsan-ni and how many lived several kilometers away.

10. Many of these landowners lived in or near the provincial town of Sŏch'ŏn, a large village in the center of the county. Despite being on the railroad line, Sŏch'ŏn never developed into a regional commercial center because the administrative offices of the county were divided between it and the nearby port town of Changhang. To this day the *Kunch'ŏng,* or county office, is located in Sŏch'ŏn, while the local *Tŭnggiso,* or county registration office, is in Changhang.

11. Residents of bustling Kunsan, only a few kilometers down the Kŭm River, did not own much land in Songsan-ni. As pointed out in Chapter 1, the lack of convenient roads hindered access to the village and made it more isolated than its location suggests.

12. No one or two individuals dominated landownership in Songsan-ni, as was the case with other villages. The largest landowners in Songsan-ni, each owning over 5,000 *p'yŏng,* were only medium-sized landowners when compared to those in Kongsu-ri and P'albong-ni.

13. In 1900 members of these three clans owned 91,575 *p'yŏng* of arable land out of a village total of 196,257 *p'yŏng* of privately held land. For the clan makeup of Korean villages, see *Chōsen no sei* (Seoul: Chōsen sōtokufu, 1934), 191.

14. This concentration of local landownership among fewer families tends to support Chong-sik Lee's suggestion that "local gentry" acquired land from small-scale farmers during these years. See Chong-sik Lee, *The Politics of Korean Nationalism* (Berkeley: University of California Press, 1963), 94.

15. Korean surveyors in 1900 also registered Songsan-ni land as higher quality than land in the other villages. Colonial-period statistics for agricultural production show higher rates of productivity in Sŏch'ŏn-gun, confirming that agricultural land in the region was more fertile than most other regions in the country. See Ansai Kado, *Chūsei nandō hatten-shi,* 135.

16. The average for assessed value of upland in the village was 7.3 *sen* per *p'yŏng* in 1914; average assessed value of land owned by the largest landowners was 7.4 *sen.* Owners of large amounts of land in Songsan-ni owned considerably more paddy land than upland, since it was the land of choice. Of the 42,435 *p'yŏng* owned by individuals owning over 5,000 *p'yŏng* each, only 5,263 *p'yŏng* was upland.

17. It is possible that powerful landowners had sufficient influence to have their land undervalued and thereby subject to less taxation. I have seen no evidence to indicate that such fraudulent land evaluations occurred, and former assessors asserted in personal interviews in Seoul that such cases were extremely rare. One assessor stated he had heard of no such instance (interview with Kim

Chŏng-su, former assessor with the Chōsen shokusan ginkō). Additional evidence that this land was accurately assessed comes from the changes in the average assessed values over time. Later in the colonial period this group of large-scale landowners acquired more land of higher assessed value.

18. Japanese-owned paddy land was assessed at 17.0 sen per *p'yŏng* and upland at 6.0 sen. Due to the small number of Japanese-owned plots (only four), however, these statistics must be used with caution. However, a similar pattern is seen in the other villages as well.

19. In 1900 ten individuals owned residential plots but no arable land. The 1914 *t'oji taejang* lists seven such owners, but they were not the same individuals as in 1900.

20. There was a small, gradual decline in the number of homes owned by the residents of Songsan-ni during the colonial period. In 1944, forty-seven different owners owned the sixty-one residential plots in the village. The difference between 1914 and 1944 was slight because Songsan-ni was never dominated by outside, principally urban, economic forces as were the other villages studied.

21. The smallest residential plot was only 37 *p'yŏng,* or about 1,300 square feet, including house and courtyard. Actual living space was probably similar to modern Seoul apartments—very cramped. Japanese travelers in Korea at this time were surprised at how small Korean homes were. See Tokunaga Isami, *Kankoku sōran,* 381.

22. For example, on the *yang'an* from Songsan-ni, the name of one of the largest landowners in the village, Yi U-hyŏn, appears in three different forms: 祐鉉, 右鉉, 宇鉉. Another common example was the interchangeable use of characters pronounced *sŭng* and *sŏng.* About one-third of all names on the *yang'an* from each of the villages appear in at least two forms, complicating identification. Kim Yong-sŏp also found the same phenomenon in the villages he studied. See *Han'guk kŭndae.*

23. In 1900 two plots of paddy land were classified as *p'oryangjŏn,* or land used to support local military artillery units in the Yi dynasty. Following the Japanese cadastral survey this land was registered in the name of Songsan-ni and was used to support local government operations.

24. Between 1908 and 1913 the Oriental Development Company bought a total of 4,320 *chŏngbo* in South Ch'ungch'ŏng province (mostly paddy land) and a total of 43,097 *chŏngbo* of arable land nationwide. See Takahashi Tomozō, *Tōyō takushoku kabushiki kaisha nijūnenshi,* 35–36.

25. Since Land Survey Bureau personnel started from Seoul and worked south, the two northern villages in this study were surveyed first: Kongsu-ri in 1912–1913 and Paeksŏng-ni in 1913. Songsan-ni and P'albong-ni were surveyed in 1914. In the case of Se-ri, the northernmost village examined, ownership declarations were distributed and compiled in 1911, and the village was surveyed in 1912. As noted earlier, however, none of the *t'oji taejang* from Se-ri survived the Korean War.

26. Ansai Kado, *Chūsei nandō hatten-shi,* 14.

27. Kunitake began buying agricultural land in Korea in 1906. Its principal operations were in South Chŏlla province, where it established the Kunitake nōjō. The Kunitake lands in South Ch'ungch'ŏng province were managed from

its branch office in Kanggyŏng, established in October 1910. In 1930 Kunitake owned 550 *chŏngbo* of paddy land and 140 *chŏngbo* of upland in South Ch'ungch'ŏng province, for a total of approximately 1,700 acres. See Ansai Kado, *Chūsei nandō hatten-shi*, 293. The corporation's total arable landholdings nationwide were approximately 1,900 *chŏngbo* (over 4,000 acres) by 1929. See Asada Kyōji, *Nihon teikoku shugi to kyūshokuminchi jinushisei* (Tokyo: Ochanomizu, 1974), 283.

28. For example, the railroad through the Nonsan plain between Taejŏn and Iri was completed in 1911. This enabled Paeksŏng-ni's producers to market their agricultural products much more widely. As a result, the role of Seoul investments in Paeksŏng-ni landownership gradually increased. By 1945 residents of Seoul (including the Oriental Development Company) owned over 16 percent of village paddy land.

29. Once land was appraised at the time of the cadastral survey, the entire country was not systematically reappraised until 1943. In addition, the land-tax rate did not change during the colonial period. Agricultural improvements and increased productivity meant higher profits, not higher taxes, for the landowner. See Sang-Chul Suh, *Growth and Structural Changes*, 83–84.

30. See Han Woo-keun, *The History of Korea*, 467–468.

31. See *Chōsen no kōsaku kanshū* (Seoul: Chōsen no sōtokufu, 1972), 93–95.

32. Prior to the construction of the railroad station at Ch'ŏn'an, only a tiny village along the road between North and South Ch'ungch'ŏng provinces existed where Ch'ŏn'an emerged. No such place appears on any map of the region until after 1905. As late as 1908, fewer than five hundred persons lived in Ch'ŏn'an, 170 of whom were Japanese. By 1913 the town's population had soared to about 3,500. See Zenshō Eisuke, *Chōsen no jinkō genshō*, 268–270. According to another contemporary source, the population of Ch'ŏn'an was about 2,300, but in either case its population increase during these years was staggering. See Kawashima Masaru, *Chūsei nandō annai* (Tokyo: Hōnan nippōsha, 1915), 51. Onyang, only several kilometers to the west of Kongsu-ri, reportedly had a population of about five hundred, seventy of whom were Japanese at the time of the cadastral survey.

33. See Fujii Kantarō, "Tōsen yori nōjō," and Kobayashi Fusajirō, *Kankoku tochi nōsan*, 725–737.

34. Grades for upland ranged from six (highest) to ten (lowest). Paddy land grades in the villages studied ran from eight (highest) to eighteen (lowest). For a discussion of this grade system, see the internal journal of the Chōsen shokusan ginkō, *Kaishin* 1:6 (November 1920): 16.

35. As a good example of this type of transfer, the extensive landholdings that had been registered in the 1900 *yang'an* in the name of Yun Il-tan were owned by Yun Pog-yong in 1913.

36. Land owned by Yi Ŭl-gi was transferred to Yi Po-sang; land owned by the landlord Yi Ch'ung-dŏk was owned in 1913 by Yi Kap-sang.

37. Yi Chae-gak (1873–19?), a descendent of Changjo, was an official in the royal household ministry in the 1890s. He served briefly as minister to England in 1902 and as minister to Japan in 1905, for which he was decorated by the Japanese government. He received a peerage when Korea was annexed in 1910. See

Ōmura Tomonosuke, *Chōsen kizoku retten* (Seoul: Chōsen sōtokufu, 1910), pp. 37–39. How Cho's extensive (almost 30,000 *p'yŏng*) paddy lands were transferred to Yi is unknown, but presumably they were sold. No information on Cho is available.

38. Pak, a Seoul druggist, received a stipend from the government-general as compensation for palace land that had been classified as state land during 1908–1910. See *Chōsen shōkō taikan* (Keijō: 1929), 812; and Arai Kentarō, *Rinji zaisan.* We know this land was sold because Pak registered the sale in the *t'oji tŭnggibu,* the register of legal transactions affecting pieces of land.

39. According to the *Chōsen shōkō taikan,* Pak lived in Seoul's Ch'ŏngjin-dong, did not have a telephone, and paid eighteen yen in taxes in 1929. See page 1005.

40. Andō and Nagaya jointly owned a great deal of land in South Ch'ung-ch'ŏng province (over 200 *chŏngbo* in 1925). See *Chōsen no nōgyō* (Seoul: Chōsen sōtokufu, 1925), 167. Andō later worked as an executive in the Kanaya shōkai, a dry goods business in Ch'ŏn'an.

41. Kawashima Masaru, *Chūsei nandō annai,* 12 of the Appendix.

42. The Oriental Development Company land was concentrated on the west side of Iri, near the village of Osan. The small Oriental Development Company holdings in P'albong-ni (actually less than any of the other villages studied) suggests that representatives of the corporation did not fan out into the nearby countryside and purchase agricultural land. Instead, the Oriental Development Company negotiated with urban Korean landlords and acquired title over the landlords' scattered holdings. The two plots of Oriental Development Company land in P'albong-ni, totaling 1,204 *p'yŏng,* were clearly not chosen based on a careful scrutiny of village land. The plots were of poor quality and at the margins of the village.

43. See Tani Genji, *Taishū jinjiroku,* overseas vol. (Tokyo: Kokusei kyōkai, 1940), 38 of the Korea section; Nakamura Sukeyoshi, *Chōsen ginkō kaisha kumiami yōroku* (Seoul: Tōa keizai shihōsha, 1933), 217. The Takase nōjō reportedly owned over 1,000 *chŏngbo* of land in South Chŏlla province in 1925. See *Chōsen no nōgyō,* 174.

44. For Ōhashi, see Abe Hiroshi, *Chōsen kōrōsha meikan* (Seoul: Minshū shironsha, 1935), 681. For the others, see Abe Hiroshi, 446; *Chōsen no nōgyō* (1932), 185; *Daijinushi-chō* (South Chŏlla Province: Taejŏn Zenra nandō, 1931), 10.

45. See Ōgaki Masuo, *Chōsen shinshi daidōfu* (Seoul: Seibunsha, 1913), 827.

46. See *Chōsen no kōsaku kanshū,* 29–30.

47. See Arai Kentarō, *Rinji zaisan,* 77–136.

48. See *Iwasaki Hisaya-den* (Tokyo: Iwasaki Hisaya-den hensan iinkai, 1961), 242–255; and Wada Ichirō, *Chōsen tochi chizei,* 183–184.

CHAPTER 6

1. For statistics on rice production and imports into Japan, see the *Nihon tōkei nenkan* for this period; Lockwood, *Economic Development of Japan,* 89; George O. Totten III, *The Social Democratic Movement in Prewar Japan* (New Haven:

Yale University Press, 1966), 35–36; Borton, *Japan's Modern Century*, 300; Sang-Chul Suh, *Growth and Structural Changes*, 20; and Kobayakawa Kuro, *Chōsen nōgyō hattatsu-shi*, 116.

2. Ho, *Economic Development of Taiwan, 1860–1970*, 73.

3. Toranuma Ryōsan, *Chōsen kōgyō kabushiki kaisha nijūnen-shi*, (Tokyo: Chōsen kōgyō kabushiki kaisha, 1929), Tables 1, 3, 5, and 6 in the Appendix.

4. See Lockwood, *Economic Development of Japan*, 98–99; James Nakamura, *Agricultural Production and the Economic Development of Japan 1873–1922* (Princeton: Princeton University Press, 1966), 159–163; Palais, *Politics and Policy*, 62; Tokunaga, Isami, *Kankoku sōran*, 668.

5. Moriya Yoshio, *Chōsen shokusan ginkō jūnenshi* (Tokyo: Chōsen shokusan ginkō, 1928), 15.

6. See *Chōsen tōkanfu shokuminroku* (1910), 812; *Chōsen sōtokufu shokuinroku* (1915); Ansai Kado, *Chūsei nandō hattatsu-shi*, part II, 36; and *Chōsen shōkō taikan*, 1027.

7. One can only speculate on why Kim sold his land to Kitagawa, perhaps it was to repay personal, unguaranteed loans. Charles Goldberg observed this pattern in these years in his village study in North Ch'ungch'ŏng province.

8. See Kita Tadamori, *Chōsen jinji koshinroku* (Seoul: Chōsen shinbunsha, 1935), 792; *Chōsen ni okeru naichijin* (Seoul: Chōsen sōtokufu, 1924); *Chōsen no nōgyō* (1925), 171; *Naisenjin jinushi shōyūchichō* (Kunsan: Zenra hokutō nomuka, 1928), 189.

9. See Tani Genji, *Taishū jinjiroku*, 38 of the Chōsen section; *Chōsen no nōgyō* (1932), 174 and 189; *Daijinushi-chō* (Zenra nandō, 1937), 2; Nakamura Sukeyoshi, *Chōsen ginkō kaisha*, 251–252.

10. See *Naisenjin jinushi shōyūchichō*, 25.

11. Biographical data on Kanehira come from the following sources: Abe Kaoru, *Chōsen kōrōsha meikan*, 198; Kawashima Masaru, *Chūsei nandō annai*, Appendix, 161; Ansai Kado, *Chūsei nandō hattatsu-shi*, 294; *Chōsen no nōgyō* (1932), 181.

12. Biographical data on Satō Seijirō come from the following sources: Abe Hiroshi, *Chōsen kōrōsha meikan*, 605; Tani Genji, 28; *Naisenjin jinushi shōyūchichō*, 2; *Chōsen no nōgyō* (1925), 166; *Chōsen tōkanfu shokuinroku* (1910), 808.

13. See Ōgaki Masuo, *Chōsen shinshi daidōfu*, 827.

CHAPTER 7

1. See Lockwood, *Economic Development of Japan* 63; and Shujiro Sawada, "Innovation in Japanese Agriculture, 1880–1935," in *The State and Economic Enterprise in Japan*, edited by William Lockwood (Princeton: Princeton University Press, 1965), *A Short Economic History of Modern Japan*, 2d rev. ed. (London, 1962), 344.

2. See Hechter, *Internal Colonialism*, 79–126.

3. See Lockwood, *Economic Development of Japan*, 56–57; George C. Allen, 109; Hishimoto Chōji, *Chōsen mei no kenkyū* (Tokyo: Chikura shobō, 1938), 600, 603.

4. Matsumura Takao, "Manshūkoku seiritsu ikō ni okeru imin rōdō seisaku no keisei to tenkai," in *Nihon teikokushugi-ka no manshū* (Tokyo: Manshū-shi kenkyūkai, 1972), 218ff.

5. Hishimoto Chōji, *Chōsen mei no kenkyū,* 659.

6. *Chōsen no nōgyō,* (1932) 211–212.

7. Takahashi Kamekichi, *Gendai chōsen keizairon* (Tokyo: Chikura shobō, 1935), 197–200.

8. Hisama Kenichi, "Chūsei nandō ni okeru kōsaku seido no kenkyū," in *Kinen ronbunshū* (Seoul: Chōsen sōtokufu suigen kōtō nōrin gakkō, 1932), 56–61.

9. Lee, *Land Utilization,* 173–176.

10. Matsumura Takao, "Manshūkoku seiritsu ikō," 227–234.

11. For biographical data on Pak Ki-hong, see *Chōsen shōkō taikan,* 812.

12. Biographical data on Kim Hŭng-in is not available beyond information on mortgages recorded on the *t'oji tŭnggibu.* For information on Takahashi, see *Chōsen shōkō taikan,* 1002. According to this source, Takahashi had a telephone in 1929 and paid twenty-four yen in taxes that year. According to maps printed during the colonial period, Takahashi lived in a very modest house in the heart of the Seoul business district.

13. For data on Ōgiwara, see Kameoka Eikichi, *Chōsen tetsudō ensen yōran,* (Seoul: Chōsen takushoku shiryō chōsakai, 1927), 1020.

14. For data on Anseki, see *Chōsen oyobi mammō ni okeru hokurikudō jinshi.*

15. For biographical data on Kim Han-gyu, see Abe Kaoru, *Chōsen kōrōsha meikan,* 217; *Chōsen shōkō taikan,* 1146; *Taehan cheguk kwanwŏn iryŏksŏ,* 127, 497, 519, 532.

16. For information on Im Man-je, see the *Kwanbo* of May 16, 1898; Miura Torahira, *Keijō kyōsan kaikokuhō,* 42. Im Tae-sun lived in Kwansu-dong in Seoul.

17. See Nakamura Sukeyoshi, *Chōsen ginkō kaisha,* 252; Abe Hiroshi, *Chōsen kōrōsha meikan,* 675.

GLOSSARY

chijŏkto (地籍図) Cadastral maps drawn up after the 1910–1918 land survey

cho (租) Payment made by cultivator to individual or institution in the Yi dynasty for right to cultivate land

chŏngbo (町步) Land measurement equaling 2.45 acres

hakchŏn (学田) Land from which produce supported local schools in the Yi dynasty

hyanggyo (郷校) Rural schools in the Yi dynasty

Kongsu-ri (公須里) Village in South Ch'ungch'ŏng province

kŭmyung chohap (金融組合) Local credit union

kun (郡) County

kungbangjŏn (宮房田) Land from which produce supported a royal palace in the Yi dynasty

Kwajŏnbŏp (科田法) Legal code for land distribution promulgated at the outset of the Yi dynasty

Kwangmu yang'an (光武量案) Last Yi dynasty land survey extending from 1898–1903

kyŏl (結) Yi dynasty measure of land productivity

mun'gi (文記) Collection of land documents used in the Yi dynasty to prove ownership

myŏn (面) Subcounty administrative division

Paeksŏng-ni (白石里) Village in South Ch'ungch'ŏng province

P'albong-ni (八峰里) Village in North Chŏlla province

p'yŏng (坪) Land measurement equaling 35 square feet

se (税) Tax paid to the central government

Se-ri (細里) Village in Kyŏnggi province

sijak (時作) Tenant

siju (時主) Landowner, usually used for landlords

Songsan-ni (松山里) Village in South Ch'ungch'ŏng province

sujogwŏn (受租權) Right to collect percentage of produce from cultivators

tojang (導掌) Local agents of landlords

t'oji taejang (土地臺長) Cadastre created after the land survey of 1910–1918

t'oji tŭnggibu (土地登記簿) Legal land registry under the court system

turak (斗落) Land measurement based on the amount of seeds needed to plant a field

BIBLIOGRAPHY

ENGLISH LANGUAGE SOURCES

Allen, George C. *A Short Economic History of Modern Japan.* 2d rev. ed. New York: Praeger, 1962.

Birnberg, Thomas B. *Colonial Development.* New Haven: Yale University Press, 1975.

Borton, Hugh. *Japan's Modern Century.* New York: Ronald, 1970.

Brandt, Vincent. *A Korean Village.* Cambridge: Harvard University Press, 1971.

Choe, Ching Young. *The Rule of the Taewŏn'gun.* Cambridge: Harvard University Press, 1972.

Chow Tse-tsung. *The May Fourth Movement.* Stanford: Stanford University Press, 1960.

Clark, Allen, and Donald Clark. *Seoul Past and Present.* Seoul: Hollym Publishing Company, 1969.

Conroy, Hilary. *The Japanese Seizure of Korea: 1868–1910.* Philadelphia: University of Pennsylvania Press, 1960.

Dore, R. P. *City Life in Japan.* Berkeley: University of California Press, 1958.

Fairbank, John K., and Edwin O. Reischauer. *East Asia: The Great Tradition.* Boston: Houghton, Mifflin, 1960.

Furtado, Celso. *Economic Development of Latin America.* Cambridge: Cambridge University Press, 1976.

Han Woo-keun. *The History of Korea.* Seoul: Eul-yoo Publishing Company, 1970.

Hatada Takashi. *A History of Korea.* Santa Barbara: ABC Clio, 1969.

Hechtor, Michael. *Internal Colonialism.* Berkeley: University of California Press, 1975.

Ho, Sam P. S. *Economic Development of Taiwan 1860–1970.* New Haven: Yale University Press, 1975.

Hoshino Tokuji. *Economic History of Chosen.* Seoul: Bank of Chosen, 1920.

201

Hulbert, Homer. *The Passing of Korea*. New York: Doubleday, Page and Company, 1906.

Imperial and Asiatic Quarterly Review 8:10 (January/April 1910): 308–337.

Iriye Akira. *After Imperialism: The Search for a New Order in the Far East, 1921–1931*. Cambridge: Harvard University Press, 1965.

Kang Man-gil. "Sirhak Thought and Its Reflection in Politics." *Korea Journal* 14:1 (May 1974): 5–7.

Kim, C. I. Eugene, and Han-kyo Kim. *Korea and the Politics of Imperialism 1876–1910*. Berkeley: University of California Press, 1968.

Kim Hyun Kil. "Land Use Policy in Korea: With Special Reference to the Oriental Development Company." Ph.D. dissertation. University of Washington, 1971.

Korea Review. Seoul.

Krumm, Raymond Edward Leo. Last Will and Testament, 1948.

Laslett, Peter. *The World We Have Lost*. New York: Scribners, 1965.

Lawton, Lancelot. "Prince Ito: His Life Work and His Influence Upon the National Policy of Japan." *Imperial and Asiatic Review* 29:57 (January/April 1910): 308–337.

Lee, Chong-sik. *The Politics of Korean Nationalism*. Berkeley: University of California Press, 1963.

Lee, Hoon K. *Land Utilization and Rural Economy in Korea*. Chicago: University of Chicago Press, 1936; New York: Greenwood Press, 1969.

Lenin, Vladimir I. *Imperialism, the Highest Stage of Capitalism*. New York: International Publishers, 1939.

Lockwood, William. *The Economic Development of Japan*. Princeton: Princeton University Press, 1968.

McKenzie, F. A. *Korea's Fight for Freedom*. Seoul: Yonsei University Press, 1969.

Moskowitz, Karl. "The Creation of the Oriental Development Company: Japanese Illusions Meet Korean Reality." *Occasional Papers on Korea* 2 (March 1974): 73–121.

Myers, Ramon. *The Chinese Peasant Economy*. Cambridge: Harvard University Press, 1970.

Nakamura, James. *Agricultural Production and the Economic Development of Japan 1873–1923*. Princeton: Princeton University Press, 1966.

Pak Pyŏng-ho. "The Legal Nature of Land Ownership in the Yi Dynasty." *Korea Journal* 15:10 (October 1975): 4–10.

Palais, James. *Politics and Policy in Traditional Korea*. Cambridge: Harvard University Press, 1975.

Peterson, William. *Japanese Americans*. New York: Random House, 1971.

Sawada Shujiro. "Innovation in Japanese Agriculture, 1880–1935." In *The State and Economic Enterprise in Japan*, edited by William Lockwood. Princeton: Princeton University Press, 1965.

Suh, Sang Chul, *Growth and Structural Changes in the Korean Economy, 1910–1940*. Cambridge: Harvard University Press, 1978.

Shin, Susan. "Land Tenure and the Agrarian Economy in Yi Dynasty Korea: 1600–1800." Ph.D. dissertation. Harvard University, 1973.

Shin Yong-ha. "Landlordism in Late Yi Dynasty." *Korea Journal* 18:6, (June 1978): 22–29.

Smith, Thomas C. *The Agrarian Origins of Modern Japan.* Stanford: Stanford University Press, 1959.

Stein, Stanley, and Barbara Stein. *The Colonial Heritage of Latin America.* New York: Oxford University Press, 1970.

Totten, George O. III. *The Social Democratic Movement in Prewar Japan.* New Haven: Yale University Press, 1966.

Waswo, Barbara. "Landlords and Social Change in Prewar Japan." Ph.D. dissertation. Stanford University, 1969.

JAPANESE LANGUAGE SOURCES

Abe Hiroshi. *Chōsen kōrōsha meikan.* Seoul: Minshū shironsha, 1935.

Ansai Kado. *Chūsei nandō hatten-shi.* Taejŏn: Hōnan nippōsha, 1932.

Aoyagi Tsunatarō. *Chōsen tōchiron.* Seoul: Chōsen kenkyūkai, 1923.

Arai Kentarō. *Rinji zaisan seiri-kyoku jimu yōkan.* Seoul: Chōsen sōtokufu, 1911.

Asada Kyōji. *Nihon teikoku shugi to kyūshokuminchi jinushisei.* Tokyo: Ochanomizu, 1968.

Bōeki. Tokyo: 1907.

Chōsen shōkō taikan. Seoul: Chōsen shōkō kenkyūkai, 1929.

Daijinushi-chō. South Chŏlla Province: Taejŏn, 1931.

Dainihon teikoku gikaishi. Tokyo: Dainihon teikoku gikaishi kanbōkai, ca. 1932.

Fujii Kantarō. "Tōsen yori nōjō keiei chakushu made." Memoirs of Fujii Kantarō, ca. 1932.

Fujisawa Seitarō. *Chōsen kinyū kumiai to jinbutsu.* Seoul: Tairiku minyūsha, 1936.

Gaikō shikō. Tokyo: Gaimushō (Ministry of Foreign Affairs) 1900–1907.

Hara Kei nikki. 9 vols. Tokyo: 1951.

Hattori Shisō, ed. *Heimin Shimbun.* Tokyo: Heimin Shimbunsha 1903–1904.

Hayashi Ichizō. "Chōsen no nōgyō imin." *Tōyō shihō* 151 (April 1911): 22–30.

Hisama Kenichi. "Chūsei nandō ni okeru kōsaku seido no kenkyū." *Kinen ronbunshū.* Seoul: Chōsen sōtokufu suigen kōtō nōrin gakkō, 1932.

Hishimoto Chōji. *Chōsen mei no kenkyū,* Tokyo: Chikura shobō, 1938.

Hori Wasei. "Nihon teikokushugi no chōsen ni okeru nōgyō seisaku." *Nihon-shi kenkyū* 171 (November 1976): 1–35.

"Imin shūchūshugi." *Chūō Kōron* 25:3: 177–178.

Im Pyŏng-yun, *Shokuminchi ni okeru shōgyōteki nōgyō no tenkai.* Tokyo: Tokyo University Press, 1971.

In Chŏng-sik. *Chōsen no nōgyō kikō.* Tokyo: Hakuyōsha, 1939.

Inoue Kiyoshi. "Nihon no chōsen shinryaku to teikokushugi." *Chōsen to teikokushugi.* Tokyo: Kyokutō Shoten, 1968.

Inoue Sojin. *Shokumin tochiron.* Seoul: Takumu hyōronsha, 1932.

Itō Seizō. *Kankoku shokumin kanken.* Tokyo: Zenkoku nōjikai, 1907.

Iwasaki Hisaya-den. Tokyo: Iwasaki Hisaya-den hensan iinkai, 1961.

Jigyō gaikyō. Seoul: Tōyō takushoku kabushiki kaisha, 1912.

Kaishin. Seoul: Chōsen shokusan ginkō, 1932.

Kajikawa Hansaburō. *Gendai no chōsen.* Tokyo: Rokugokan, 1927.

Kambe Masao. *Chōsen nōgyō iminron.* Tokyo: Yūhikaku shobō, 1910.

Kameoka Eikichi. *Chōsen tetsudō ensen yōran.* Seoul: Chōsen takushoku shiryō chōsakai, 1927.

Kankoku chūō nōkaihō. Seoul: Kankoku chūō nōkai, 1904–1910.

Kankoku sangyō shisatsu hōkokusho. Osaka: Osaka Chamber of Commerce, 1904.

Katō Masanosuke. *Kankoku keiei.* Tokyo: Shitsugyō no nihonsha, 1905.

Kawashima Masaru. *Chūsei nandō annai.* Tokyo: Hōnan nippōsha, 1915.

Kim Chŏng-ju, *Chōsen tochi shiryō.* Tokyo: Kankoku shiryō kenkyūjo, 1970.

Kim Chŏng-myong, ed. *Nikkan gaikō shiryō shūsei.* 10 vols. Tokyo, 1975.

Kimishima Masahiko. "Tōyō takushoku kabushiki kaisha no setsuritsu katei." *Rekishi hyōron* 282, 285 (November 1973, January 1974): 35–51.

Kita Tadamori. *Chōsen jinji kōshinroku.* Seoul: Chōsen Shinbunsha, 1935.

Ko Sŭng-je. *Shokuminchi kinyū seisaku no shiteki bunseki.* Tokyo: Ochanomizu, 1972.

Kobayakawa Kurō. *Chōsen nōgyō hattatsu-shi.* Tokyo: Yūhōkyōkai, 1960.

Kobayashi Fusajirō. *Kankoku tochi nōsan chōsa hōkoku.* Tokyo, 1905.

Kuroki Yukichi. *Komura Jutarō.* Tokyo: Kōdansha, 1968.

Kusakabe Kagekatsu. *Keijō shimin meikan.* Seoul: Chōsen chūō keizaikai, 1921.

Maejima Seizō. *Nihon teikokushugi to gikai.* Kyoto: Mineruba shobō, 1976.

Mansei daidōfu. Seoul: Mansei daidōfu kakkosho, 1932.

Matsumura Takao. "Manshūkoku seiritsu ikō ni okeru imin rōdō seisaku no keisei to tenkai." *Nihon teikokushugi-ka no manshū.* Tokyo: Manshū-shi kenkyūkai, 1972.

Miura Torahira. *Keijō kyōsan kaikokuhō.* Seoul: Keijō kyōsan kaizen toriatsu-kaijo, 1916.

Miyajima Hiroshi. "Chōsen kōgō kaikaku igo no shōgyō-teki nōgyō: sannan chihō o chūshin ni." *Shirin* 57:6, 38–77.

———. "Tochi chōsa jigyō no rekishi-teki zentei jōken no keisei." *Chōsen-shi kenkyūkai ronbunshū* 12 (1974): 61–97.

Mizuta Naomasa. *Tōkanfu jidai no zaisei.* Tokyo: Yūhōkyōkai, 1974.

Moriya Yoshio. *Chōsen shokusan ginkō jūnenshi.* Tokyo: Chōsen shokusan ginkō, 1928.

Nakamura Sukeyoshi. *Chōsen ginkō kaisha kumiai yōroku.* Seoul: Tōa keizai shihōsha, 1933; revised 1937.

Nitobe Inazō zenshū. Tokyo: Nitobe Inazō zenshū henshūiinkai, 1970.

Ōgaki Masuo. *Chōsen shinshi daidōfu.* Seoul: Seibunsha, 1913.

Ogino Katsushige. *Chōsen oyobi mammō ni okeru hokurikudō jinshi.* Tokyo: 1927.

Ōmura Tomonosuke. *Chōsen kizoku retten.* Seoul: Chōsen sōtokufu, 1910.

Pak Kyŏng-sik. *Nihon teikokushugi no chōsen shihai.* Tokyo: Aoki shoten, 1973.

Pak Mun-gyu. "Nōson shakai bunka no kiten toshite no tochi chōsa jigyō ni tsuite." *Chōsen shakai keizaishi kenkyū.* Seoul: Seoul University, 1933.

Rekishi hyōron. Minshushugi Kagakusha kyōkai 282, 285 (November 1973, January 1974).

Saitō sōtoku no bunka tōchi. Tokyo: Yūhōkyōkai, 1970.

Segai Inoue-kō den. Tokyo: Inoue Kaoru-kō denki hensankai, 1968.

Shikata Hiroshi. *Chōsen shakai keizaishi kenkyū.* Tokyo: Kokusho kankōkai, 1976.

Shimonaka Kunihiko. *Seijigaku jiten.* Tokyo: Heibonsha, 1970.

Shinobu Seizaburō. *Nichiro sensō-shi no kenkyū.* Tokyo: Kawade shobō, 1973.

Takahashi Kamekichi. *Gendai chōsen keizairon.* Tokyo: Chikura shobō, 1935.

Takahashi Tomozō. *Tōyō takushoku kabushiki kaisha jūnenshi.* Tokyo: Tōyō takushoku kabushiki kaisha, 1928.

Takazaki Sōshi, "Uchimura Kanzō to chōsen." *Shisō* 9:639 (September 1977): 78–94.

Tanaka Ichinosuke. *Chūnan sangyō-shi.* Taejŏn: Taiden shitsugyō kyōkai, 1921.

Tanaka Shinichi. "Kankoku zaisei seiri ni okeru 'chōsei daichō' seibi ni tsuite." *Tochi seido shigaku* 63 (April 1974): 1–20.

Tanaka Shōhei. *Tochi chōsa to jinushi.* Tokyo: Ganshōdō, 1915.

Tani Genji. *Taishū jinjiroku.* Tokyo: Kokusei kyōkai, 1940.

Tani Toshio. *Kimitsu nichiro sensō-shi.* Tokyo: Genshōbō, 1966.

Togo Minoru. *Nihon shokumin-ron.* Tokyo: Bunseidō, 1906.

Tokunaga Isami. *Kankoku sōran.* Tokyo: Hakubunkan, 1907.

Tomimura Rokurō. *Chūnan ronsan hatten-shi.* Tokyo, 1913.

Toranuma Ryōsan. *Chōsen kōgyō kabushiki kaisha nijūnen-shi.* Tokyo: Chōsen kōgyō kabushiki kaisha, 1929.

Tōyō keizai zasshi. Tokyo: 1908.

Tōyō shihō. Tokyo: Tōyō kyōkai, 1898–1906.

Tsurumi Yūsuke. *Gotō shimpei-den.* Tokyo: Taikeiyō kyōkai, 1943.

Ugaya Ramon. *Chōsen e yuku hito ni.* Tokyo: 1914.

Wada Ichirō. *Chōsen tochi chizei seido chōsa hōkokusho.* Seoul: Chōsen sōtokufu, 1920.

Wakatsuki Yasuo. *Kaigai ijū seisaku shiron.* Tokyo: Fukumusa shuppansha, 1975.

Yamaguchi Atsumizu. "Yonjūichinen ni okeru kankoku keizaikei." *Chōsen* 2:5 (January 1909):102–103.

Yamaguchi Sei. *Chōsen sangyōshi.* Seoul: 1910.

Yamaguchi Toyomasa. *Chōsen no kenkyū.* Tokyo: Ganshōdō, 1911.

Yamamoto Kotarō. *Chōsen ijū annai.* Tokyo: Minyūsha, 1904.

Yi Chae-mu. "Chōsen ni okeru 'tochi chōsa jigyō' no jittai." *Shakai kagaku kenkyū* 7:5 (1955).

Yokoyama Ippei. *Kankoku shisatsu-roku.* Tokyo: Fukuoka shoten, 1904.

Zenshō Eisuke. *Chōsen no jinkō genshō.* Seoul: Chōsen sōtokufu, 1927.

OFFICIAL PUBLICATIONS IN JAPANESE

Chōsen sōtokufu. *Chōsen chishi shiryō.* Seoul: 1919.

———— *Chōsen ni okeru naichijin.* Seoul: 1924.

———— *Chōsen no kōsaku kanshū.* Seoul: Chōsen no sōtokufu, 1929; Tokyo: Gannandō, 1972.

———— *Chōsen no nōgyō.* Seoul: 1925, 1932.

———— *Chōsen no sei.* Seoul: 1934.

———— *Chōsen sōtokufu shokuin-roku.* Seoul: 1939, 1940.

────── *Chōsen tochi chōsa jigyō hōkokusho.* Seoul: Rinji Tochi Chōsa kyoku, 1918.

────── *Chōsen tochi kairyō jigyō yōran.* Seoul: 1937.

────── *Suigen kōtō nōrin gakkō yōran.* Seoul: 1933.

────── *Tōkei nempō.* Seoul: 1920.

Chōsen tōkanfu. *Kankoku nōgyō sankō jikō.* Seoul: 1909.

Chōsen tōkanfu. Seoul: Chōsen tōkanfu shokuminroku, 1910.

Gaimushō. *Nihon gaikō bunsho.* Tokyo: Nihon kokusai rengō kyōkai, 1961.

Nōshōshō. *Chōsen nōgyō gaisetsu.* Tokyo: 1910.

Zenra hokutō nomuka. *Naisenjin jinushi shōyū chichō.* Kunsan: 1928.

KOREAN LANGUAGE SOURCES

Ch'ŏn Kwan-u. "Pan'gye Yu Hyŏng-wŏn yŏn'gusang." *Yŏksa hakpo* 3 (January 1953): 87–139.

Chosŏn munje sajŏn. Seoul: Sinhaksa, 1948.

Han U-gŭn (Han Woo-keun). *Han'guk kyŏngje kwan'gye munhŏn chipsŏng.* Seoul: Tong'a munhwa yŏn'guso, 1966.

Ilche ch'imnyakha Han'guk samsimnyungnyŏnsa. Seoul: Kuksa p'yŏnch'an wiwŏnhoe, 1971.

In Chŏng-sik. *Chosŏn nongch'on munje sajŏn.* Seoul: Sinhaksa, 1948.

────── *Chosŏn nong'ŏp kyŏngje-ron.* Seoul: Pangmun ch'ulp'ansa, 1949.

Kim, Chin-bong, "Imsul millan ŭi sahoe hyŏngch'ejŏk paegyŏng," *Sahak yŏn'gu* 19 (April 1967).

Kim Yong-mo. *Hanmal chibaech'ŭng yŏn'gu.* Seoul: Han'guk munhwa yŏn'guso, 1972.

Kim Yong-sŏp. *Chosŏn hugi nong'ŏpsa yŏn'gu.* Seoul: Ilchogak, 1971.

────── *Han'guk kŭndae nong'ŏpsa yŏn'gu.* Seoul: Ilchogak, 1975.

────── "Hanmal ilche ŭi chijuse." *Han'guksa yŏn'gu* 8 (1972): 149–180.

────── "Kojong si ŭi kyunjŏn sudo munje." *Tong'a munhwa* (August 1968).

────── "Sut'alŭl uihan ch'ŭngyang: t'oji chosa." in *Han'guk hyŏndae-sa,* edited by Sin Sŏk-ho. Seoul: Sin'gu munhwasa, 1971.

Kojong sidaesa. Seoul: Kuksa p'yŏnch'an wiwŏnhoe, 1971.

Kojong sillok. Part of *Yijo sillok.* 10 vols. Beijing: Chosŏn kwahagwŏn and Chung-kuo k'o-hsueh yuan, 1959.

Kuhan'guk pŏmnyŏng mongnok. Seoul: Pŏmmubu, 1970.

Kwanbo. Seoul: Taehan chejuk, 1894–1910. Reprinted in Seoul: Asea munwhasa, 1974.

Kyujanggak tosŏ Han'gukpon ch'ongmongnok. Seoul: Tong'a munhwa yŏn'guso, 1965.

Namgung Ŏk, ed. *Hwangsŏng sinmun.* Published daily 1898–1901. Seoul: Han'guk munwha kaebalsa, 1971.

Pak Pyŏng-ho. *Han'guk pŏbche sago.* Seoul: Pŏmmunsa, 1974.

────── *Han'guk ŭi pŏp.* Seoul: Sejong taewang kinyŏm saŏphoe, 1974.

Pibyŏnsa tŭngnok. 28 vols. Seoul: Kuksa p'yŏnch'an wiwŏnhoe, 1959–1961.

Shin Yong-ha. *Chosŏn t'oji chosa saŏp yŏn'gu.* Seoul: Han'guk yŏn'guwŏn, 1979.

────── *Tongnip hyŏphoe yŏn'gu.* Seoul: Ilchogak, 1976.

Taehan cheguk kwanwŏn iryŏksŏ. Seoul: Kuksa p'yŏnch'an wiwŏnhoe, 1972.

Tong'a munwha. Seoul: Seoul University.

Wŏn Yŏng-hüi. *Han'guk chijŏksa.* Seoul: Pomun ch'ulp'ansa, 1972.

Yi Ch'ŏl-wŏn. *Wanggungsa.* Seoul: Tongguk munhwasa, 1954.

Yi Hong-jik. *Kuksa taesajŏn.* Seoul: Chimungak, 1971.

Yi Hüi-süng. *Han'guk inmyŏng taesajŏn.* Seoul: Sin'gu munhwasa, 1972.

——— *Kugo taesajŏn.* Seoul: Minjung sŏgwan, 1974.

Yi Ki. *Haehak yusŏ.* Seoul: Kuksa p'yŏnch'an wiwŏnhoe, 1974.

Yu In-ho. *Han'guk nongji chedo ŭi yŏn'gu.* Seoul: Pangmundang, 1975.

Yu Kil-jun p'yŏnch'an wiwŏnhoe, ed. *Yu Kil-jun chŏnsŏ.* Seoul: Iljogak, 1971.

Yu Wŏn-dong. *Yijo hugi sanggong'ŏpsa yŏn'gu.* Seoul: Han'guk yŏn'guwŏn, 1968.

Yun Pyŏng-sŏk. "Ilbonin ŭi hwangmuji kaech'ok yogu e taehayŏ 1904 nyŏn Nagamori myŏng'ŭi ŭi wiim kyeyak kidorŭl chungsimŭro." *Yŏksa hakpo* 22 (January 1964): 25–72.

INDEX

Agricultural banks and credit unions, 117–118, 125–130
Agricultural reform: Yi dynasty, 21–26
Agricultural school: in Suwŏn, 17

Cadastral survey: Japanese (1910–1918), 71–72, 74
Chijŏkto (cadastral maps), 7–8
Chōsen kōgyō kabushiki kaisha, 113
Chōsen shintaku kabushiki kaisha, 146, 148–150
Chōsen shokusan ginkō, 116–119, 125–128, 146, 150, 155
Colonial agricultural policy: Japanese in Korea, 58–62, 68–71, 115–120
Colonialism, 1–3, 54; Japanese, 1–4, 54–68
Colonial settlement, Chinese in Manchuria, 56; Japanese in Korea, 55–63, 66–68, 121, 124–131
Corporation (company) law, 113, 124
Credit unions, 118, 128–130

Depression, impact on Japan, 137–140; impact on Korea, 140–142

Economic reform: of Yi dynasty, 19

Fish scale system, Chinese, 21

Hakchŏn, 47
Hayashi Gonsuke, 58–61
Hyanggyo, 47

Inoue Kaoru, 55, 64
Ireland, 54–55; potato famine in, 138
Irrigation: and importance in agriculture, 13–15, 18
Itō Hirobumi, 66–67

Japanese economic policies, 1914–1929, 112–115; 1929–1933, 137–140

Kabo Reforms, 20
Kankoku ginkō, 117
Katsura Tarō, 63–64
Kim Hong-jip, 26
Kojong, King, 23, 26, 66
Komura Jutarō, 57–62, 70
Kongsujŏn, 12
Kongsu-ri, 9; landownership (1890s), 36–43, 45, 48–51; landownership (ca. 1914), 75–79, 95–102; landownership (1914–1929), 120–136; landownership (1929–1935), 142–158; village location and description of, 10–13
Korean resistance, 66–68, 70
Krumm, Raymond Edward Leo, 20, 28
Kungbangjŏn, 22–23, 32–34; in villages studied, 45–46
Kunitake gōmeikaisha, 92, 94, 107
Kwajŏnbŏp, 16, 30–36
Kwangmu *yang'an:* type of data recorded in, 5–6, 9, 20–21, 29, 48–49, 52, 75, 86–87, 163

ABOUT THE AUTHOR

Edwin H. Gragert, who received his Ph.D. from Columbia University, has lived for extended periods in Korea and Japan. Dr. Gragert has served on the Committee on International Relations of the House of Representatives and on Congressional observation delegations to Korea. He is currently Director of Programs for the Copen Family Fund, which pioneered the field of international telecommunications in education, and lectures on Korean and Japanese history.

STUDIES OF THE EAST ASIAN INSTITUTE

SELECTED TITLES

The Origins of the Korean War: Liberation and the Emergence of Separate Regimes, 1945–1947, by Bruce Cumings. Princeton: Princeton University Press, 1981.

The U.S.–South Korean Alliance: Evolving Patterns of Security Relations, edited by Gerald L. Curtis and Sung-joo Han. Lexington, MA: Lexington Books, 1983.

The Foreign Policy of the Republic of Korea, edited by Youngnok Koo and Sung-joo Han. New York: Columbia University Press, 1984.

Japanese Culture, third edition, revised, by H. Paul Varley. Honolulu: University of Hawaii Press, 1984.

Shamans, Housewives, and other Restless Spirits: Women in Korean Ritual Life, by Laurel Kendall. Honolulu: University of Hawaii Press, 1985.

Urban Japanese Housewives: At Home and in the Community, by Anne E. Imamura. Honolulu: University of Hawaii Press, 1987.

Kim Il Sung: The North Korean Leader, by Dae-Sook Suh. New York: Columbia University Press, 1988.

Race to the Swift: State and Finance in Korean Industrialization, by Jung-en Woo. New York: Columbia University Press, 1991.

Sowing the Seeds of Change: Chinese Students, Japanese Teachers, 1895–1905, by Paula S. Harrell. Stanford: Stanford University Press, 1993.

Social Mobility in Contemporary Japan, by Hiroshi Ishida. Stanford: Stanford University Press, 1993.

Driven by Growth: Political Change in the Asia-Pacific Region, edited by James W. Morely. Armonk, NY: M. E. Sharpe, 1992.

Schoolhouse Politicians: Locality and State During the Chinese Republic, by Helen R. Chauncey. Honolulu: University of Hawaii Press, 1992.

Pollution, Politics and Foreign Investment in Taiwan: The Lukang Rebellion, by James Reardon-Anderson. Armonk, NY: M. E. Sharpe, 1993.

Japan's Foreign Policy after the Cold War: Coping with Change, Gerald L. Curtis, ed. Armonk, NY: M. E. Sharpe, 1993.

Landownership under Colonial Rule, by Edwin H. Gragert, Honolulu: University of Hawaii Press, 1994.

Production Notes

Composition and paging were done on the
Quadex Composing System and typesetting
on the Compugraphic 8400 by the design
and production staff of University of
Hawaii Press.

The text typeface is Sabon and the
display typeface is Garamond ITC.

Offset presswork and binding were done by
The Maple-Vail Book Manufacturing Group.
Text paper is Writers RR Offset,
basis 50.